# Amon's Secret

## Also by Arnold Ytreeide

for Advent

*Jotham's Journey*

*Bartholomew's Passage*

*Tabitha's Travels*

*Ishtar's Odyssey*

for Easter

*Amon's Adventure*

# Amon's Secret

*A Family Story of the First Christians*

Arnold Ytreeide

KREGEL
PUBLICATIONS

For Thorin—
A blessing beyond all understanding,
a joy beyond belief.

*Amon's Secret*


Published by Kregel Publications, a division of Kregel Inc., 2450 Oak Industrial Dr. NE, Grand Rapids, MI 49505. www.kregel.com.



The artist is represented by the literary agency of WordServe Literary Group, Ltd., www.wordserveliterary.com.

**Library of Congress Cataloging-in-Publication Data**
Names: Ytreeide, Arnold, 1954- author.
Title: Amon's secret : a family story for the church's beginning / Arnold Ytreeide.
Description: Grand Rapids, MI : Kregel Publications, [2023]
Identifiers: LCCN 2022029752 (print) | LCCN 2022029753 (ebook) | ISBN 9780825447709 (print) | ISBN 9780825469671 (kindle) | ISBN 9780825470127 (epub)
Subjects: LCSH: Church history--Primitive and early church, ca. 30-600--Juvenile literature.
Classification: LCC BR165 .Y77 2023 (print) | LCC BR165 (ebook) | DDC 270.1--dc23/eng/20220725

ISBN 978-0-8254-4770-9, print
ISBN 978-0-8254-7012-7, epub
ISBN 978-0-8254-6967-1, Kindle

Printed in China
23 24 25 26 27 28 29 30 31 32 / 5 4 3 2 1

# Before the Story

## *An Important Note to Parents and Teachers*

No matter how you look at it, this is a tough story for kids. The early days of the Christian church were full of relentless persecution, barbaric punishment, and cruel death. All simply because some people believed that Jesus was their Savior and wanted to spread his message of forgiveness and salvation. For that, they were whipped, stoned, beheaded, and crucified.

It's just a tough story for kids.

But it's a true story, and a story full of truth, so it's a story kids need to understand. They need to understand—at appropriate levels for appropriate ages—that our faith must not be frivolous; it must be deep, dominant, determinate. They need to understand that each of us must be ready to defend our faith.

When I sat down to write this book, I struggled with how to present that part of the story for a wide range of ages in a way that would inform but not traumatize children. My answer to that dilemma is *Amon's Secret*.

Stories are built on drama, though, and drama is based in conflict. Sometimes conflict is upsetting to children. While there is no graphic violence "on screen" in this story, the plot does lead us through some scary territory. If you have a child who is very young, or particularly sensitive, I urge you to pre-read each chapter and leave out or soften any parts you feel would be too frightening.

But still, *Amon's Secret* is a story with meanings at many levels—more, probably, than even I am aware. It is my prayer that your children—and you—will find a new and deeper appreciation for, and understanding of, this thing we call the church and the faith in each of us that brings it to life.

### *How to Read This Book*

All the previous books in this series were built around a particular time of year—Advent, Christmas, Lent, and Easter. Each chapter of those books was timed to coincide with the events of those celebrations. *Amon's Secret* has no such temporal connection other than a momentary mention of a church holiday called Pentecost, which is traditionally celebrated 50 days after Jesus's resurrection.

How should you read this book? I think the answer must be, "Any way that works for you."

Like its earlier companions, *Amon's Secret* is broken into short chapters, each of which ends with a devotional thought. At whatever time of year works for you and your family, you could choose to read one chapter each morning or evening as a family or personal devotion for a month.

But because there are no external connections to think about, you can also just sit down and read it or give it to your children to read. Whatever works for you and your family.

## *Pronunciation Guide*

Biblical names can be difficult to pronounce. In reality, no one knows what the proper pronunciations are. If you grew up in a Western culture, your mouth may not even be *capable* of pronouncing these names correctly. But for those who would like to conform to at least a pretense of a guide (admittedly inaccurate), here is how we have chosen to pronounce some of the names you'll encounter in *Amon's Secret*:

Amon = uh-MAHN
Caiaphas = KYE-uh-fuss
Cornelius = core-NEEL-yus
Gamaliel = GAM-uh-leel
Jadon = JAY-duhn
Jotham = JAW-thum
Raphu = rah-FOO
Tamar = TAY-mar
Uri = YER-ee

You can also visit the website listed below to hear pronunciations of these names.

## *Online Extras*

Bonus Features for this title include:

- facts about life in Jerusalem during the time of this story
- a floor plan of Amon's house, the temple, the Antonia Fortress, and the house of Caiaphas

- maps of the markets and other locations inside Jerusalem
- drawings of the temple
- photos of Jerusalem today

You can access all of these for free at www.JothamsJourney.com.

## Chapter One

# Celebration

*This must be what it feels like after you get kicked in the head by a mule*, Amon thought. He had seen such a thing once, and afterward the man had walked around in a daze, not knowing what was going on, where he should go, or even who he was. *I feel like a thousand bees are buzzing in my head.*

Amon walked through the crowded streets of Jerusalem with his father, Jotham, his mother, Tabitha, and his younger brothers, Jadon and Uri. At thirteen he had already been declared by the rabbis to be a man, but at the moment he felt very much like a child.

*Everyone else must be feeling the same way*, he decided. It seemed as if the entire city of Jerusalem was celebrating. In a courtyard on one side street, women in colorful scarves danced. On another street a man from the east threw into a fire some kind of powder that exploded in flashes and smoke to the cheers of a crowd. And everywhere Amon looked, people were eating and singing and celebrating.

"I do not believe I have ever seen such a big grin on your face," Amon's father said as they walked.

"Nor have I ever been accused of having a big grin," Amon laughed with an even bigger grin. He had always been known as a serious boy, and now a serious young man—always inventing, always creating, always thinking serious thoughts. "Do you not see, Father, how the entire city of Jerusalem is celebrating?"

Jotham scanned the streets. "I believe, my son, that most of Jerusalem is simply doing what they do every day. It is only you and I and a few others who are celebrating."

As Amon checked all the streets again, he realized his father was probably right. While many friends and families had been at the Mount of Olives and were indeed celebrating, most of the people in Jerusalem were merely going about their business. How could they not know and not be excited about what he and the others had just witnessed?

*I just saw a man, a human being, rise into the air and enter the kingdom of heaven*, he thought for the thousandth time since it had happened an hour before. *How is that possible?*

He knew the answer, of course. Knew it was a miracle of God, and the man—Jesus—was himself God. But it was all so impossible to think about with his logical, rational mind. Jesus, first rising from the dead, then ascending into heaven. How could such a thing be true?

*I just have to accept it, even if it seems impossible*, Amon thought. And that's what brought the huge grin to his face and the faces of certain others in the city. They seemed to make little circles of excitement wherever they gathered.

But then there were the others in Jerusalem. The priests, the Sadducees, the Pharisees, and many of the common Jews. They made a much bigger circle. They didn't believe Jesus was the Messiah, hadn't been there to see him walking and talking and ascending to heaven. They couldn't accept the miracles he worked. All this brought a bit of a frown to Amon's face.

Amon forced thoughts of those doubters aside and the grin returned.

This was the day that Jesus had proven himself to be the Messiah, the Savior of the world, and nothing at all could spoil that.

"Father, maybe we could *not* take our sheep to market today?"

Jotham laughed. "No, my son, we will not be going to market today. This is a day of celebration, because"—and here he threw his head back and yelled, not caring who heard him—"Jesus is the Messiah!"

The whole family cheered, then Tabitha said to Jotham, "Your aunt was so happy."

Amon looked from his mother to his father and back again. "*Whose* aunt?"

"My aunt," his father said. "Mary."

Amon gasped. "Mary, the mother of Jesus? She's your aunt? How can that be?"

"Joseph was my father's brother, so his wife is my aunt."

"No, I mean how can we be related to Mary and I not know it?"

"You've just forgotten," Tabitha said as they continued walking.

"But you never *talked* about it."

Jotham and Tabitha exchanged a look, then he gently said to Amon, "We tried. When you were young you didn't care, and when you got older you wouldn't listen because you thought we were . . . 'sick in the head' is how you put it."

Amon's face grew red and he turned away, saying only, "Oh."

They walked up through the center of the big city, past the Hippodrome where Roman-style chariot races and other games took place, and Herod's theater, a huge semicircular building for entertainment.

As they passed the Pool of Siloam, Amon noticed a small crowd gathered at the edge of the water, including Peter, one of the disciples of Jesus. Uri ran over and hugged him, and Amon shook his hand, saying, "Isn't it miraculous?"

Peter laughed and roughed up Amon's hair. "It is indeed, my young friend." Then turning to Amon's father, he said, "We have just baptized a dozen people into The Way of Jesus. Is your family ready to make such a public statement?"

Jotham looked at his wife, then at Amon, Jadon, and Uri. All of them nodded, but he knelt down in front of Uri. "Do you understand what we're talking about, Uri?"

"No. But it sounds like fun."

Amon had a sad feeling inside, watching Uri. Even though the boy was eight years old, he had trouble understanding much of the world. He was happy, though, and just needed a little extra time and patience.

"Do you remember who Jesus is?" Jotham asked the boy.

"Of course. He's the one we saw go into the sky today."

"Well, what we're doing here is called baptism, and it's a way we can show ourselves and others that we believe Jesus is God. Would you like to do that?"

Uri frowned. "Will we still be home in time for lunch?"

Jotham turned away, and Amon wasn't sure if he was smiling or crying. Uri seemed to have that effect on people. Jotham looked back at him. "Yes, we will be home long before lunch."

Uri shrugged his little shoulders. "Okay."

Peter led them back to the pool. When it was Amon's turn, he stepped into the cool water up to his waist. Peter put one hand behind his head, and one in the small of his back, then spoke the words, "I baptize you in the name of God the Father and Jesus the Christ, his only son, the Messiah."

Amon kept his eyes open as Peter laid him back into the water—water that flooded across the life he'd always known—and it washed away the stains of his sin. When he emerged from the waters a moment later, he knew his life would never be the same.

Once the entire family had been baptized, Jotham gathered them and prayed. Then he turned to Peter and said, "Thank you, my friend."

"It is my great honor. Now, if I may ask for your hospitality, could we perhaps use your upper room once again?"

Amon's father quickly agreed, and they all walked up the steep streets to Amon's house, close to where the Essene Gate created a passage through the tall stone wall that surrounded the entire city. Amon watched as all eleven remaining disciples of Jesus, including Matthew and Bartholomew,

entered the house. Behind them followed Jesus's mother, Mary, several other women, and James and the other brothers and sisters of Jesus. Amon had met James on many occasions already but had only seen the other siblings of Jesus from afar. As they filed past him up the stairs, he wondered what it must have been like to have Jesus as an older brother.

Amon sat on the stairs and listened as the apostles prayed for God's guidance and elected Mathias as a new disciple to replace Judas Iscariot, who had betrayed Jesus. The other Judas, who remained faithful to Jesus, kept begging everyone to refer to him as "Judas *not* Iscariot," or by his other name, Thaddaeus, so people didn't get him mixed up with the betrayer.

After the meeting, the believers spent the rest of the day celebrating in the streets with friends and neighbors. Even as the sun began to set, the excitement through much of the city did not. The laughter and stories and speculation simply moved indoors. Amon's own house filled with people. Families brought food, lamps, and oil, and kept streaming through the door. As he climbed from the bottom floor to the upper room, then up to the open rooftop, Amon was amazed at the bright light from all those lamps and at the plates of meat, cheese, and bread. Dozens of small groups of people talked and laughed.

Amon looked over the edge of the roof. The children of all those families played in his father's sheep pens behind the house. Tamar and Benjamin approached the back door, so Amon ran down the stairs to greet them.

"My friends!" he said as they entered the house, "I thought I had lost you forever. Where have you been?"

Benjamin, a year younger than Amon and not yet a man, spoke up. "We were at my house, trying to tell my father what happened today."

"And he wouldn't believe a word of it," Tamar added. She was only slightly younger than Amon, and they had come to be good friends during their earlier adventures trying to save Amon's father. She was the daughter of Bartholomew, the disciple of Jesus, and a woman named Muriel, who died of a fever when Tamar was quite young. When Bartholomew and Amon's parents were children, they had all been present the night Jesus was born in Bethlehem. "Why are men so stubborn?" Tamar asked, shaking her head.

Amon grinned. "I think *everyone* is stubborn sometimes, especially about things we've been taught all our lives." Tamar slumped, and Amon added, "Besides, it is stubborn men who will carry the message of Jesus across the entire world."

"You mean, men *and* women." Tamar straightened her shoulders.

Amon frowned. He didn't want to get in another argument about girls being as capable as boys, so he tried to put an end to it before it began. "I'm just saying that Jehovah has always used *men* to do his work."

The scowl on Tamar's face said that the argument was far from over.

"If you two are going to start this again, I'm leaving." Benjamin's voice made a funny squeak, and he blushed.

"Your body is telling you it is time to become a man," Amon said. "Now your *head* must decide the same thing."

Benjamin just frowned and walked off.

Amon sighed. "It is just a fact, Tamar, that girls aren't important to Jehovah. Everyone knows that. It is clear in our laws."

Tamar pursed her lips but kept her anger under control. "I don't believe your mother would agree with that thought. Nor Mary, Jesus's mother, nor any of the other women who've supported his journey."

Even as a young girl, Tabitha, Amon's mother, had fought against the Romans and King Herod to save her father.

"And where in the words of Jehovah did he ever say he had no use for women?"

Amon's eyes widened in surprise. He wasn't used to having his words questioned by those younger than himself, at least not on matters of Jewish law. "There are many examples throughout Jewish law where Jehovah speaks to us through our rabbis."

"Words from our rabbis, yes. Through *men*. But are they really the words of Jehovah? Are there not many places in the laws where the rabbis do not even agree with each other? Or where they admit they do not know a thing? If Jehovah is always speaking through the rabbis, how could they disagree or not know? Is Jehovah confused? Is he unsure of himself?"

Amon frowned and looked toward the floor to avoid her eyes, afraid her words were close to blasphemy. "These things are very complicated," he said finally. "Men must study them for many years before . . ."

Tamar ignored Amon's stammering. "Our great father Moses told us the words Jehovah spoke to him on Mount Horeb, correct?"

Amon nodded his head slowly. "Yes, of course, but . . ."

"And he spoke to Ezekiel about the sins of Jerusalem, correct?"

"Yes."

"And we know what he said about Jonah and Hosea and Zechariah because those words were written down for us by our prophets, correct?"

Amon simply stared at her.

"Then where, please tell me, in all of the Torah, did Jehovah ever say, 'And beware the woman—she is an inferior creature, stupid in the mind and evil in the heart. Do not listen to her for she is not to be the leader of men.' Where in all of Scripture did he say such a thing? I'll answer that for you. He did *not* say such a thing! Only the priests and rabbis—old men, all—ever said that women may not serve Jehovah."

Amon noticed others starting to stare at them. "Shhh!" He looked around nervously, then pulled Tamar into the room where his mother stored their food. "Take caution," he whispered. "You must not speak such things. The high priest has many ears."

Tamar lowered her voice. "What about Ruth? Esther? Miriam? Rahab?" She looked Amon straight in the eye. "I am correct, no? And what of Mary of Magdala, Mary and Martha of Bethany?"

Amon fidgeted. "I do not yet know," he whispered finally. "But my mind will think on these things."

~

As the evening flew by and the plates of meat and cheese and bread emptied, the small groups talking excitedly melted into one large group listening quietly to many stories from those close to Jesus. People sat on the floor, stood against the walls, and sat on the stairs leading to the upper room. Stories of the day were shared, but also stories of the past, of the words they'd heard Jesus speak, and the things they'd seen him do. Mary told about the angel that had visited her, about raising Jesus as a child, and about always knowing in her heart that he was the Son of God.

A few of the children had already fallen asleep when one man, a friend of Amon's father, said, "Jotham, you, Tabitha, and Bartholomew were all there on the night Jesus was born. Tell us what you saw."

Amon's father looked nervously to his wife and Bartholomew, and Amon could see they all came to a silent agreement. He knew this had always been a sensitive subject for the three of them because no one ever believed their stories. Even Amon had thought his father sick in the head when Jotham claimed to have seen angels and miracles. But now, Amon knew, all those stories had been true.

Those sitting at the table quickly moved to make room for the three. Slowly, Tabitha, Bartholomew, and Jotham came from where they had been standing around the edges of the room and sat at the table. Jotham was the first to speak. "For me," he said softly, and everyone leaned in to hear, "it started when I was ten years old and ran away from my father's tents."

And with that, Jotham, Tabitha, and Bartholomew each told long and amazing adventures of how they had met and how they had each been present when the Messiah, Jesus, was born.

As the stories continued, Amon noticed Levi, one of the disciples, who was also called Matthew. He sat on a stool in the corner under the light of an oil lamp, writing on a parchment.

Amon worked his way through the crowd and stood next to Matthew. "What is it you write?" he whispered.

Matthew looked up and smiled. "Sorry, it is just my way. All my life I have kept records and ledgers of people's affairs."

Amon considered this. "So you would know how much to tax them."

Matthew turned away as if ashamed.

Amon knew from stories he'd heard that the man had once been a tax collector and was one of the men most hated by the other Jews.

"Until Jesus saved me from myself," Matthew whispered, "I was a wretched man. But when I started following him and saw a new way to live, I used my skills to record the things he said and did. Mary, over there"—he gestured toward the mother of Jesus sitting on the other side of the room—"even told me some stories about his childhood. Did you know that when he was twelve, Jesus once left his parents and went to the temple, where he taught the rabbis?"

Amon's mouth dropped open. "Jesus wasn't even a man yet, but he could teach the rabbis?"

"That's what she said. In any case, I've been keeping all these notes about Jesus from the beginning. I just can't help thinking that someone, someday, can make these things into a book, so those who come after us can know that Jesus is the Son of God."

Amon's father was just telling how *his* father, a shepherd, had been camped outside Bethlehem one night and how they all witnessed a host of heavenly angels announce the birth of Jesus.

Matthew went back to scribbling down the stories as fast as others could tell them, and Amon wandered back over to his friends. He leaned over to Tamar and whispered, "I think we might be witnessing the beginning of something big."

The look on Tamar's face said, "Like what?"

"I think," Amon answered the look, "that the men—I mean, the people—in this room are going to change the world."

Tamar scanned the crowd, her gaze passing over the people telling stories, the people listening. "Wouldn't that be just amazing." Then she turned to Amon. "When do we start?"

✦ ✦ ✦

What must that day have been like! To see Jesus—a man of flesh and blood—rise into the air and change into a glorious form to rejoin God the Father. What a sight it must have been, and what an electrifying event.

All those who saw it must have shouted and cheered and cried and then told everyone who would listen what they had seen. There must have been parties that night and excited talk about a new way of living, a new future.

For those involved, it must have changed their lives forever. Their heads must have been buzzing as if full of a thousand bees, and all of life must have seemed strange and new and exciting.

What must that day have been like.

I think I know.

I think it must have been exactly like the day I decided to give my life to Jesus, confess my sins, accept his forgiveness, and follow his example of selflessness, kindness, and love. Not that I've mastered any of those things yet, but I'm trying. And ever since that day, nothing has seemed the same. Life has been strange and new and exciting.

Because of Jesus.

Chapter Two

# Teachings

Someone was crying. A child, maybe a baby. No, not just a child, but several children. All crying at once, as if no one had fed any of the children in all of Jerusalem. It made Amon want to shout from his rooftop, "Will someone please feed the sheep!"

Amon's eyes flew open. It was morning. The sun was on his bed mat on the roof of the house, the place he most liked to sleep. And the sheep were bawling. Amon raised his head and looked around. His parents were still asleep, also on the rooftop, but their beds were in the shade. He sighed, then forced himself to get up and go tend to the sheep.

The events of the day and night before were still as clear as a mountain brook in Amon's mind: Jesus ascending into heaven and the celebration and stories afterward. It was all fresh and wonderful. He thought about all these things as he fed and watered the flock, until he heard his father's voice.

"Amon, you should have woken me." His father came out of the house, stretching in the sunlight.

"I was awake, you were asleep, and I saw no reason to disturb you. I am certainly old enough to care for the sheep."

Jotham laughed and hugged his son. "That you are. And your mother and I thank you for the extra rest. Yesterday was thrilling, but also exhausting."

Amon poured the last bucket of water into the sheep trough. "I still can't believe we're related to Jesus. And Mary."

"Yes," Jotham said. "Joseph was my favorite uncle, and he married Mary. That makes her my aunt and your great-aunt. And, of course, Jesus was my first cousin. *Is* my first cousin," he corrected.

Amon shook his head in disgust. "All that time, I was related to the Messiah and wouldn't even let you tell me about him. I was such a fool."

"Not a fool, just young."

"I am still young," Amon answered, "so please tell me anytime I am acting like a fool." He saw his father looking off into the sky. "What is it?" he asked. "What are you thinking?"

"I was just remembering," Jotham said slowly, "a fool I used to know in my youth." He looked back at Amon. "One of the many people I met on my amazing journey was an Essene named Nathan. He pretended to be a fool and saved me from being sold into slavery."

"Is that why you chose to live near the Essene Gate when you came to Jerusalem?"

Jotham smiled. "It may have had something to do with it. But the point is"—he patted Amon on the back—"sometimes one who appears foolish is really being wise in another way."

After the rest of the family got up, they all had a breakfast of bread and honey, then Amon walked across the upper part of Jerusalem, looking out over the entire city and the huge temple on the opposite hill. Finally he arrived at the house of his teacher, the rabbi Gamaliel.

"If a Jew is brought before the Sanhedrin and convicted of blasphemy," Gamaliel asked without even looking up from the parchment he was reading, "what will be the judgment?"

Amon gaped at the elderly man in surprise for several seconds, not because his teacher had greeted him with a question, but because it was such a simple question. In five years under his teaching, Amon had gotten used to the fact that Gamaliel always seemed to know who was approaching without even looking. He'd also gotten used to not being greeted in the traditional way, but with a question of the law.

"Death by stoning, of course," Amon said.

Still without looking, Gamaliel asked, "And what if the one so accused and convicted is a close friend or relative of one of those sitting in judgment, or even a member of the Sanhedrin itself?"

Amon thought carefully, knowing there was a trick to this question. What was *written* in the law was often not what was *practiced* in the law, especially when the guilty one was a member of the Sanhedrin—the court that made such decisions. His own father had been a victim of that fact just a few months before. But what answer did Gamaliel really want from him at this moment? "The same sentence, of course," Amon finally answered, "though what the law says and what men do is often different."

Gamaliel pulled out a cloth and wiped his nose. "Then, when the Messiah returns to judge all men, who will be judged most severely—the one who committed the offense, or the one who failed to carry out the law?"

Instantly Amon realized he had been skillfully led into a trap. It should have come as no surprise, since the same thing had happened just about every day of his lessons for years, but usually he came prepared for the verbal battle. Today he had other things on his mind and had forgotten to prepare.

Finally, with a sigh and knowing he was beaten no matter what, Amon said, "The man who failed to carry out the punishment shall be found twice as guilty as the original offender because he takes upon himself both the original offense and the additional offense of disobeying a law of God."

Gamaliel smiled. "Very good, Amon. Completely wrong, but very good." He went back to his parchments.

"That is all you will say? Why am I wrong? My logic, my understanding of Scripture, and my knowledge of the law are all flawless."

Gamaliel turned back, still with a smile, but now one that said, "Did you really just say that?"

"Alright, maybe not flawless," Amon admitted, "but I am still correct."

There was a long pause, during which Amon pulled up a stool and sat down, then Gamaliel said, "You are thinking of the law in two dimensions only, Amon. You think in past and present, but not *future*."

Amon's mouth opened and closed several times. "Future?" he finally wheezed.

Gamaliel nodded. "Think with me. When will Jehovah sit in judgment on us?" Amon stared at him blankly, so the teacher answered the question himself. "After the Messiah has come, correct?"

"Uh, yes, I suppose . . ."

"And will the law at that time be the same law you and I study today?" Still Amon's mouth moved without speaking, so once again Gamaliel answered his own question. "It will not. I do not know particularly *what* it shall be, but I know that in all likelihood the teachings of the Messiah and the glory of Jehovah shall both bring things to light that you and I cannot yet see. So the correct answer to this question, my young student, should be, 'I do not yet know.'"

Amon sat, stunned, for several moments.

Gamaliel went back to his studies.

They were sitting in the outer courtyard of the rabbi's house, surrounded by a short stone wall and tall stands of grape vines. When finally he had gathered his wits, Amon replied. "Yes, I can see why you would say that. But the truth is, my teacher, that the Messiah has already come, so we *can* answer the question."

Gamaliel's head snapped up and he spun quickly, as if searching to see who may be passing by on the street. Then he stood, grabbed Amon by the tunic, and ushered him inside the house. "Amon!" he hissed. "You must not say such things where others might hear. It is terribly dangerous."

"But rabbi, it's true. Have you not heard what happened on the Mount of Olives yesterday?"

Gamaliel waved his hands in the air in dismissal. "Yes, yes, I have heard the stories. But they are fabrications, fantasies, lies even. We must not—"

"Rabbi!" Amon took the old man by the shoulders and stared him in the eyes. "I was there. I was on the Mount of Olives, and I watched as Jesus of Nazareth, *in the flesh*, rose into the air, and angels were with him. I am not fabricating this, I am having no fantasies, and I do not lie. Jesus of Nazareth is the Messiah."

Gamaliel turned his back toward Amon and pulled away, pretending to sort some parchments on a table. "I will not hear such blasphemy," he said. "I am a member of the Sanhedrin, do not forget, and by law should report your words."

Amon walked up behind his teacher and spoke softly. "I know you have doubts yourself, my teacher."

Gamaliel stopped sorting and listened.

"I know you are tied to past traditions, but I also know you see truth in the words and actions of Jesus. Allow yourself to believe."

The rabbi didn't reply.

Amon stood silent for a time, then quietly slipped out and headed home. Along the way he ran into Tamar and Benjamin, and together they decided to climb to one of their favorite places, the Garden Gate, in a wall that used to form the edge of the city but now ran through the middle of it. They entered the tower next to the gate and climbed the stairs. Once out on top of the wall, they could see all of Jerusalem to their left and right, the towers of Herod's palace behind them, and the temple in front.

"By tomorrow," Benjamin said, "the whole city will know that Jesus is the Messiah."

Amon sighed, thinking about Gamaliel. "I'm not sure everyone will accept it quite that quickly."

"But the last words Jesus spoke," Tamar said, "told us to go out and tell the whole world about him. How long could that take?"

Amon did some calculations in his head. "I would say that if we all did our part, we should be able to tell the whole world about Jesus in about a year."

"A *year*?" Benjamin cried. "Why so long?"

"Remember Benjamin, a man of God learns to be patient," Amon said, repeating what both his parents and Gamaliel had told him many times. "A year seems a terribly long time to wait, but it will go quickly. And in that time, everyone everywhere will hear the good news of Jesus and choose to follow him, and we'll all be living in a new world where there's no hate, no war, no anger—just the love of God flowing between us. And then Jesus will return."

"So let's get busy and start telling everyone," Tamar said.

Instead, Amon gasped and took off running.

"Wait!" Tamar yelled after him. "Where are you going?"

"I just remembered," he shouted back. "I haven't yet told my friend Saul."

✦ ✦ ✦

Imagine you walk in the door of your favorite restaurant. Suddenly a siren sounds, lights flash, confetti falls, and balloons are released into the air. The owner of the restaurant comes over and pats you on the back saying, "Congratulations! You're our one-millionth customer, and you've just won free meals for you and all your friends and family for the rest of your life!"

What do you think your friends would say when you told them?

Some might doubt at first, but then they'd quickly check the internet, find out you're telling the truth, and gladly accept the news.

So why is it so difficult to get people to accept the best news ever known to humankind, news that will nourish them for the rest of their lives and bring them *eternal* life?

Amon calculates that it should take about a year to spread the news about Jesus and assumes everyone will accept that news as soon as they hear it. Obviously, that didn't happen, and still doesn't happen today.

Just as it took Amon a long time to believe the truth about his parents' experiences with Jesus, most people today are reluctant to believe in Jesus. It took several miracles before Amon would finally believe, and many of us who call Jesus our Savior had to have a miraculous encounter as well.

Here's my question: What if *you're* the miracle someone is waiting for before they can accept Jesus?

## Chapter Three

# Stephen

Tamar and Benjamin ran to catch up with Amon, who was already inside the tower and halfway down the stairs. "Amon! Wait up," Benjamin yelled.

Amon stopped, waiting on the stairs as his two friends pushed their way down through people on their way up. Then they all headed down to the street again and out into the sunshine.

Tamar asked, panting, "What . . . what will you say to him?"

"To Saul?" Amon asked.

She nodded.

"I will tell him the wondrous things we have seen and heard, so that he will believe as well."

"But remember, Saul was against Jesus from the beginning. He may not like what you say."

"How could he not like it? He is an intelligent and logical man. I will tell him the truth I have seen, and he will believe it."

Tamar's eyebrows raised. "I'm not so sure. You yourself told me just last night that it takes some people a long time to accept what is obvious to others."

"Like my father, who says he'll never believe in 'this Jesus person,'" Benjamin said.

Amon scoffed. "Nonsense. Saul is my friend and he will trust what I say." With that, he walked quickly through the narrow, winding streets toward Saul's house, glancing back once in a while to make sure Tamar and Benjamin were keeping up.

Saul was several years older than Amon, and also a student of Gamaliel. The two had been friends for years, spending much time in debate over questions of law.

The trio passed a street corner where several merchants had set up wood-and-cloth stalls selling leather, jewelry, and perfume. The perfume vendor was talking excitedly to the jewelry vendor, but Amon didn't pay much attention until the man said the word "Messiah."

Amon skidded to a stop and listened.

"I'm telling you, I saw it with my own eyes," the man said. "He rose straight into the clouds, and two angels joined him!"

"You've been telling me stories for years," the jewelry vendor answered as he rearranged some necklaces. "Why would I believe you now?"

"Because," the leather vendor joined in, "this time he's telling the truth. I saw it myself."

The jeweler sat on his stool with a thump. "You mean . . . *the Messiah has really come?*"

"That's what I've been telling you all day," the perfume vendor said. "And now I'll tell the whole world." He ran toward Amon and his friends. "Children! Have you heard? The Messiah has come to us, from Nazareth of all places!"

"Uh, yes, we know," Amon said. "We were there too."

The perfume vendor was so excited he ran up to the next people that passed by.

Benjamin crossed his arms. "Are you going to tell him you're a man, not a child?"

Amon shook his head. "No, his news is more important than my pride."

As the three moved more slowly through the upper city crowds, people here and there talked excitedly about Jesus, going door-to-door, telling their neighbors, even stopping strangers in the street. Some people listened politely and then moved on, others accepted the news with joy, but a few got angry and threatened all who believed such nonsense.

They passed a darkened alley running off to the right, between a woman selling bread and a man selling figs.

Amon held out his arm to stop the others. "We should check on Leshem." Without waiting for them to agree, he bought a loaf of bread and a dozen figs and entered the alley.

At the far end, a young blind man sat alone in a corner, dressed in a tattered tunic and resting his head against the stone wall. He was scratching the few whiskers on his chin, then his head snapped up. "Who is that? Who's there?"

Amon approached the young man slowly. "I can answer your questions, or I can share with you our lunch. Which would you prefer?"

"Amon? Blessings on you, my friend." Leshem reached out with his hands, searching the air. "I shall gladly share a meal with you. And those are the footsteps of Tamar and Benjamin I hear, are they not?"

"Greetings, Leshem." Tamar grinned.

Benjamin sat in the dirt in front of Leshem. "Yes, it is I, soon-to-be-a-man Benjamin."

Leshem laughed.

The others sat, then Amon tore off a piece of bread and placed it in Leshem's hand. "And we have figs as well," he said, holding up one finger to Tamar and Benjamin.

They nodded and took one fig each.

As he chewed his food, Leshem asked, "What's been happening in the city? I've heard happy shouting and angry shouting and singing but can make no sense of it."

"Have you heard the name 'Jesus'?" Amon asked.

Leshem shook his head.

"Then let me tell you."

Leshem ate most of the bread and all his figs in the time it took Amon to explain. He was chewing his last bite when Amon finished. "You say these men are healing people? In the name of this Jesus?"

"Yes, it is so. At least that's what people are reporting."

Leshem jumped to his feet, putting a hand against the wall to steady himself. "I must go find them."

"We can lead you," Tamar said, also standing.

"No, no," Leshem said. "There is no need. I've traveled this city without sight all my life. I can find my way. Thank you for the meal." Leshem hurried up the alley as if he could see.

Amon and the others followed, yelling their goodbyes as Leshem headed toward the temple, then continued on their own mission. They reached a large square surrounded by merchant stalls and saw a crowd gathered. In the center of the crowd, a man stood on the edge of a well, shouting. The blinding sun was directly behind the man so that Amon couldn't see who it was. He took a few steps to his right, then his eyes widened in surprise.

"Who is it?" Tamar asked.

"A friend of my father's. His name is Stephen," Amon said. "He always says whatever he thinks."

As if to prove Amon right, Stephen said to the crowd, "You stubborn people. Must you forever resist the Holy Spirit? That's what your ancestors did, and so do you. Name one prophet your ancestors didn't persecute. They even killed the ones who predicted the coming of the Righteous One—the Messiah, who was betrayed and murdered right here in Jerusalem." He then went on to tell about the death and resurrection of Jesus, and his return to heaven.

Some people in the crowd started shouting "Hallelujah," but others walked away grumbling. One of those passed Amon on his way out of the square. Amon heard him say, "The Sanhedrin should put a stop to all this blasphemy."

Amon turned to his friends. Benjamin's eyes were so wide open they looked like little moons, and Tamar's scowl said she was ready for a fight. Amon just frowned. "Like I said, it will probably take a whole year before everyone in the world believes in Jesus."

They started to walk away but were stopped by the shout of "Amon!" They turned and saw that Stephen had left his perch and was trotting their way. "Amon!" he said again as he caught up with them. "It is good to see you. I spoke with your father this morning, but you were at your lessons."

"Actually, my visit to Gamaliel was social." Amon kicked at some stones in the street. "Although, with Gamaliel, there's always a lesson regardless. What were you talking to my father about?"

"Some of the followers have been talking," Stephen said, "and we think it is time for those of us who believe to start meeting together. Your father agreed and is going with me to speak to the apostles of Jesus."

"What a wonderful idea," Tamar said. "When will we start?"

Stephen shrugged. "I do not know. The apostles will have to approve and organize such a gathering. In the meantime," he said, turning to the vendor behind them, "allow me to buy a treat for the three of you." He picked up three pieces of sweet fruit from the booth.

Amon took half a step away and put his hands behind his back. "It would be a most welcome kindness for you to give the children a treat."

Stephen blushed. "Of course," he said with a bow of his head. "You are a man now. No offense intended."

Amon bowed his head. "Of course not, and none taken."

Once Stephen had paid for two pieces of fruit, he said goodbye.

"But please do let us know any news of meetings," Amon called.

"That's one really nice adult," Benjamin said, smacking his lips.

Amon grabbed the fruit from his friend's hand and snitched a bite.

"Hey!" Benjamin cried. "I thought you were too old to accept gifts."

"I am." Amon sucked on the sweet juice of the fruit. "But I'm not too old to steal it from a friend."

They both laughed, and Tamar too. Amon handed back the rest of the fruit and they continued up the street.

Saul was on the roof of his house with a bucket. A strong smell floated through the air, stinging the nostrils of the three friends.

"What is that smell?" Tamar pinched her nose closed.

"Oh, hello, friends." Saul looked down at them.

Amon and Benjamin both yelled, "Hello, Saul."

"It's just pitch," Benjamin said to Tamar, as though it was something everyone should know. "We all use it on our roofs to keep water out of our houses."

"I'm a shepherd girl, remember? We don't *have* roofs." She looked upward and said, "Hello, Saul."

Saul wiped his hands on a cloth and climbed down a ladder. "What brings a young man and his friends to my house on such a pleasant day?"

Amon waited until Saul was all the way down. "We have come to talk to you about the events of yesterday," he said. "And about what we are to do next."

Saul led them inside and poured water into four clay mugs, then passed them out. Amon was just taking a sip when Saul said, "Yes, a most disgusting thing, isn't it?"

Three heads jerked up at once and stared at Saul. Amon made eye contact with Tamar and Benjamin, and shook his head slightly, warning them not to say anything. "Well," Amon said slowly, "that's why we came here. To get your opinion."

"It's hardly opinion," Saul snapped. "The Torah warns us about false prophets, and it's just shameful that some people in Jerusalem are claiming this . . . this . . . Jesus . . . is the Messiah!"

As Saul paced, glaring his angry thoughts at the floor, Amon spoke carefully. "So, you are of the opinion that Jesus is *not* the Messiah?"

"Of course. It's a fact, just as I've told you before. He is a false prophet who caused his own death by believing his own lies."

Amon realized he had thought exactly the same thing until he saw Jesus risen from the dead. Hadn't Saul also seen the error of his thinking? Obviously not, Amon decided. "It seems there are many in the city who find the story to be true—that Jesus truly is the Messiah."

Anger filled Saul's face. "Do not speak such words in this house!" he snarled, and Amon took a step back. "I will not hear of false gods, no matter who is speaking."

"I—I only came to hear your thoughts." Amon bowed his head. "I did not mean to bring anger into your home."

Saul let out a deep breath. "Forgive me, my friend. The anger was already here, hiding behind my sacks of flour. You merely invited it out into the open. However," he said, now with a smile, "I have swept it back where it belongs and shall keep it there."

Amon tried to smile, then asked what plans Saul had for the coming spring, and what questions of the law he had been working on. Saul told them what he was planning to plant, and about three parchments he'd been reading from three rabbis.

"But lately," he said in conclusion, "my work with the Sanhedrin has kept me very busy. It seems there are many heretics in the city these days, and I believe the elders will soon take action against them."

"You mean, heretics like those who believe Je— those men who worship that carpenter's son as the Messiah?"

Saul smirked. "Yes, that's exactly what I mean. And the Sanhedrin surely cannot allow it to continue for much longer."

Amon took a step toward the door. "I think it is time for us to go home. We will talk more of this when we meet again." They all thanked Saul for the water and headed back toward Amon's house.

"Sooo, now what?" Tamar asked as she and Benjamin tried to keep up with Amon.

Amon was silent for several moments. "I think we now have a mission."

"A mission?" Benjamin asked.

Tamar finally pulled alongside Amon. "What sort of mission?"

Amon stopped, spun around, and looked at his two friends. "This mission: We will not stop, and we shall not rest, until Saul of Tarsus falls on his knees and worships Jesus of Nazareth as his Messiah!"

✦ ✦ ✦

The trouble is most people—at least in the western world—have at least *heard* of Jesus. And the vast majority even have some idea of what he did. Or at least what those crazy Christians say he did. But their knowledge of Jesus is incomplete and tends to be full of assumptions. Like Saul, they think they know things about Jesus, but the things they know aren't true.

People have lots of good reasons to *not* believe in Jesus—the world is full of self-declared saviors who just want power over others, or want money, or need to be famous, so try to trick or force people into following them. To many, just as to Saul, Jesus sounds like just one more trickster trying build an audience.

But like Amon and his friends, you and I know the truth. How can we help others see that truth, the truth that Jesus really is God, the Savior, the Messiah?

Chapter Four

# Pentecost

A little more than a week later, everything was different.

Almost all the apostles had moved out of the upper room of Amon's house and into a much larger space, because so many people came to them for advice and judgment that the house had started to sag. Bartholomew remained, along with Tamar, which Amon was surprised to discover made him exceedingly happy. Out in the streets, people were talking about Jesus as the Messiah, not in timid and scared ways like before but with boldness and courage, talking out in the open and not caring who heard them. And the city was full of travelers as Jews gathered for Pentecost, the harvest festival.

As with all the festivals, the streets of Jerusalem were crowded, smelly, and loud during Pentecost. People came from as far away as Egypt, Rome, and Pamphylia. Amon could speak Greek, Hebrew, Aramaic, Persian, and Latin, but as he pushed through the masses of people, he heard many languages he couldn't even identify. Simply trying to get home through the congestion, he pulled Tamar by the hand so they wouldn't get separated, and she in turn grasped the hand of Benjamin. Amon's mother had sent them out before sunrise to buy some of the first of the wheat harvest, but so many people wanted wheat that they'd had to go to the other end of the city to find any.

"I went to see Gamaliel last night," Amon yelled.

Passing between a mob trying to buy the last of the sacrificial doves, a mob trying to rent the last room available in Jerusalem, and a mob arguing about the power of the chief priest, Tamar couldn't hear him. "You did what?"

"I said I talked to Gamaliel last night. About Saul."

"What did he say?"

"He's worried Saul has let his zeal for the law overrule his compassion for people."

From the end of the train, Benjamin yelled, "What are you talking about?"

Tamar looked at the screaming crowds, shook her head, and yelled, "I'll tell you later!"

Finally they burst through the door of the house and collapsed around the table. "Your wheat, Mother," Amon panted, holding out a full bag.

Tabitha took the bag and frowned. "I don't believe this will be enough. I'll need a half-weight more."

Amon stared at his mother, his mouth hanging open, but then she laughed. "A joke only," she said. "This will be fine." She returned to her baking.

The three friends slurped up a drink of water from a thing called a "pipe" sticking out from the wall—a Roman invention Amon had adapted to make his mother's life easier. Then they ran up the stairs to the upper room. Since the apostles had moved out, the family had returned their own belongings to the room, including Amon's wicker chest holding all his tools for writing, scientific research, and inventing.

Amon pulled out his tablet. "All we need to do," he said, while digging in the chest for his stylus, "is make a logical diagram of all the prophesies about the Messiah." He found the stylus—a length of bone that was carved to a point at one end and flat at the other—and began erasing. The tablet was a board of apple wood as long as Amon's forearm. It narrowed down to a handle at one end and was covered in a thick layer of beeswax. With the flat end of the stylus, he smoothed out the wax from the last time he'd used the tablet.

"Don't you think Saul already knows the prophecies?" Tamar asked.

"Of course. He has simply never put them all together in his mind correctly. We will help him do that."

Tamar looked doubtful, but Amon finished smoothing the wax, then sat on the table with his feet on the bench, holding the tablet in one hand and the stylus in the other, waiting.

Benjamin's mouth opened, but it was Jotham's voice Amon heard, coming up from below. "Amon, your mother and I are taking a special order to the temple for morning prayers. Watch your brothers."

Amon frowned to his friends, but yelled down the stairs, "Yes, Father." He heard the door below close, then turned to his friends. "Now, give me prophesies."

"I think it would be Jehovah's words to Abraham," Benjamin said. "'I will bless those who bless you, and whoever curses you I will curse; and all peoples on earth will be blessed through you.'"

"Very good, Benjamin," Amon said as he began writing. "You have learned much from your rabbi. Give me another." Amon wrote down several more passages from the Torah which clearly said that the Messiah would descend from Abraham through David. He ran out of room on his apple tablet, so pulled out his sycamore tablet, which was made of two boards covered in wax and hinged together like a book. "What else?"

Tabitha spoke up. "'Therefore the Lord himself will give you a sign: The virgin will conceive and give birth to a son, and will call him Immanuel.'"

"Excellent." Amon etched the verse in the wax. "From our father Isaiah."

"'But you, Bethlehem Ephrathah,'" Benjamin said, "'though you are small among the clans of Judah, out of you will come for me one who will be ruler over Israel, whose origins are from of old, from ancient times.'"

Twice as they worked, Amon went downstairs to check on his brothers. When they were done an hour later, the three friends had collected over fifty prophesies of the Messiah from the Torah. "And every one of these was fulfilled by the birth, life, death, and resurrection of Jesus." Amon scanned the verses that covered four tablets and a piece of parchment. "When Saul sees this, he'll *have* to believe."

"Tamar doesn't think so," Benjamin said.

Amon looked at him, then at Tamar, then back to Benjamin. "What do you mean?"

Benjamin in turn looked at Tamar, who hesitated. "I just think Saul already knows all of this." She waved her hand across the tablets. "I don't think it's his head that doesn't believe, I think it's his heart."

Amon scoffed and picked up the stack of tablets. "Saul and I are both logical thinkers. We do not act on emotion, but on facts and reason. Once he sees this evidence, he will understand and change his mind."

Tamar was about to say something when Amon's brother Jadon came running up the stairs. "Amon! Amon! Come quick. Peter has called for an assembly."

"What is it you say?"

"Peter has sent word through the streets—he has called an assembly. He wants all believers to meet at the house of Omar the spice merchant. Come on!"

Amon glanced at the others. Leaving the tablets, they scurried down the stairs. His parents still weren't home, so Amon took both of his brothers by the hand and headed out into the chaos with Tamar and Benjamin close behind.

It took twenty minutes of pushing and shoving—and another five to find Uri once when his hand slipped out of Amon's—but finally they arrived safely at the house of Omar. It was huge, having a large open court with a pool and tables and benches outside, and tapestries and tables of food inside. All the doors and windows to the house were open, and Amon could see people standing around and talking.

"There must be a hundred people here," Tamar said, gawking.

Amon did a quick estimate in his head. "More than that, I think."

"Father, Mother!" Uri screeched in delight and ran to his parents.

"How did you know to come here?" Amon's father asked, even as Uri was still pulling at him.

Amon was relieved to be free of his brother-watching duties. "Jadon heard the call. And you?"

"I'm not sure—the word just spread from street to street."

Amon saw Stephen inside one window of the house, and James the brother of Jesus talking with some women. The apostles Philip and James the Younger were also in the house, as was Barnabas, a trusted friend to many. Amon was sure the other apostles were somewhere inside as well.

At the edge of the courtyard, off by himself near some bushes, lurked Nicodemus, one of the rulers of the Jews and a member of the Sanhedrin. Was he trying to hide, or at least not be noticed? Amon elbowed his father, then pointed.

"Ah yes, Nicodemus," Amon's father said. "I heard that he and Joseph of Arimathea provided a wealth of spices and a tomb for Jesus. I wonder what he's doing here."

Before Amon could respond, a man's voice shouted, "Shalom. Shalom, my friends."

Everyone quieted down, then Amon saw that the call came from Peter, inside the house but visible through the open windows and doors.

"Please, everyone," Peter said, sweeping his arms across the assembly, "gather in close."

The crowd edged forward—all except Nicodemus—squeezing into the house as best they could. Amon's family and many others were still outside but could see and hear quite easily.

"My friends," Peter said when all were quiet, "I have invited you here for no other reason than to pray together. There is a burning in my soul, a desperate longing to see and touch God's Spirit, and to do so with all those who believe. This, I think, must become a pattern for us, to meet together to seek his face. Come now, pray with me."

Peter began to pray, but soon Bartholomew took over, then James and many others. Jadon and Uri grew restless, but Tabitha held a firm hand on their shoulders keeping them still.

Amon wondered how long the prayers would go on. His father's sheep needed to be watered and . . .

Suddenly a strange sound filled the air.

All praying stopped.

All movement stopped.

Puzzled, people looked around as if trying to locate the sound that seemed to come from all around.

*It sounds like a windstorm*, Amon thought, *but the trees do not move*.

The noise grew louder until many of the children, and even some adults, covered their ears. It sounded exactly as if they were inside the mightiest windstorm ever to hit Jerusalem.

But the air was still.

Suddenly, the house was on fire.

But no, not the house, Amon realized, the *people*!

Everywhere he turned, tongues of fire were dancing on the head of each woman, man, and child. Slowly he rolled his eyes back and saw the edges of a flame on his own head. Before he could even think more about this, a strange sensation flooded his body. His skin tingled, and his lungs filled with ticklish air, even as his whole being seemed to inflate with a wondrous sense of joy.

He checked to see if his feet were still on the ground and was surprised to see them firmly planted on the courtyard stones.

And then he began shouting.

He couldn't help himself. The words came pouring out of his mouth as if the words themselves were alive and had to escape out into the open.

"Praise God from whom all blessings flow," he yelled. "Hear, O Israel: The LORD our God is one LORD."

On and on it went, the words flowing like rain in a storm. And not just Amon, but every child, man, and woman inside and outside the house, lifting endless praises to God in a constant uproar.

A different noise coming from the street drew Amon's attention. From all directions, attracted by the noise, filling the streets and surrounding the courtyard, were hundreds of other people, some who lived in the city, others visiting from elsewhere.

One man ran up to Amon in the courtyard and shouted in his face, "What is going on here, friend? What is happening?"

Amon tried to answer over the din of other people asking the same question. "It is the Holy Spirit of God," Amon yelled with a grin. "God himself has come to each and every believer!"

The man looked around, confused. "I am not from this place. Is this what usually happens here?"

Amon laughed. "No, it has only just happened today. And where are you from, my friend?"

The man looked puzzled. "You speak to me in my language, yet you do not know that I come from Cappadocia?"

Amon frowned. "I am speaking to you in Aramaic. I do not know Cappadocian."

The man stared, then burst out laughing. "You just said that perfectly in my language."

Amon stared back, then started to speak. As soon as he did, he realized the words coming out of his mouth were not Aramaic—and he didn't know *what* they were. He saw many other people, including his parents and brothers, also appeared confused.

His father was just then saying something to another man. The words his father spoke sounded foreign to Amon's ears, and yet he understood them.

"What is this that is happening?" the Cappadocian man said, looking back and forth across the crowd. "What does all of this mean?"

Amon suddenly understood and grinned. "It is a miracle of our God," he said, though his mouth felt funny pronouncing the unfamiliar words.

He heard men laughing and looked out toward the crowd in the street who were watching.

"These Jerusalem Jews," one of the laughing men yelled out. "They are all drunk—even the children!"

The crowd mocked the Jews again, and another man shouted, "This must be some new kind of religion that worships strong drink."

Amon felt a stab of pain in his chest and wondered how such a glorious day had suddenly turned so mean.

✦ ✦ ✦

It's easy to think of God as the Father living in heaven, far beyond our ability to see or hear him, distant and unreachable other than through his word. This is what we call the "transcendent" God, the God of glory and power and majesty, that we can know only from a great distance. We know this God from the words he spoke to just a small number of people over the centuries. This is the only God most humans knew for thousands of years.

We can also think of God as the Son, living here on earth in a flesh-and-blood body two thousand years ago, helping us understand who God the Father is and teaching us by example how to live unselfish lives and care about others. This is what we call the "immanent" God—"Emmanuel," God with us. This is also the God who demonstrated just how far he's willing to go to save us, even to the point of dying a cruel, unjust death on a cross. We know this God from the stories of him that were written down and passed down from the many people who knew him personally.

But we can also think of God as the Spirit living inside us, helping us through the joys and sorrows of life, guiding us in decisions, working through us, even demonstrating his power through us. This is what we call the "indwelling" God, the God of comfort, who communes with us moment by moment, the God who first filled believers on the day of Pentecost a short time after Jesus ascended to heaven. We know this God through the thousand ways we feel him inside us, prompting and prodding us, giving us strength and wisdom we didn't know we had, doing the impossible in and through us.

Of course, in reality there is only one God. But in a mystery that people still debate today, he shows himself to us in three distinct ways: transcendent (distant and mighty), immanent (here with us), and indwelling (inside us). All three are available to all believers all the time.

That, of course, includes you and me.

## Chapter Five

# Siloam

Most of the people in the courtyard and house were now quiet as the group of men in the street pointed and laughed at them.

"Please, let us have some of this liquid god you are drinking," one of them shouted.

Anger built inside Amon's chest, but then another voice came from behind him.

"My friends," Peter said, coming out of the house with the other eleven apostles. "Fellow Jews and all of you who live in Jerusalem, let me explain this to you; listen carefully to what I say." Peter climbed atop a stone table and the crowd quieted. "These people are not drunk, as you suppose. It's only nine in the morning! No, this is what was spoken by the prophet Joel: 'In the last days, God says, I will pour out my Spirit on all people. Your sons and daughters will prophesy, your young men will see visions, your old men will dream dreams. Even on my servants, both men and women . . .'"

Amon grinned as Peter preached to the crowd. Some of the men who had been laughing now listened closely. Others just waved their hand at Peter in disgust and walked away.

"Everyone who calls on the name of the Lord," Peter shouted, "will be saved. Fellow Israelites, listen to this: Jesus of Nazareth was a man accredited by God to you by miracles, wonders and signs, which God did among you through him, as you yourselves know. This man was handed over to you by God's deliberate plan and foreknowledge; and you, with the help of wicked men, put him to death by nailing him to the cross. But God raised him from the dead!"

For a moment, Amon felt a stab of pain in his heart. He himself had been one of those calling for the punishment of Jesus before his death. He thought about all that had happened since then and about his own conversion.

Peter finished his sermon. "Therefore let all Israel be assured of this: God has made this Jesus, whom you crucified, both Lord and Messiah." Peter still stood atop the table, breathing hard.

A woman in the crowd called out to the apostles, "Brothers, what shall we do?"

Peter jumped on the question as if he'd been waiting for it. "Repent and be baptized, every one of you, in the name of Jesus Christ for the forgiveness of your sins. And you will receive the gift of the Holy Spirit. The promise is for you and your children and for all who are far off—for all whom the Lord our God will call."

Chaos erupted again as the people in the crowd pushed forward, begging to be baptized. When Amon saw how many were in the streets, he began to panic. How could they baptize all these people in Omar's tiny pool?

But Peter called for anyone wanting to follow Jesus to meet the disciples at the Pool of Siloam. As he climbed down from the table, Peter grabbed Amon by his cloak. "Come with us and keep a tally."

Amon gulped at the task he'd been given, but quickly formed a plan. "Benjamin!" he shouted to his friend, who a few moments before had been speaking in some strange language. "We must go to your house and gather all the tablets we can find."

Benjamin followed Amon without arguing. The two ran through the crowded streets, up back alleys, and even splashed across one small pond of water. They jumped over carts, slid under camels, and ran through the arena of the empty Hippodrome until at last they jumped over the low fence around Benjamin's house.

His parents were cleaning some animal hides and looked up. "Greetings, Amon." His father waved with the bloody knife he was using. "Benjamin, what's happening?"

The two friends slammed through the door as Benjamin called over his shoulder, "Amon and I are working on a project."

As they ran through the house, Benjamin collected several tablets and stacked them in Amon's arms. Then they ran back out the front door.

Benjamin's mother looked up as Amon ran by. "I trust you will keep him out of trouble as always."

"On my honor as a man of God," Amon answered as he pushed through the gate.

The Pool of Siloam sat inside the walls of Jerusalem in the southeast corner of Jerusalem. It had been built by King Hezekiah many years before and provided water for all the city. It was cut out of the limestone and surrounded by steps on three sides. By the time Amon and Benjamin arrived, out of breath, the entire area was already packed with people.

Then the crowd parted as Peter and the other eleven apostles approached. Tamar was with her father to help organize the people. Each of the twelve took up a position on the bottom step around the pool, about waist deep in the water. John, Matthew, and Andrew were directly in front of Amon. Just as Peter helped the first woman step into the water, Amon turned to Benjamin and, still panting, said,

"Now, please help me. Watch the six apostles on the other side of the pool and make a mark for each person they baptize. I'll do the six on this side."

For the rest of the morning and far into the afternoon, the apostles baptized one person after another in what seemed like an endless stream. Every so often the apostles would take a bite of bread or a handful of grapes to keep their strength up. Toward the end, they all were moving much more slowly, and their voices were raspy. *I hope they can survive this*, Amon thought.

Throughout the day, Amon watched for Nicodemus, wondering if he had been a part of the miracle, but he couldn't find the old Pharisee in the crowd. When the last person seeking Jesus had been baptized, all twelve apostles collapsed onto the steps, praising God for this miracle.

Tamar came and sat with Amon and Benjamin, also worn out from the hours of work in the sun. She, Amon, and Benjamin moved down a few steps, took off their sandals, and soaked their feet in the water.

From where he lay across the steps like a wet blanket, Peter called to Amon in a ragged voice. "How many?" he asked. "How many were baptized today?"

All six tablets were filled with marks, but the boys had grouped them in hundreds. A few minutes later Amon had them added up. "Over three thousand."

Now the apostles sat up, and some jumped to their feet. "Three *thousand*?" Peter whooped. Then he and all the others danced and praised God.

Stephen arrived carrying a cloth bag full of bread and cheese and began passing it out to the apostles. "I saw that you missed the midday meal," he said. When the Twelve had been fed, he came and sat next to Amon and his friends.

"You three worked hard too," he said with a smile, handing them each a piece of cheese. He then sat at the edge of the water and tore off chunks of bread for each. "You have each served Jesus well today."

All three looked at him in surprise.

"What?" he answered their looks. "You don't think supporting the apostles is serving Jesus?"

Amon turned to his friends, then back to Stephen. He swallowed the bite he'd been chewing. "I guess I didn't think of it like that."

"Whatever you do to further the kingdom of heaven is ministry, my friend. So whatever you do, do it boldly and without fear."

Amon remembered the wounds he'd seen on the hands and feet of Jesus and thought about how much the Lord suffered as the price of every person's sins. "I will."

"Good." Stephen stretched and yawned. "Now I just have one last question—have you been baptized?"

"Yes, we all have," Amon answered.

Stephen shook his head. "Well, I do not think it was done correctly."

"What?" Amon wondered if he had misunderstood the process.

"No, no, no, I'm sure of it," Stephen said. "We need to do it again." And with that, Stephen pushed Amon, then Benjamin, then Tabitha into the water.

At first the three screamed and sputtered, splashing about as they got over the shock of it. But soon they had organized revenge and pulled Stephen into the water.

Then most of the twelve apostles joined in, which seemed a perfect way to celebrate the miracles of the day.

When they had all climbed back up on the steps, laughing and exhausted, it was Tamar's father Bartholomew who smiled at Stephen and said, "You know, that's exactly the kind of thing Jesus would have done. He was always so full of joy."

"He still is, my friend," Stephen answered.

Bartholomew grinned. "Yes, of course. I wasn't implying he's still dead, only that we don't see him quite as easily now as when he walked among us."

~

The next day, Amon, Benjamin, and Tamar headed toward Saul's house, carrying Amon's tablets. They were shouldering their way through the fish market. Fish sellers yelled about their catches, fish buyers yelled out offers to buy, and everyone else yelled just because everyone was yelling.

"Turn here," Amon tried to say to the two friends behind him. They couldn't hear at all but understood where he was pointing. Three streets over, it was still crowded but much quieter.

"I should have known better than to try to get through the fish market at this time of day," Amon said. It was always late afternoon by the time a fish was caught in the Sea of Galilee to the north, salted and preserved, then carried all the way to Jerusalem.

"What are you going to say to Saul?" Tamar asked.

Amon thought all the way to the end of the block before answering. "I will act as if I am simply trying to solve a puzzle. Saul and I have had arguments like that all our lives. Well, at least for the last five years. We often debate a thing as if we actually believe it, simply to find the truth." Having spent some time with Saul themselves while Amon crawled through tunnels beneath the temple to save his father, Tamar and Benjamin knew that Saul was as smart as Amon, having traveled through many countries with his father, who was a Roman citizen as well as a Jew.

They arrived at Saul's door and Amon knocked.

The door flew open. Saul's eyes glared and his mouth twisted into a snarl. "What?"

Amon stepped back. "I—I have come for a small debate—"

Saul went back in the house, leaving the door open. "I have no time for debates," he growled.

Amon stared as Saul disappeared into the house. He had never seen his friend this angry before. He stepped inside slowly, followed by the others. "What has you so troubled, my friend?"

Saul paced back and forth across the room. "Did you not hear?" he spat. "Are you the only one in Jerusalem deaf to the cries?"

Amon swallowed hard, afraid he knew what Saul was talking about. "Hear what? What cries?"

"There was a riot yesterday," Saul screamed, then lunged at Amon as if it was the young man's fault. "Thousands of people screaming 'Jesus is the Messiah!'"

Amon backed up against the wall, Saul's face only inches from his own. "I . . . I know there was a celebration . . ."

"It is disgusting," Saul ranted as he returned to pacing. "Who do these people think they are? Who do they think this *Jesus* was? Why can't they see he was an imposter, just like all the others?"

In the corner, beside the now closed door, Tamar and Benjamin stood close together, their eyes wide, holding hands and watching the scene.

Amon was silent, and finally Saul began calming down. "Forgive me, my friend," he said more quietly, but still full of anger. "This new cult has me concerned for all Jews. It is not your fault."

Amon took a deep breath. "Perhaps we should talk about it, friend?"

Saul paced slower now and shook his head. "No, no. I have heard all their lies and arguments. There is nothing to their story." He stopped suddenly and stared straight at Amon. "Do you know that some of them are even claiming this Jesus fulfills all the prophecies of the Torah?"

Automatically, Amon's eyes darted to the tablets held by Benjamin and Tamar, up to Tamar's eyes, then back to Saul. "Uh, yes, I have heard that argument."

Saul got a funny look on his face, then stepped a little closer, his eyes locked on Amon's.

"Why did you come here today?"

Amon gulped. "Just for a small debate on a minor topic, like we always do."

Saul took a step closer. "You have never before brought an audience for one of our debates." He pointed at Tamar and Benjamin. In one swift motion Saul grabbed Amon by the front of his tunic and slammed him against the hard stone wall. His eyes glared, his nostrils flared, and he breathed hard and fast. He leaned close and whispered, "Amon? You are not one of those followers of Jesus, are you?"

✦ ✦ ✦

I wonder why baptism is so important for Christians. Jesus was baptized, of course, and said we should "make disciples of all nations, baptizing them in the name of the Father and of the Son and of the Holy Spirit" (Matt. 28:19).

But why? Why is it so important?

First, I don't think it's magical—there's nothing special about the water or the words that somehow takes away selfish thoughts or our ability to act sinfully.

Second, it's not *required* for salvation. Jesus obviously felt it was important, but I don't see anywhere in the Bible that baptism is a requirement of salvation. In fact, Jesus said to the thief hanging on the cross next to him, "Today you will be with me in paradise" (Luke 23:43). Obviously the man did not have time to be baptized before he died.

Third, it's not just symbolic. Yes, there is a definite benefit to proclaiming your faith to other believers, announcing to them that you have accepted Jesus as your Lord and Savior. But I think there's something more important than that.

The real *why*, the real power of baptism, is that it forces us to make a decision. It's too easy to simply say, "I've accepted Jesus." Those are words we can speak without really meaning them. But to be baptized, I have to make a conscious decision to allow another person to dunk me into (or sprinkle or pour on) the water, getting me wet and somewhat uncomfortable in front of others. But more than that, I have to decide to let my self-sufficient ego publicly admit to others that I'm submitting to a higher authority. I'm giving up power over myself.

A decision. That's the real power of baptism.

Over three thousand people made that decision after hearing Peter preach at Pentecost.

And every one of us gets to show others we've made that same decision by being baptized.

Chapter Six

# Signs & Wonders

Amon couldn't stop the worms from squiggling inside his stomach, and his head hurt where it had hit the wall. Drops of sweat broke out across his forehead and nose. And he couldn't make his face stop wrinkling up in fear.

"You're not, are you?" Saul hissed, this time louder, and it sounded very much like a threat instead of the sincere concern of a friend.

He swallowed and forced his mouth to speak. "Have I said anything to make you think I am?"

Saul continued to stare into Amon's soul, and it felt to the younger man as if his insides were being torn to pieces. Finally Saul's shoulders relaxed, he let out a long breath, released Amon, and stepped back. "Forgive me, my friend," he said, now putting his hand on Amon's shoulder. "The events of the last few weeks have made me suspicious of even my closest companions."

Amon stepped closer to the door as Saul paced the room more slowly and thoughtfully. "Perhaps—perhaps we will come back another day for our debate."

Saul drew another deep breath and seemed to be fully himself now. "That might be best." He looked to Tamar and Benjamin as well. "There is much on my mind these days, and I'm afraid I would not be much of a sparring partner right now." Then his head jerked up, suddenly remembering. "Besides," he said, quickly gathering his cloak and walking stick, "I almost forgot about the Sanhedrin."

Amon knew that Saul often worked for the ruling body of the Jews, and that they met almost every day except the Sabbath. Considering the recent events in Jerusalem, they'd have much to discuss.

"We have had many conversations about the Jesus problem in the Sanhedrin." Saul pulled the door open and let them out.

The bright sunlight made Amon squint, and he held the tablets against his chest so Saul couldn't see them.

Saul kept talking as he pulled the door closed. "If it continues, we will soon need to take action to squash this movement before it leads astray any more weak-minded Jews."

Amon tried to smile at his friend and nodded slightly. "Good fortune," he said, then turned and walked the opposite direction. *Why did I say such a thing?* he wondered. *Saul should have bad fortune if he's going to work against The Way of Jesus!*

"Now what?" Tamar asked when they had turned a corner and collapsed in the shade.

Amon looked at her as he leaned against the building. "You are kind not to ridicule me."

"Why would I ridicule you?"

"Because you were right, and I was wrong. I was very, very wrong. About Saul listening, I mean."

Benjamin said, "You weren't wrong. Saul is wrong. That he thinks with his anger instead of his mind is not your fault."

"Maybe, but I misjudged him. I thought his mind, not his emotion, was in control of his thoughts."

Tamar sighed. "Perhaps there are times when all of us think with our emotions instead of our minds. Remember, you didn't believe the facts about Jesus for a long time."

"Fair point," Amon conceded.

"Either way," Benjamin said, "our mission has failed."

"Not yet, it hasn't. That was only the first battle. We will try as many times as it takes to make Saul see the truth."

Over the next several days, the Jesus movement grew. Omar the spice merchant opened his house and property to any believers who didn't have a home of their own. "Take whatever you need," he said over and over to all the believers. Others did the same, so that those who had more were taking care of those who had less, sharing their homes and food and clothes—whatever was needed. Amon's father also invited in all who were needy, and soon their upper floor was once again filled with people. His mother, meanwhile, set to work making clothes for as many poor widows as she could.

Reports came in continually that the apostles were performing signs and wonders in the name of Jesus, though Amon hadn't witnessed any.

And every day, groups of believers gathered together to teach and discuss the ways of Jesus, sometimes in their homes over a meal, sometimes on a street corner, often in the temple itself. Not knowing what else to call themselves, they soon began referring to this collection of believers as "The Way," since Jesus had referred to himself as "the way and the truth and the life."

One morning Amon looked out over the city just as a small caravan approached the gates. He recognized it instantly, then ran through the streets, grabbing Benjamin along the way.

"What is it?" his friend asked.

"My glass merchant has finally returned," Amon hollered. They made their way through the gates in the city wall and out to the Kidron Valley, then worked through the line of camels. About two thirds of the way back, Amon found the glass merchant and was happy to hear that the man had brought Amon's full order. The glass was wrapped in many layers of cloth and leather. Amon paid him, then he and Benjamin carried the packages—which each seemed to weigh as much as a horse—up the hill to the Roman Praetorium. The rough ropes securing the packages cut deeper into Amon's flesh with every step. Sweat dripped from his nose, and his chest was heaving for air by the time they reached the palace.

"We can put them here." Amon set his down in a small room on the outside of the mansion. He stopped to catch his breath. "No one would dare steal anything from the Roman palace." He wiped his face on his sleeve. "Please tell my parents I will be working here the rest of the day."

"I'll see you later then." Benjamin headed for home, giving Amon a slap on the shoulder as he passed.

Amon had been hired by the governor, Pontius Pilate, to install "rocks you can see through" in all the windows of his great throne room, in exchange for Pilate letting Amon's father live. Amon had already installed one of his other inventions—a wind machine over Pilate's bed—then had finished about two-thirds of the window job when he ran out of glass. The long, tall throne room was empty since Pilate was not in the city, so Amon pulled out a ladder he had built just for this job and spent the day carrying panes of glass high up to the open windows near the top.

Sometime in midafternoon, Amon looked down and saw the head of a small child peeking through the grand doorway to the hall. "Hello, is there something you need?"

The boy looked up. "Dancin' camels, this place is *huge*!"

Amon recognized the boy as his brother Jadon and laughed. "Yes, that it is. I'll be right down." He finished installing the pane he was working on, then descended the ladder. "Is that food I see in your hand?"

Jadon stopped gawking at the room as he remembered why he was there. "Oh, yes. Mother thought you would need some lunch."

Amon sat on the stone floor and scarfed down the meat, olives, and bread.

Jadon sat next to him, still scanning the hall. "Can I climb the ladder?"

"No."

"Why not?"

"You're too young, it's too tall, and I'm too busy."

"It's no fair! You always get to do the fun things."

Amon swallowed a drink of water. "You have not yet figured out the secret about being a little brother."

"What secret?"

"Mother and Father make all their mistakes on me, so life is much easier for you."

"Really? Mother and Father makes mistakes?"

Amon answered around the olive in his mouth. "Yesh, menny." He swallowed. "For years I had to go to bed much earlier than my friends, but you get to stay up until dark every night. So you see, your life is easier because I did all the work of training them."

Jadon smirked. "Okay, I get it. But I'd still like to climb the ladder."

"Someday you will."

Amon finished his lunch, thanked his brother, then worked late into the night. The job was almost complete, but the torches were failing, and he was so tired he felt it would be dangerous to climb the tall ladder even one more time. He decided to stop after he heard the late-night shift change of the sentries outside. With his tools back in the storeroom, he dragged himself home and was asleep almost before he got to his bed.

~

After lunch the next day, Amon headed to the temple with Peter and John for the afternoon prayer time. Peter had made it clear that he would still be attending synagogue, still saying his prayers, and still observing the Sabbath. "If Jesus taught at synagogue and kept Sabbath," Peter kept telling everyone, "why wouldn't we?"

As they entered through the Beautiful Gate, a lame man was being carried in by friends so that he might beg for donations. When they passed, the lame man called out, begging Peter and John for some money. Peter stopped abruptly and spoke to the man as easily as if he'd just asked for directions to the nearest bread merchant. "Silver or gold I do not have, but what I do have I give you. In the name of Jesus Christ of Nazareth, walk."

"And the man just jumped up and started leaping around the courtyard!" Amon told his parents at dinner that night. "It was old Silas. You know, the man lame from birth."

Jotham stopped eating and looked at his son. "Silas? The truth you tell!"

"And nothing but the truth."

"Forty isn't so old," Amon's mother said.

"Forty is waaay old," Jadon said.

Amon's father shook his head. "I've been giving Old Silas—I mean, Silas—alms as long as I can remember."

"And then what?" Tabitha urged Amon on.

"Well"—he took another bite of stew—"you know Peter. He couldn't pass up an opportunity to preach."

"In the temple?" Tabitha gasped, and suddenly started coughing.

"Yes," Amon said. "Right there at Solomon's Colonnade."

"Anything else?" Amon's father asked as he patted his wife's back.

"Nope. A lot of people came to Jesus, Peter and John were arrested, then I came home."

"Wait. What?" Tabitha coughed. "Peter and John were *arrested*?"

Amon nodded as he took the last bite of his stew.

Tabitha and Jotham looked at each other, then at their son, and said at the same time, "Tell us!"

Amon dished another helping of stew. "Tell you what? They were arrested, that is all there is to it."

"Are you not concerned?" Amon's father asked.

Amon went back to eating. "Nope. Jehovah will take care of them."

"How many?" Jotham asked, wheezing just a bit. "How many came to Jesus?"

Amon shrugged. "I don't know, a couple thousand."

~

The next morning Amon and his father went to listen as Peter and John were brought before the Sanhedrin. After ritual baths, they passed through the gates that only Jews could pass, walked through the Court of Women with Solomon's Colonnade along one side, then into the Court of Prayers, where only Jewish men were allowed. Off to the left side was the Chamber of Hewn Stone where the seventy-one members of the Sanhedrin met. Those not members of the Sanhedrin, like Amon and his father, weren't allowed into the chamber but stood outside the doors, listening.

Several other cases were discussed and decided, then Peter and John were brought out. Annas, the high priest, asked many questions, as did other judges, including Saul. Then Peter said, "If we are being called to account today for an act of kindness shown to a man who was lame and are being asked how he was healed, then know this, you and all the people of Israel: It is by the name of Jesus Christ of Nazareth, whom you crucified but whom God raised from the dead, that this man stands before you healed. Jesus is 'the stone you builders rejected, which has become the cornerstone.'"

"That's one of the prophecies I used," Amon whispered.

"What's that?" his father asked.

"I used that prophecy to help convince Saul of Jesus. At least, I was going to. It actually didn't work out so well."

Jotham and Amon turned back to the trial. Peter kept preaching about Jesus, and it was obvious the judges weren't sure what to do. Clearly the lame man standing before them had been healed, so they couldn't exactly argue that point. But neither could they accept that the man was healed in the name of Jesus. So they sent Peter and John out, shut the door, and talked about how to stop the spread of this new belief. When they called the two apostles back in, the high priest gave them a stern warning not to preach in the name of Jesus any longer.

John replied, "Which is right in God's eyes: to listen to you, or to him? You be the judges! As for us, we cannot help speaking about what we have seen and heard." Then they walked out into the sunshine of the temple courts and kept on preaching about Jesus.

"Saul was even angrier than when we talked to him last," Amon told Tamar and Benjamin as they walked slowly past the Hippodrome an hour later. Once in a while, they could catch a glimpse of the Roman chariots practicing, each pulled by a white horse inside the great coliseum. The speed of the chariots was fascinating, but the stories his father told of men and animals dying in the Hippodrome for the entertainment of the Romans sickened Amon. Herod the Great, he knew, had arranged and approved of such games simply to maintain his friendship with Rome.

"I don't understand why he's so blind to the truth," Benjamin said as they started up the hill.

"Who, Herod?" Amon asked, still thinking of his father's stories.

Benjamin looked at him like he was crazy. "No, not Herod, Saul!"

"Oh. I guess we are all blind to the truth sometimes. Maybe it's part of being human."

"Or maybe it's just part of being male," Tamar said with a smile. "We women are much better at discerning truth than you men."

Benjamin shouldered her in fun but answered seriously. "I believe that might often be true, but there were still many women screaming for Jesus to die when he carried his cross through the streets."

This gave Amon two thoughts: *I wish I hadn't been stuck in the tunnels under the temple while all that was happening* and *When did Benjamin start sounding so grown up?* But he asked, "How will we convince Saul about Jesus?"

Before the other two could answer, Leshem, their blind friend, came running up the street from the direction of the temple. "They healed me!" he yelled. "They healed me!" He ran up to just about everyone he met and looked them in the eyes as he told them of his miracle. Suddenly he grabbed Amon by the shoulders. "Did you hear? They *healed* me!"

Amon was shaken. He had known Leshem for years and had never seen him running or looking at *anything* before. "Who—who healed you?" he stuttered.

"Amon? Is that you?"

Instantly Amon realized his friend had never seen him before, and only knew him by his voice. "Yes, it's me. And this is Benjamin and Tamar. Who healed you?"

"Peter," he shouted. "John. James. Half of those Jesus followers were there," the young man laughed. "I've been blind since the day I was born," he said, "but now I can see! And I must tell everyone about it." He then ran to the next person up the street, proclaiming, "Praise Jesus, I'm healed!"

~

Over the next week there were many reports of the apostles healing people right in the middle of the temple courts, even in the Court of Women. Wherever the three friends went, people openly talked about the signs and miracles done in the name of Jesus, and they often heard that it was Stephen and other followers of Jesus who administered those miracles.

So many new people were added to The Way every day that it was difficult to keep track of them, and new believers kept pouring into the city—some rich, some poor, but all seeking others who knew Jesus. The apostles did their best to keep things organized and collected food and clothes from the established followers to give to those in need.

One afternoon while Jotham and Tabitha were out distributing food and clothing to widows, Tamar and Benjamin helped Amon water his father's sheep in the pens by their house. Every few minutes, someone—often a stranger—would come up to them asking for information, directions, or food for their family. "I think when we're done here," Amon said as another lost person headed in their direction, and as he poured water into a trough from an urn, "we should hike into the hills and get away from all this noise."

"And smells," Benjamin added.

"And smells," Amon agreed.

Tamar sighed a big sigh. "It *would* feel good to run out in the open air for a time."

"Running isn't quite what I was thinking." The other two turned to Amon and he answered their unasked question. "I was figuring it might be easier to think up a plan to convince Saul to change his mind if we weren't around all this noise and chaos and constant interruptions."

Benjamin shook his head slowly. "That's my friend. Never spend a moment in fun if you can spend it thinking hard about something."

Amon laughed and started to speak, but before any words came out, Stephen ran up to them, huffing and puffing. "I found you," he wheezed. "We've been looking everywhere." He grabbed Tamar's shoulders. "The Sanhedrin has arrested the apostles again, but this time *all* of them—including your father!"

✦ ✦ ✦

It's very difficult for me not to judge others.

When I read in the Bible of all the things the Sanhedrin did, as well as the other Pharisees and Sadducees and religious leaders, it makes me sick. They had people arrested and thrown in jail, ordered people severely beaten, and even had people killed.

How dare they! They must have been truly evil men to do such horrible things.

But then I wonder, am I really any different?

Most of the men of the Sanhedrin were simply trying to follow the laws God had given them, the laws of what we call the Old Testament that had been taught them since they were young.

Imagine if someone walked into your church or school or home and started shouting that you needed to forget everything you were ever taught and start following some guy you've never heard of. How would you react?

I think that's how the Sanhedrin reacted (though, like everything, it's more complicated than that).

So I've decided, to the best of my ability, to let God the Father worry about who needs to be punished or rebuked, to follow the example of God the Son, who simply loved on everyone he met even if that person was shunned by society, and to allow God the Spirit to help me not be ashamed of where God's love leads me.

Does that sound like a plan?

Chapter Seven

# Arrested

They were just jealous is all," Benjamin said, trying to keep up. "I watched them yesterday—every time Peter or James healed someone, the priests just got redder in the face."

Amon, Tamar, Stephen, and Benjamin pushed through the crowded streets as they headed toward the temple. There were many groups of three or four making music, entertainers balancing things on the ends of sticks, and so many vendors Amon couldn't keep track of all the different foods. Of course, there were also plenty of Roman soldiers about to keep the peace.

"Why would they be jealous?" Amon asked no one in particular.

Stephen answered. "The chief priest's whole family, in fact, most of the men in the Sanhedrin, see themselves as closer to God than anyone else. They can't figure out how the apostles are able to heal people when they themselves cannot."

A man lost his balance and stepped on Amon's foot.

"Ow!" Amon grabbed his foot and scowled at the man, who was walking away unaware. "Why are there so many people here?" he spat out, letting his pain control his words for a moment.

Stephen looked at him as if he had just asked what city they were in. "Because of the apostles, that's why. The word is spreading from town to town, and everyone is coming here to see for themselves."

Tamar had to step over a goat that suddenly appeared. "Especially the ones who are sick or injured."

"Well, they should all go home and wait for the apostles to come to *them*," Amon shouted. Instantly he was filled with shame for his selfish remark. "Or at least someone should organize the whole thing so there's not so much chaos."

Stephen stopped the group at a cheese vendor. "It may be a long day, and we may not have an opportunity to eat later." He bought them all a few bites of goat cheese. Since Stephen was eating, it was correct for Amon to accept the charity as well.

"Thank you," Tamar said.

"Yes, thank you," Benjamin added.

They both looked at Amon.

"Amon!" Tamar chastised. "Do you not thank one who has done you a kind deed?"

Amon looked up as he swallowed. "Oh—yes, of course. Thank you, Stephen."

Stephen licked the last of his cheese from his fingers. "And what has captured your thoughts?"

"What if Saul were to watch the apostles, to see how they heal people, and hear the words they preach? Surely he cannot deny the power of Jesus's name when he sees it in action."

Stephen shook his head slowly. "I do not believe Saul's mind will be changed by a simple demonstration. When someone continues to hold a belief even in the face of all logic and evidence, it is difficult to wake them to the truth. The lie becomes who they are."

Amon thought about this as they snaked through the crowds and finally entered the temple courts. "Maybe when Saul hears *why* the apostles were arrested, he'll realize that Jehovah is at work here."

Benjamin, being not of age, and Tamar, being female, waited in the Court of Women while Amon and Stephen entered the Court of Israel.

Amon talked to others in the crowd and went back to his friends with a report. "The apostles have been put in the jail for the night. They will face the Sanhedrin in the morning to answer the charges."

"What *are* the charges?" Tamar asked, her voice cracking and tears welling in her eyes.

"Failing to obey the orders of the Sanhedrin, I'm sure. They were told not to preach about Jesus, yet they did."

Tamar clenched her fists. "But Jesus *is* the Messiah!"

Amon cocked his head. "The Sanhedrin does not believe so." He stared at her, then said, "I'm sorry, that sounded very cruel. I only meant that the Sanhedrin does not share our beliefs. I'll go to Gamaliel and see if he has any ideas on how to help your father. Benjamin will stay with you, if you'd like."

Benjamin nodded, Tamar thanked them both, and Amon left the temple.

The climb up the hill was slow. All the streets in this part of town were lined with sick people on blankets and healthy people taking care of them. Every thirty paces or so, someone would grab his sleeve and ask, "Have you seen any of the apostles of Jesus? My son (or daughter or husband or wife) needs healing!" Each time, Amon would patiently explain that the apostles had been arrested, which caused such sorrow that by the time he reached the top of the hill, the street behind him was filled with the wails of the brokenhearted.

Finally he turned down the short side street that led to Gamaliel's villa. He passed under the archway of grapevines and entered the courtyard to find the elder pacing nervously across the stone pavement.

"Amon," he said when he saw his student, and rushed over to him. "I am so pleased to see you. Tell me the news."

They sat on a stone bench, and Amon reached for a handful of grapes. "I think you know all," he said, quenching his thirst with the fruit. "Our friends have been arrested again and are held in the public jail."

The white-haired man shook his head in despair. "We must do something to help them. Whether I agree with them or not . . . that is . . . ever since I watched what the high priest did to that Jesus . . . but I am at a loss as to what."

Amon stopped chomping and stared at him, one eyebrow raised. "You must stand and speak at their trial in the morning, of course!"

Gamaliel looked at him with sad eyes. "I have no words. What could I possibly say that would persuade the Sanhedrin?"

Amon closed his eyes and sat very still. "I shall pray to Jehovah tonight that wisdom will fill your mind by morning." Amon waited, then opened his eyes. "Now, have you found a solution for *my* problem?"

Gamaliel looked up at him. "Saul?" Off Amon's nod, the elder stood and paced again. "He is the other reason I walk these stones. I am afraid, *very* afraid, that my friend and former student has been led astray by the angel of darkness, and I do not know how to help him find his way back."

Amon hung his head in disappointment. "Then we will do that which we know to do and that which works more than any other thing—we will continue to pray to Jehovah." He stood to leave but stopped, his back still to the old teacher. "By the way, you have no *former* students. We will all follow and look up to you always, even after your body has finished its work here."

Gamaliel smiled his thanks at the words as Amon turned back, waved once, and took his leave.

There was much unrest in Amon's house that night. Many people of The Way stopped by to hear some words of wisdom from Jotham and Tabitha, and some even from Amon. But there were no answers to be given, and though much food and drink were consumed, it was consumed in sorrow, as if a bite of bread or a dish of figs could make things right.

Amon's mother spent much time with Tamar, who feared greatly for her father. Many of the women who came by expected the girl, as the daughter of an apostle, to have some wisdom, causing her to climb to the roof to get away from it.

Mary, the mother of Jesus, stopped by to see if she could help. Since everyone else was busy, Amon quietly greeted her and told her there wasn't much to be done. Mary sat next to him at the table. "I think I'll stay a while, just in case someone needs comforting."

"Oh, if that's what you're looking for, you can start with me."

Mary put her arm around him. "Yes, I'm sure this has been a terrible ordeal, even for a man." She gave him a hug, then leaned back, her eyes watching his face. "We haven't really talked since that morning at the well," she said, referring to the morning they found the tomb of Jesus empty. "Much has changed since then."

Amon stared at the floor. "Indeed. Much has changed, and I most of all, it seems. I can't believe I was so blind to the truth. All my life my father tried to tell me I'm related to the Messiah"—he looked at Mary—"and his mother. But I thought his stories to be fantasies. Jesus showed me how wrong I was."

Mary laughed softly. "Jesus showed us *all* how wrong we could be. But don't feel too bad—your father had the benefit of seeing things for himself that are just history to you."

"Do you remember my father being there that night? The night Jesus was born?"

"Oh yes, how could I forget? There was much excitement among the shepherds, and with Jotham most of all. He was one of the first to see Jesus, and as I recall, the very first to hold him besides Joseph and me."

Amon shook his head in wonder. "And I thought him a fool." He was remembering times he was so embarrassed by his father that he kept friends away from him. Times he was so angry at his father's impossible stories that he'd storm out of the house. And one time in particular when he denied he was the son of Jotham. *I was just a child*, he reminded himself, then brought his mind back to the present and sighed. "If you really want to comfort someone, Tamar is up on the roof, and I believe she would appreciate your company."

Mary stood, patted Amon on the shoulder, and climbed the stairs.

~

Early the next morning, as the sky was just turning pink, Amon's entire family, Tamar included, left for the temple. They stopped along the way to pick up Benjamin, who had gotten up early to finish his chores. By the time they arrived in the Court of Women, a crowd had already gathered, most of them around the center of the court. Normally there were only scattered groups of three or four people. As they drew closer, Amon could hear someone talking. He led the family around to the other side, where it wasn't as crowded. Standing in the middle of the court, preaching about the power of Jesus, stood Peter and the rest of the apostles.

As soon as she saw him, Tamar ran to Bartholomew and hugged him tightly. She trembled a bit, her hands grasping the folds of his tunic. "What happened? How is it you are free?"

Her father held her tightly and kissed the top of her head. "An angel of the Lord. It was an angel of the Lord. He opened the door of the prison and told us to come out here and preach the good news."

The apostles spread out across the courtyard, each preaching to small groups who couldn't get close to Peter. At the far end, a column of temple guards headed out toward the jail, marching in perfect unison. As the voices of the apostles bounced around the courtyard, the soldiers ran back toward the hewn chamber and the Sanhedrin, looking completely confused and terrified. Bartholomew was on his third small group when the same guards came out to the Court of Women as if searching for something.

Seeing Peter, the guards surrounded him, looking greatly relieved. "By order of the high priest," one guard said, and Amon recognized him as Raphu, the captain he had investigated before Jesus was crucified, "you are ordered to appear immediately before the Sanhedrin to answer their questions."

Peter nodded politely and spoke for all the apostles. "Of course," he said. "We will be happy to give our message of hope to the elders."

Bartholomew and the others started to follow Peter, but Tamar held onto her father's cloak and dug her feet in.

"Do not fear, daughter," Bartholomew said as he pulled her clutched hand from his cloak. "Jehovah is with us."

Surrounded by guards, the apostles walked calmly into the Court of Israel.

Most times, Amon and his father could get close enough to the Chamber of Hewn Stone to hear what was going on inside through an open door or window. Not this time. The hall was closed up tightly, and the guards kept everyone back. After an hour, the doors opened and the apostles came out again.

"We are to wait out here while the elders decide our fate," Peter said to the men surrounding him.

A cold stab of fear shot through Amon's body. Often, when one waited for the Sanhedrin to decide a thing, the decision was death.

After a time, the doors opened again, and the apostles reentered the hall.

This time the men outside waited for hours. As the sun reached the top of its arc, Amon tapped his father on the shoulder. "I'm going to tell the others what's happening." Leaving his father, he returned to the Court of Women and found them finishing off some bread and cheese his mother had purchased. He took a few bites himself as he gave them the little news he had to share. Just as he was about to ask for a drink of water, a cry swept across the crowd.

Everyone looked toward the top of the steps leading to the Court of Israel.

Tamar screamed.

All the apostles were standing there, but their clothes were bloody and torn, and their faces swollen and bruised.

Tamar pushed through the crowd and Amon followed her, then moved ahead to clear a path when she got stopped behind a wall of men. Together they shoved their way up to her father. When they broke through and saw him, Amon stopped suddenly and stared. His mind could not process what he was seeing. Under his ripped and torn cloak and tunic, Bartholomew's body was cut, bruised, and bloody.

Tamar screamed and pulled back.

The wounds were still fresh and bleeding. All the apostles were in the same condition. The horror of it kept Amon's mind spinning, and all he could think of was . . . *Wait a minute, they're laughing.* He looked up at Bartholomew's face, then to all the others: the apostles were laughing, as if they had just come from a birthday celebration.

"Fa-father," Tamar stammered. "You've been terribly beaten! Why are you laughing?"

Bartholomew winced at the pain of putting his arm around his daughter. "Oh Tamar, don't you see? We are all just so happy that we have been found worthy to suffer for the name of Jesus!"

~

That afternoon Amon once again visited his teacher. He found Gamaliel hunched over a scroll in his house, his face a few inches from the writing, trying to read. Without looking up he said, "Amon, you arrive at a most opportune time." He turned to his student. "It is more difficult every day for me to read these words. Come, read to me."

Amon sat across from the elder. "I will do better than that." He pulled from his bag an angular clear rock the size of his palm and handed it to Gamaliel. "Read through that."

Gamaliel held the crystal between the scroll and his eye, then jumped up as if he'd found a snake on his desk. "What is this?" he gasped. "Is it sorcery?"

Amon chuckled. "No, rabbi, it is the work of Jehovah, not unclean spirits. Because you are old—I mean, an elder—the light from the parchment gets lost on its way to your eye. This crystal helps it find its way. I bought it from my glass merchant a few days ago but forgot to give it to you."

Gamaliel tried to hide a smile, then easily read aloud the text he had been straining to see. He set the crystal down. "But you did not come here today to help the light find its way to my eyes."

Amon shook his head. "No, I came to ask what happened in the Sanhedrin this morning."

Gamaliel slowly stood and walked to the open side of the room that looked out over Jerusalem and the temple. "The high priest was ready to have all the apostles stoned to death for preaching the name of Jesus," he said. "I suggested that it might be better to let them go and wait to see what happens." He turned to face Amon. "I reminded them that Theudas and Judas the Galilean also built up a movement of false hope, but both soon faded away on their own."

"And do you think the followers of Jesus will soon fade away?"

The elder sat again and sighed. "I—I do not yet have an opinion on that. But it is the only question I study in the Scriptures these days. That"—he tapped the scroll with the crystal—"is what I was doing when you arrived, and what your magical rock will now make much easier."

~

Amon was amazed that, even as their wounds were treated and they recovered from their ordeal, the apostles never stopped preaching. Instead of being intimidated by the Sanhedrin, the people of The Way grew bolder and louder. The city filled with the sick and the poor wanting to hear the message of salvation in Jesus, but the wealthy and powerful also came, and many were baptized.

It was after a long day of tallying baptisms that Amon came home so tired that he dropped into a chair, his arms and legs hanging limp. "Over twelve hundred today," he told his mother, who was busy sewing a new tunic for a widow across town.

She looked up. "And I saw thirty people healed this afternoon alone."

Amon flashed a giant grin. "Now nothing can stop us from spreading the word that Jesus is the Messiah."

At that moment Amon's father stumbled into the house and collapsed at the table, face ashen and eyes staring straight ahead.

The family rushed in around him, and Amon's mother sat next to him, her hand on his shoulder. "What is it, Jotham? What has happened?"

Amon's father stared at the faces around him, and, voice shaking, whispered, "They killed Stephen."

✦ ✦ ✦

Stephen's death was a shock, and it caused a great uproar in Jerusalem. But did you catch the amazing events before that? An angel of the Lord appeared in the jail, unlocked the door, and told the apostles to go out and keep preaching Jesus.

An angel!

We hear all the time about angels announcing the birth of Jesus or performing signs and wonders. But leading a jail break? In a city we can still visit today? And testified to by several witnesses?

So here's my question: Do you think angels really exist and still work in our world today?

I do.

## Chapter Eight

# Sorrow

Evening came and Tabitha tried to get her family to eat some supper. Only Uri and Jadon would take anything. Bartholomew had come home from preaching to be with Tamar, and Benjamin came straight over as soon as he heard, since no one in his house particularly cared that a Jesus follower had been executed.

*Stephen is dead*. The thought spun round and round in Amon's mind, keeping most other thoughts from forming. *Stephen is dead, killed by the Sanhedrin for preaching the name of Jesus*.

Suddenly, being a believer didn't seem like a thing to celebrate anymore. Maybe it was even something to hide.

"We must continue on," Bartholomew said as they all sat around the table. A lamp was lit in the center, and an untouched loaf of bread sat next to it. "We must continue to preach the word we know to be true, no matter the cost."

At these words, Tamar hugged her father closer.

By midmorning the next day, not much had changed, except that Jadon and Uri were their usual noisy selves. Amon came down from the rooftop wearing his cloak and carrying bag. He grabbed a bite of bread and announced to his parents that he was going over to talk with Gamaliel. Tamar still cuddled with her father, and Benjamin had gone home late the evening before, so Amon would go alone.

It struck him as soon as he stepped out of the door: the streets were empty. As Amon walked, there was an occasional worker and, as always, a few Romans about, but the crowds of the last few weeks were gone, vanished overnight.

Was everyone just indoors, hiding? No, Amon finally realized, many people of The Way had simply left Jerusalem. Hundreds, in fact. He saw the signs of it as he moved through town—empty alleyways where people had camped. The courtyard of Omar's house vacant and left a mess. The fields outside the city almost deserted, believers and their animals alike gone.

"They've run away to someplace safe," a gruff voice said behind Amon as he stared out one of the city gates.

Amon knew the voice was that of Josiah the cheese seller, one of his close friends.

"Not that I blame them," the older man added. "These walls are not safe for those who preach Jesus."

Amon wondered why Josiah was in his stall with his cheeses displayed like any other day. Although, from the look of it, he had sold much of his cheese to those who fled. "Where did they go?"

Josiah shrugged as he sliced into a block of white cheese. "Hebron. Bethlehem, Jericho. Some to far off places where the high priest will find it more difficult to stick his nose in their business."

"You mean like up north, to Galilee?"

"I mean like to Cyprus, Antioch, Rome even."

Amon's eyebrows shot up in surprise. "Rome? They would just leave their lives here and go live in a foreign country?"

Josiah slammed his cleaver into a new block of cheese. "They took their lives with them, in order to start fresh. It's not such an odd thought, you know. Remember, your own father grew up in the family of a wandering shepherd." He handed Amon a bite of cheese. "It may actually be good for your cause," he added. "All those believers traveling all over the world—they may spread your message faster than you thought possible."

"Perhaps," Amon said. "And what about you? Are you a believer?"

Josiah scoffed. "Me? No, no, no. I am much too old to change my ways now. I will leave it to you younger men to follow the latest messiahs."

Amon leaned in close. Even though they were alone on the street, he spoke softly. "What if Jesus is the *real* Messiah?"

Josiah began stacking what was left of his cheese. "Then I would have to have proof of that before I abandoned everything I have always believed."

"No, you do not have to abandon it," Amon answered, "because Jesus isn't a different thing than what you have always believed. He is the *fulfillment* of everything you have always believed."

Josiah was quiet, then took a chunk of cheese and stuck it in Amon's mouth. "Go on now," he laughed. "I might have a customer any moment."

Amon waved and walked away.

"I wasn't there." Amon hadn't even entered the door of Gamaliel's house before the old rabbi had looked up from the basin where he was washing his face and spoken the words. "I wasn't there," he said again, patting his face dry, as if Amon hadn't heard.

"I understand," Amon said quietly. He had, indeed, come to ask Gamaliel why he hadn't stopped the murder of Stephen. Now there was a new question on his lips. "Do you know what happened?"

The rabbi shook his head as if in disgust. "It was those men from that place they call the Synagogue of the Freedmen. Liars and evildoers, they are. They hired witnesses to spew lies about Stephen. Then they brought him before the high priest and Sanhedrin."

"What did they say?"

Gamaliel sat and pointed at a chair for Amon. "They claimed he preached blasphemy against Moses and God."

As Amon sat, he tried to decide if that could be true. After all, Stephen always did speak his mind. But then he decided that, no, he had never heard Stephen say a single word against the core beliefs of the Jewish faith. "Did Stephen reply?"

"Yes, yes." The rabbi nodded his head. "Nicodemus told me Stephen gave a most eloquent defense based on nothing but the Torah." He sat back and stared out over Jerusalem. "They say his face glowed as he spoke, as if God's Holy Spirit was upon him."

"But?" Amon prompted.

Gamaliel looked back at Amon. "But then he told them how they—how *we*, for I am a part of them—have continually persecuted God's messengers and even killed the one he sent to save us."

Amon hung his head. "I don't suppose that went over very well."

"No, it did not. They screamed, dragged him outside, and . . . and . . ."

"Murdered him," Amon finished the sentence.

Gamaliel stared at him. "Yes."

"And what of Saul? Was he there?"

A heavy blanket of sorrow seemed to wrap itself around the old man's shoulders. "Yes," he whispered.

Amon leaned forward to hear him.

"He held the cloaks of the other men while they killed Stephen."

Amon pursed his lips and his eyes opened wide. "Then Saul is no longer my friend," he hissed. "I shall do whatever I must to see him punished for this."

In the space of one breath, the old-man Gamaliel departed and the teacher Gamaliel returned. "Amon," the teacher said in the tone the boy had heard so many times during his lessons. "Understand that if Jesus is not the Messiah, then Saul and the Sanhedrin did exactly what the Torah demands. We must not tolerate men who claim to be of God but think only of themselves." He took a deep breath and let it out slowly. "But if Jesus *is* the Messiah, then . . ." Gamaliel's voice trailed off.

"Then we must make Saul see this," Amon finished his rabbi's sentence again. "And what of you? Do you now believe that Jesus is God's son?"

The old-man Gamaliel returned once again. "I—I do not yet know."

Amon wasn't sure if it was sorrow, guilt, or fear he heard in the old man's voice.

"But if he is," the rabbi added, "perhaps Jehovah will use you to convince Saul of it."

On his walk back home, Amon passed two relatives of Caiaphas. When they saw Amon, they stopped talking and stared. Amon quickened his pace and thought how dangerous a place Jerusalem had suddenly become. No wonder so many people of The Way had left the city to live as far away as possible.

~

Two Sabbaths passed as the believers hid their beliefs, or at least remained silent when they were out in public. "I am so tired of this," Amon complained quietly to Tamar and Benjamin as they all walked home from selling some sheep at the market. It was the end of the day, and the light from the setting sun made their faces glow. "I want to sing hymns and shout praises and scream the name of Jesus!" This last word was said more loudly.

Tamar and Benjamin both shushed him.

It felt like there were priests on every street corner listening for any clue to finding people of The Way.

"But we cannot," Benjamin said in a whisper. "The Sanhedrin has not cooled its temper toward us even since they killed Stephen. It is not likely they will any time soon."

Amon again thought how much more mature his friend sounded these days.

Lamplight glowed from the windows of the house as they approached—the only windows in Jerusalem with glass, other than those he had put in the palace of Pontius Pilate.

Amon pushed the door open and immediately stopped. Peter, James, and John all sat at the table with Amon's parents. He signaled his friends behind him to be quiet, then crept quietly into the house and headed for the stairs.

"Amon," his father called just as his son reached the first step, "do you not want to greet our guests?"

Amon stopped with his foot on the step and looked back. "Forgive me, I did not want to interrupt what must be a very important discussion."

"Very important indeed," Jotham said. "But Amon, Peter did not come to talk with your mother and me, he came to talk with *you*."

Amon sucked in his breath, confused, and returned to the table. "Oh, uh, I'm sorry, I just thought—"

"Come," Peter said, standing. "Let us speak in private."

Tamar and Benjamin sat at the table with the others as Peter and Amon stepped out the back door to the sheep pens.

"Why would you want to talk to *me*?" Amon asked.

Peter breathed a heavy sigh. "Amon, you know that so much has changed since Stephen's death." Amon didn't answer, and Peter rubbed his eyes. "Many have left the city, many have left the country, and everyone still here is afraid. We cannot talk freely, and we cannot meet or sing or preach. The Sanhedrin has made life very difficult for all of us."

Every muscle in Amon's body tightened as he tried to hold back the painful thoughts of what had happened in the last two weeks. He closed his eyes and held his breath as images of the threats, the arrests, the beatings flashed through his mind. Finally he opened his eyes and began breathing normally. "Do you think they were wrong to run away in fear?"

Peter's whole body seemed to sag in sadness. "How could I criticize their fear," he said softly, "when my own fear caused me to deny Jesus before he was crucified?"

Amon looked at him in surprise.

"That night—that horrible, dreadful night," he whispered, "after Jesus was arrested. As we stood around a fire waiting to see what would happen, a girl recognized me and told everyone I had been with Jesus. 'I don't know what you're talking about,' I snapped. 'I don't know the man.'" Peter's eyes began to water. "Three times I denied him, and those words will haunt me forever." Peter seemed lost in his memories for a few moments, then he took a deep breath and turned to Amon. "So who am I to tell others how they should act in the shadow of their fear?" He looked into the distance and leaned on the fence of the sheep pens.

Amon wasn't sure what to say. "I understand," he said at last. "Both *your* fear and theirs, as well as my own. These are very dangerous times for those who follow Jesus, and it seems wise to take extreme precautions."

"And yet," Peter said, "we still must provide a way for the people to meet and worship. We are all starving for the bread of fellowship and the living water of teaching." He turned toward Amon and said more softly, "Do you know what the people call you, Amon?"

Amon was confused. "I did not know the people call me *any* thing."

Peter smiled. "Yes, they most certainly do. They call you the Clever One."

Amon's eyes grew wide in confusion, and he shook his head slowly. "Why would they call me that?"

"Because, my young friend," Peter said, standing up straight, "you have a mind like few others. The people are in awe that you stood face-to-face with Pontius Pilate and saved your father's life. They see your inventions, they read your writings, they listen to your music, and they know that Jehovah has given you a truly amazing mind."

Amon shifted his weight, uncomfortable. Here was a man whom the Messiah had chosen and that angels served. Who could be more special than that?

"And so I have an assignment for you." Peter patted Amon on the shoulder. "I would like you to invent and put into practice some way for our people to communicate. A method or means for them to know when and where it is safe to gather. And, with the help of Benjamin and Tamar, to search the city for hidden spaces and out-of-the-way places to meet. Do you think you can do that for us?"

Amon stared at his elder in disbelief. He gulped. "If it will serve the Messiah and his people, I will do all that I can."

But inside he was thinking what an impossible task this would be.

✦ ✦ ✦

Peter denied that he even knew Jesus. Not just once, but three times.

What did Jesus do about it? He restored Peter and made him the "rock" on which he built his church.

After Stephen was killed, the followers of Jesus were understandably afraid. They lived with the very real possibility of being severely punished for their beliefs. It's no wonder they wanted to keep quiet about their faith.

But what about us? Most of us don't need to worry about being arrested or persecuted because we follow Jesus, and yet we often hide our faith as if it were something embarrassing. Many times in my life I have done just that—hidden my love for Jesus out of fear that others would ridicule me, not accept me, or think I'm dumb. Shame on me.

Yet, if Jesus were standing here in the flesh with me, I don't think he'd say, "Shame on you!" I think he'd put his arm around my shoulders and say, "Well, let's see if we can't do better next time." Just the way he did with Peter.

Fear is human. At one time or another we all fall into its trap. What if we try to do better? Try to worry less about other people's opinion of our faith and focus on the love Jesus has for us and the love we have for him.

Chapter Nine

# Greeks

Amon shivered a little. The morning air was chilly, and the sun had not yet risen high enough to peek over the walls of the city.

"Where are we going?" Benjamin yawned as they descended into the lower city. The Tyropoeon Valley separated Mount Zion, where Amon lived, from Mount Moriah, where the temple stood. It was into this "Valley of the Cheesemakers" the two friends walked. The buildings and houses they passed were mostly dark and quiet this early in the day.

"We're doing a survey." They were just passing through an intersection where later in the day many sellers of cheese would set up their booths.

"I wish the cheese market was open. I'm starving," Benjamin complained. "What's a 'survey'?"

Amon was taking some notes on his tablet as they walked and didn't respond. They were just then walking under a bridge between the two hills.

"Halt!"

The command had been yelled in Greek and both jumped and looked up.

Two sloppy and dirty Roman soldiers half slid, half stumbled down the slanted rock footing that held up the bridge. Their helmets sat crooked on their heads, and only some of the straps holding their armor together were secured, making everything rattle and sag.

As they approached, Amon noticed the soldiers seemed to be having trouble walking.

"What are you boys doing out here this early in the day?" one of the soldiers said, his hand resting on the handle of his sword. His slurred speech and the stink of his breath told Amon the two men had been drinking much wine while hiding up under the bridge.

Syrian Greeks. Amon's whole body tensed in terror, and he held his breath. One part of his mind wondered what the men were doing here—these foreign soldiers were usually only hired to be part of the Roman governor's personal guard when he came to visit Jerusalem. Another part of his mind wondered if he and Benjamin would get out of this meeting alive—Syrian Greeks were known to hate Jews, and Amon had heard many stories of pain and death at their hands.

"Uh, we were just on our way to the market for my mother," Amon answered in Greek, finding his breath again.

Benjamin gave him a sideways glance but said nothing.

"And what are you writing on your little tablet there, boy?" The man grabbed the tablet from Amon's hand, turning it every direction trying to read it. But Amon had been writing in Hebrew, and obviously this soldier didn't know that language.

"It is just a shopping list."

Again Benjamin looked at him sideways.

The soldier looked up at Amon and squinted, as if trying to make his eyes focus.

He stared for so long Amon couldn't keep his insides from shaking.

Finally the soldier said, "Well, you'd better get on with it then," and shoved the tablet so hard into Amon's chest that it bruised his bottom ribs. The soldiers' fingers were covered in a white dust. Then the two soldiers stumbled up the street toward the Roman fortress of Antonia.

Benjamin collapsed onto a wooden bench between two market stalls. "I thought we were dead," he wheezed.

Amon sat next to his friend, still trembling. "I can't believe we didn't even see them until they yelled," he answered. "We know better than to not pay attention to our surroundings."

Benjamin looked away. "I just never expected someone to be hiding under a bridge."

"Nor did I. But it could have cost us our lives. We must be more careful."

They were quiet for a moment as their breathing slowed, then Benjamin stared straight ahead as he quietly asked, "Was it wrong of you to lie to them?"

Amon's head jerked up in surprise. "What?"

"You lied to the soldiers about what you were writing. Was that wrong? You know the Torah much better than I."

"I . . . We were in danger."

"I know. But was it right or wrong? Did Jesus ever lie to get out of trouble?"

Amon shook his head slowly. "No, of course not." He didn't want to answer further but couldn't leave it at that. "I will have to think on these things."

The boys drank from their skin of water, then stood and continued their survey. Peter and John had gone to Samaria to teach—and also to warn believers about Saul—but told Amon to have a plan ready by the time they got back. Tamar had gone with her father to preach in several small towns across

Judea—and warn them about Saul—so it was up to Amon and Benjamin alone to come up with a means for people of The Way to communicate.

"What's a 'survey'?" Benjamin asked, repeating his earlier question.

"It's when you study a place or situation to see what is there."

"Huh?"

Amon laughed, which helped erase the memory of the Greek soldiers. "Say you were looking for a place to graze your sheep. Instead of taking the sheep from field to field searching for grass, it would be much faster to go alone and check to see which fields might work. That's a survey."

"Oh. So we're searching for a place to graze your father's sheep?"

"No. We're searching for a place to graze the sheep of Jesus."

Benjamin gave him a questioning look, then his face brightened. "The people of The Way!"

"Exactly." Amon walked faster.

By midmorning they had traveled all the way through the Tyropoeon Valley to the North Gate. As they walked, the city had come alive, though it was still very quiet. Shops and booths had opened, and people went about doing their daily business, but the only ones talking were the merchants and customers arguing over the price of a goat or a length of red cloth. There was none of the joyful shouting and talk of Jesus as there had been before.

They passed the beggars sitting at the foot of the Garden Gate, then climbed the stairs to the top of the wall. They sat, dangling their feet over the heads of the beggars thirty feet below, and looked out over the city. To their right, atop Mount Zion but still inside the walls, stood Herod's palace with its towers, and at the far corner Amon's home, though they couldn't see it from here. To the left was Mount Moriah, with the temple on top, also inside the walls. Even though Moriah was shorter than Zion, the temple was so tall it was higher than anything else in the city.

Outside the wall at the far end of the city, beyond Amon's house and past the Essene Gate, Roman troops practiced their marching and fighting up on a hill. As they watched from atop the wall, Amon and Benjamin could see how ten small eight-man units formed together to create eighty-man centuries, which in turn were combined to create four-hundred-eighty-man cohorts and so forth, until twenty thousand men were perfectly organized.

Amon's gaze drifted back down to the streets of Jerusalem. The usual lunchtime mob of people never developed, and many side streets were completely deserted. Jerusalem had been a busy city even before the excitement of Jesus, but now it seemed almost deserted. Here and there a handful of people shopped or conducted other business, some women hung clothes out to dry along the wall, and a few small groups of children gathered around their rabbis. But there was none of the excitement or joy of before.

"This is so strange," Amon said. "Remember how crowded it was after the Holy Spirit came to us?"

"Yes. We had to fight through crowds just to walk a block."

"How can we ever reach all the people of The Way with news about meetings without the Sanhedrin figuring it out?" Amon didn't really expect an answer from his friend, and Benjamin gave none. Amon suddenly shouted, "Benjamin!"

His friend jerked away in fear. "What? I—I do not know how we'll reach—"

"No, no, no," Amon interrupted. "I was not yelling at you to answer, I was yelling because I figured it out. Look out in front of us," he said, pointing. "What do you see?"

Benjamin scratched his head. "I—I see Jerusalem."

"Exactly. You see *all* of Jerusalem, and all of Jerusalem sees *you*."

Benjamin sat up straight and smoothed out his cloak as if everyone was watching him. "They do?"

"No, no, but they could, *if they knew to look here*."

"Why would they want to look at . . ." Suddenly it seemed Benjamin understood. "We can use some sort of signal on top of the wall to signal The Way."

Amon grinned. "Yes."

"Then we're done with our survey?"

"No, not at all. We've only figured out how we can get the message to the people. Now we have to figure out how to *form* the message, and when and where we will all meet."

Benjamin slumped. "Oh, is that all?"

The two climbed back down the stairs and headed up Mount Zion's hill to the upper city.

As they walked, Amon thought aloud. "I think we've learned something today," he said. "It is more dangerous to meet when the city is quiet than when it is noisy."

"Why do you think that?"

"Remember this morning? We were all alone, walking in the quiet, so the two soldiers under the bridge could see and hear us easily. Since there was no one else for them to look at, they noticed and bothered us. Had we been in a crowd, they wouldn't have even spotted us."

"True," Benjamin answered. "Plus, they could probably hear clearly the things we said."

"Exactly. If we hold our meetings in the middle of the day, when the city is noisy, we won't attract attention as we would in the silence of the night." Amon leaned his head back and shook the last few drops from his water pouch. "Or at least not as much."

"Very good thinking."

"Now we just need a place to meet. It must be close to or in the city, be able to hold hundreds of people, and be built so that no one outside the building can hear what's happening inside."

Benjamin looked at his friend with a doubtful face. "Where in all of Jerusalem will we find such a place?"

The two friends walked across the upper city, heading toward Amon's house. They passed the fineries market for rich people, where Tamar had once been given a small taste of a substance called "chocolate." A few streets down they passed the house of Omar, where they had received the Holy Spirit. Several workmen were going in and out of the house while Omar watched over everything they did.

Amon pulled at Benjamin's cloak, and they turned into the courtyard of the house. "Omar," Amon called. "Greetings."

Omar waved. "Greetings, my young friends. Are you thirsty?"

"Yes, thank you," Amon said.

The elder motioned for a servant to bring water. They drank gladly as Omar said, "What grace has brought me a visit from two such fine young men?"

Amon wiped his mouth. "We were just passing by on our way home. Your house seems very busy today."

"Ah, yes. It is because of this water you drink." He motioned with his hand to their cups. "My cistern has developed a leak, and all my water drained out. These men found the leak on the bottom and are repairing it."

Amon stopped drinking. "Oh! Well, we should not be drinking your water then, if you don't have much."

Omar grinned. "Nonsense. We have many urns full. Would you like to see the cistern?"

Amon had seen a cistern several years before and remembered being amazed, but Benjamin had never seen one. They both nodded and Omar led them to the rear of the house. There, in the floor, was an opening the size of a door with stairs dropping down into it. Omar borrowed a torch from a worker and led the two friends down the steps. As they descended, they entered a chamber the size of a large house carved out of the rock, and as tall as two men standing on each other's shoulders.

"Dancin' camels," Amon shouted. "This is huge!"

Several men were working in the space, plastering the walls. Torches were stationed around the chamber, lighting the whole place with bright amber light.

"What happened to the water?" Benjamin asked.

"Every few years the plaster on the wall breaks down, and the water leaks out into the ground," Omar said. "That happened again this winter."

They watched, gawking, as one workman mixed a powder into the plaster and the other men spread it on the rock walls, making sure to fill in all the cracks and holes. After a few minutes, Omar led Amon and Benjamin back upstairs and offered them some sweet bread.

"How does the cistern get filled?" Benjamin asked.

"Rain," Omar said, "and a small spring that trickles in."

Amon imagined the cistern full of water and tried to picture people in it. "Perhaps we could use this as a secret place to baptize believers. Once it is again full of water, I mean."

Omar thought that an excellent idea, offered them some smoked deer meat and bread for lunch, then invited them to visit anytime.

On their way out they passed the workers, and Amon stopped to talk with one who introduced himself as Eli. "I was just wondering," Amon said, always anxious to learn, "what you use to seal the cisterns. I thought it would be some kind of tar or pitch, but it doesn't look like that."

Eli wiped his hands on a rag. "Yes, you'd think so, wouldn't you? But we use a mixture of lime, sand, and water that makes a very solid and long-lasting seal."

Amon had many more questions, which Eli answered before he and Benjamin headed up through the market again. They quietly greeted several merchants who were followers of The Way, one of whom was a woman named Maacah they knew well. For a time, when they were younger, both boys had worked for her, collecting a small insect she used to dye cloth red for her wealthy customers.

"Where have you been all day?" Tamar demanded as they entered Amon's house. "Father and I returned this morning, and I couldn't find you."

Amon apologized and gave her a quick summary of their day. "And was your own journey successful?" She frequently got to travel, while Amon remained in Jerusalem. But travel made him nervous, and he was very happy to stay safe inside the city walls.

"Yes, very. Father and the others made many converts to The Way."

An entire account of the trip was given by Bartholomew at dinner.

Amon invited Benjamin to stay for the night, and his mother said it was okay. With Tamar, they spent the evening hours in the upper room, empty of visitors now, trying to come up with a plan for communicating to the believers. Peter would be home any day and would expect Amon to have some clever answer, but so far he didn't feel very smart.

~

Late that night, as Amon and Benjamin snacked on leftover dinner, Amon asked his father the question Benjamin had asked him in the morning about lying.

Jotham leaned back on his stool and rested against the wall. "That is a difficult question. I suppose there might be times when a lie told in defense of someone else would not violate the law. And I myself have told your mother, on occasion, that a meal she has prepared was delicious when it really wasn't. But overall, I would say you must never lie. If it is a matter of your safety, perhaps simply not answering the question would be a better path to take. But you should ask Gamaliel."

Up on the rooftop that night, Amon lay sleepless on his bed as Benjamin breathed heavily next to him. He was staring at the stars when several thoughts came together in his mind. He sat up straight, quickly examining the ideas, and instantly deemed them to be excellent. He shook Benjamin. "Wake up," he whispered.

"What?" Benjamin blurted.

Amon put his hand over his friend's mouth. "I have discovered the answer to our problem!"

✦ ✦ ✦

Is a lie ever not a sin? Are there circumstances when a lie spoken for a good cause is okay?

This is a question that has puzzled Christians from the very beginning. Joshua 2 tells the story of Rahab, who lied to save the lives of two men doing God's work. The writers of Hebrews (11:31) and James (2:25) say very clearly that she had faith and should be honored. Yet neither of those verses specifically approves of the lie she told to accomplish her goal.

Perhaps the more compelling example from Scripture is the nurses of Exodus 1:15, who ignored Pharaoh's order and then lied to him about it to save the lives of newborns. How did God respond? Verse 20 reports, "So God was kind to the midwives."

Elisha told a blatant lie in 2 Kings 6:19–23, when he said to his enemies he would take them to one place but actually took them to another where they were captured. God even assisted in the deception by temporarily blinding the enemy. Elisha's lie led to good when the enemies were treated well, and it brought peace between the parties without anyone being killed.

Yet Augustine, one of the early Christian leaders, declared Rahab and the others absolutely sinned when they lied. Many people across the centuries, and even today, still believe the same. On the other hand, Luther, another church leader, said "a good hearty lie for the sake of the good and for the Christian Church, a lie in case of necessity, a useful lie, would not be against God."

Amon is still struggling with the answer to Benjamin's question. He has asked his father and will ask Gamaliel, but in the end, he must seek the guidance of God's Holy Spirit in deciding this for himself.

Chapter Ten

# Limestone

"Ow, that *hurts*!" Benjamin yelled.

He was hanging upside down from a rope around his ankles into a hole in the rock at the back of a house in the upper city. "And the torch is burning my face."

"Then drop it," Amon commanded as he and Tamar held the other end of the rope.

"Okay," Benjamin called. "Pull me up."

Amon and Tamar slowly tugged on the ropes, being careful not to drop Benjamin. A moment later Benjamin was facedown on the ground outside the hole with no torch in his hand. "No good," he said, spitting dirt from his mouth. "You couldn't fit two goats in that thing."

They were talking about an old cistern that the owner of the house had told them was cracked and empty. It was the third such cistern they'd checked that morning. Amon thanked the owner, and the three headed up the street.

"This could take a year," Amon said. "There are just too many houses in Jerusalem for us to check out."

"Maybe there's someone who already knows all the cisterns in Jerusalem," Tamar said.

Amon and Benjamin stopped suddenly and looked at each other. "Eli!" they yelled.

"Who?" Tamar asked.

"Eli. He's the man working to fix Omar's cistern." They ran home, asked Amon's mother for a basketful of lunch, quickly answered her questions, then Amon and Benjamin headed back to Omar's house. Tamar stayed to help Tabitha grind more wheat for bread for the widows and poor, since they all agreed it would be a little suspicious for her to join the "boys."

Amon and Benjamin arrived at Omar's and whispered their plan to him.

He was just leaving for an appointment, which worked out perfectly. "Alas, I cannot have lunch with you," he said loudly, just as Eli and the workers came up from the cistern, "since I'm meeting with my rabbi."

As Omar departed, Amon looked at Eli. "Well, we have an awful lot of lunch here. Would you and your men care to eat with us?"

Eli looked at the basket, then at the scrap of bread in his hand. He scowled and rubbed his head as if thinking. "Hmm, let me see. Stale bread or a basket full of delicacies. That's a difficult decision." His scowl became a grin. "Oh alright, we accept your kind offer."

The other men echoed Eli's decision and they all sat around one of the tables in Omar's courtyard.

As they ate salted fish, fresh bread with olive oil, olives, and figs, Amon struck up a conversation. "Have you always been a repairman of cisterns?" he asked Eli.

Eli licked some salt from his fingers. "Yes. Since at least my father's father, our family has taken care of all the cisterns in Jerusalem."

Amon and Benjamin gave each other a look as if to say "Perfect!"

Benjamin pulled an olive pit from his mouth. "How long will your repairs last? Must Omar have his repaired again soon?"

"Not soon," Eli said as he popped three olives in his mouth. "About every eight to ten years."

"It must be very difficult work," Benjamin added as he dipped a piece of bread in the olive oil.

Eli shook his head. "Actually, it is quite pleasant. We spend our days in cisterns, out of the cold of winter, the heat of summer, and the wet of rainy days. We can talk and laugh, and nobody is bothered because nobody can hear us."

Finally Amon felt he could ask the question he really wanted answered. "And I suppose they never wear out—you can always add another layer of plaster?"

Eli shook his head. "No, eventually most cisterns develop such deep cracks that they will no longer hold water."

Amon's mouth desperately wanted to smile, but he held it in check. "Oh, really? Are there many such dry cisterns in Jerusalem?"

"Yes, indeed," one of the other workers said around a fig in his mouth. "Most are small, but there are several very large ones right here inside the city walls."

Amon's smile was almost winning its battle for control of his mouth. He decided he'd better not ask more about this for fear of losing the battle and making the workmen suspicious. They finished their meal talking about the upcoming chariot races in the Hippodrome, then Amon and Benjamin packed their basket and headed home.

"Wait!" came a yell as they reached the street. Eli ran up. "I did not properly thank you," he shouted. But as he got close, he put a hand on each of the boys' shoulders and spoke quickly and quietly.

"Remember these names," Eli whispered, and gave them eight names. "Each of these people have houses with large cisterns that are dry, and each of them are people of The Way."

Amon's mouth dropped open. "How did you know—"

Eli cut him off. "I figured out what you were doing before you pulled the first olives out of your basket." He smiled. "I am glad to be of help, Clever One."

Amon gasped, then he and Benjamin walked away dazed and amazed. *Perhaps I am not such a Clever One if Eli saw through my plan in seconds.* But they ventured on and spent the afternoon talking with each of the eight people Eli had mentioned.

~

For the next three days, the boys and Tamar were hidden away in the upper room whispering and completing the plans for the believer meetings, or they were out in the streets talking with certain people and experimenting with certain things. Finally they were ready, and Amon reported to Peter, who had just returned to Jerusalem. Peter in turn called a secret meeting at Amon's request, inviting the other apostles who were in town as well as a dozen prominent men and women among the faithful.

The next day at midday, each of them wandered the streets near Omar's house and, when it seemed no one was watching, entered the courtyard. Once inside the walls, they scurried to the back of the house and descended the stairs into the newly relined cistern. In all, there were about thirty people seated on the floor, including Amon's parents, Tamar's father, Tamar, and Benjamin. Torches around the walls of the cistern provided light, just as when the workers had been there. One old man at the far end of the cistern was already asleep, leaning against the wall.

*This is going to be a long afternoon*, Amon thought.

"Greetings in the name of our Lord and Savior Jesus Christ," Peter began, "and thank you all for coming. No doubt you are wondering why we are in a place such as this in the middle of the day. All of that will be answered momentarily. But first, let me say this: You all know that, ever since the death of Stephen, and even before, it has become increasingly dangerous for us to meet. So I asked Amon to develop a plan that would allow us to meet safely for teaching and worship. He has now completed that task. He is, after all, the 'Clever One.'"

Most everyone in the chamber, including Amon's parents, grinned.

"Therefore"—Peter looked toward the end of the chamber—"I now invite Amon to come forward and present his plan."

Amon's mouth dropped open, and he felt as if he'd just seen Jesus appear in the flesh once again. "Me? I thought *you* were going to explain it."

Peter smiled and shook his head. "No, no, this is *your* plan. You explain it."

Everyone shifted their attention from Peter to Amon, and the young man began to sweat.

"Uh, alright," he stammered as he stood. Amon was used to reciting poems and oratory before an audience, but that was just repeating memorized words. This was actually *talking*, and it made his stomach quiver just a bit. "First, I should tell you this will take some time."

Most everyone shifted positions to get comfortable.

"When Peter gave me this task, I soon realized there was no place in all of Jerusalem where we can all meet at the same time. At least, not that I can think of or find. Then one day Benjamin and I were watching the Romans practicing their maneuvers, and it struck me that we need that same kind of organization."

Several faces around the rock chamber showed concern, as if wondering about Amon's intentions.

"Not that we are an army." He held up his hands to calm the speculation. "But when a Roman general wants something to happen, he only tells one man. That man tells ten others, then each of those tell ten more, and so on, until the whole legion has the order in a matter of minutes. I propose we do the same. Peter will be the 'general.' When he needs to send a message to all people of The Way, he will tell a few of us here. Those few will tell others, who will tell ten or so others. In that way, we will have an entire communication network that can spread news all across Jerusalem in just minutes."

There were many nods of approval as the people considered the plan. Peter himself beamed as if he were proud of Amon.

"Next, we thought about the time of day we should hold meetings. At first I was thinking we would all sneak out in the quiet of the night to gather." Amon stepped over next to Benjamin and looked down to acknowledge his friend. "But one morning Benjamin and I were walking through the city while it was still dark and quiet. Suddenly two Roman soldiers"—he looked up again—"Syrian Greeks, confronted us."

At this Amon's mother gasped, and many of the others showed concerned.

Amon avoided his mother's gaze. "We were able to get away safely, but it made me realize that the quiet of the night is a bad time to try to hide. If we'd been walking through town in the middle of a busy day, the soldiers never would have bothered us. Well, not as likely anyway."

Murmurs of agreement swept across the chamber.

"So we decided that, just like this meeting today, we should gather at midday. Many people go inside to sleep or escape the heat every day, so it will not be suspicious if we are not seen for an hour or are seen entering a house. We decided the best time to meet would be while the Sanhedrin is in session each day. After all, it is the Sanhedrin and its members and guards that we must escape the attention of, and they can't very well pay attention to us if they are all locked away in the temple to meet."

"A very wise plan," Peter said, clapping his hands together softly.

"But then we faced the problem of *where* to meet. As I said, there is just no place large enough to fit all the hundreds of believers at the same time. But that's when it struck me: the Sanhedrin meets in a room cut out of rock. Perhaps we should do the same. And so, here we are."

Some of the people glanced at the walls of the cistern, many with concern on their faces.

"We first discovered this one, but then found there are many more throughout the city. They're cool in the summer, warm in the winter, and buried deep enough in the rock that no sound should escape through the walls. All we must do is cover the entrance, and any sound of singing or preaching we make should just blend in to the noise of a busy city in the middle of the day."

"That's absolutely brilliant!"

Amon looked toward the voice.

It came from the old man he had thought was sleeping. The man opened his eyes, his bushy gray eyebrows pushing up into his thick, gray hair. "That's probably the most clever thinking I've ever heard."

Everyone started talking, but then Peter held up his hand to quiet them.

Amon wasn't sure if he should acknowledge the old man's compliment but decided to just continue. "We will divide all people of The Way into smaller congregations of twenty or thirty. Each group will meet twice a week on assigned days in one of three cisterns so they're not always meeting at the same time and same place every day, which might attract attention."

"Brilliant!" the old man said again.

Amon checked his mental list to make sure he had covered everything else before saying, "Finally, there is the matter of communication. It would be awkward if Peter had to pass on by word of mouth to each group when and where to meet every day, so we need one central message that reaches every believer in the city at the same time."

"Perhaps Peter could stand atop the temple and blow a horn," Omar joked.

Everyone laughed.

Even Amon chuckled. "That's actually pretty close." He waited until the chamber was quiet again before saying, "It all starts with some dirty laundry."

✦ ✦ ✦

Was it just a coincidence that Amon and Benjamin happened to meet Eli? Was it a coincidence that Eli knew all the cisterns in the city, or that Eli was himself a believer in Christ?

There have been many times in my life when strange circumstances came together to create a good outcome. Some of those were probably just coincidence—like the time I lost a contact lens on a hike and found it a quarter mile back. A coincidence. Probably.

But there have been many times in my life when an amazing, impossible set of circumstances came together for some good—like God saving my life, the way I met my wife, or doors of opportunity opening.

I've learned a new name for those kinds of events. Instead of "coincidences," I call them "miracles," because I'm convinced they were orchestrated by God's Holy Spirt, though I certainly didn't earn or even deserve those things.

Amon likes to think up plans and have everything work out exactly the way he's designed it. But he's beginning to learn that when his plans aren't perfect, or when he just can't pull off another amazing feat himself, God has miracles large and small ready to help.

## Chapter Eleven

# The Plan

Does this mean you're doing our laundry now?" Amon's mother asked.

Amon grinned and covered his face with his hand. "Uh, no, that's not exactly what I meant."

Laughter filled the cistern.

"Instead, I've asked Maacah to help."

All eyes turned to the seller of fine cloth, who sat at the far end of the cistern with a basket in front of her.

"Maacah has agreed to donate twelve lengths of cloth to help all believers in Jerusalem communicate." Amon led the group in applause, then started digging in his backpack. "And this is how we will signal."

He pulled out several colored sticks as Maacah pulled out two samples of the cloth, each about as wide as her forearm and many feet long. One cloth was black, the other red.

"Every day except the Sabbath or holidays," Amon said, "my mother, Tamar, and some of the other women will take turns going in pairs to a different place on the city wall where people have already hung their clothes to dry. There they will hang six of these cloths in a pattern that will tell everyone of The Way when and where to meet that day."

General mumbling swept across the group as people said to their neighbor things like, "How could this work?" or "What is he saying?"

"Please," Amon said, "let me demonstrate." He took the sticks painted black and red, and laid six of them at random on the ground representing six lengths of cloth. "Suppose Caleb goes out three days after the Sabbath," he said, pointing to a man named Caleb, "which is one of the days his congregation meets. He sees these six strips of cloth hanging on the wall: black, red, red, black, red, black. He knows, because I'm telling him"—Amon looked up and smiled at the milk merchant—"that black means the number zero, and red means the number one. So he sees in the cloths the number zero, one,

one, zero, one, zero. It's just a number, but with only the digits zero and one. You could call it a binary number or something, I suppose."

Some people seemed confused, but others whispered explanations to them until they understood.

"Now, Caleb knows, because I'm telling him"—Amon smiled again—"that the first three digits are the time of today's meeting, and the second three are the place. He also knows, because he has memorized it, that 'zero, one, one' means the fourth hour of the day, and that for his particular congregation 'zero, one, zero' means the cistern at Elam's house."

Grins erupted on most faces as people finally understood the plan.

"What appears to be just some cloth drying in the sun"—Amon paused, hoping all of this made sense—"will actually tell all the believers at a glance when and where to meet, if it is their day to meet."

"Doesn't that mean everyone will show up at the same place?" Amon's mother asked.

Amon shook his head. "No, because each congregation has a *different* 'zero, one, zero.' We have eight total cisterns, and each congregation will be assigned to three of them. So your 'zero, one, zero' will be different from that of someone in a different congregation."

| Binary Number | Hour of Day | Cistern (for example) |
|---|---|---|
| 000 | 1 | Boaz |
| 001 | 2 | Giliad |
| 010 | 3 | Elam |
| 011 | 4 | Gehazi |
| 100 | 5 | Hirma |
| 101 | 6 | Jubal |
| 110 | 7 | Uriah |
| 111 | 8 | Jcssc |

Time in the New Testament was a relative thing and changed slightly every day throughout the year. It started with the "first hour" of the day, which began with the breaking of dawn. The remainder of the daylight up until the third medium-sized star was visible in the evening was broken into twelve equal parts with the "sixth hour" being noon. Thus the "third hour" of the day would be a different length in winter than in summer, and from day to day. This sounds confusing to those of us with modern timekeepers, but it was just part of life and education for the people of the ancient world.

There were a few moments of silence as people stared at the black and red sticks, then suddenly the cistern was filled with applause as they grasped Amon's complete plan.

"Just brilliant," the old man shouted again.

"You truly are the Clever One, Amon," a woman said.

The excitement built as they decided who would lead which groups, worked on memorizing the numbers of each cistern for their congregation, and figuring out who would decide which groups would meet on which days.

Amon was given the job of deciding, at random, which cisterns would be used each day, so that there would never be a pattern that someone could notice.

The meeting had lasted well over an hour by now, and the air inside the cistern was getting thick and stale. Because of this, it was decided that congregational meetings should only be about an hour long, depending on the size of the chamber and number of people.

There were two days left until the Sabbath, so it was decided those days would be used for explaining the system to all the believers, quietly and mouth-to-ear.

~

On the day after the Sabbath, before dawn, Amon's mother, Tamar, and two other women each took baskets of cloth and walked along the wall toward the gate of the Essenes. When they found a section where women had already hung laundry high on the wall, they arranged six strips of cloth for the day, then hung them up in the correct order, being careful not to make them look *too* arranged. Their task complete, they walked home quietly, talking among themselves to seem like any group of women on any other laundry day. They even stopped and talked with another group of women headed to a well.

Tabitha and Tamar entered their house, where Amon was playing King's Ransom with Jadon and Uri as he anxiously waited, having already made the boys' breakfast.

"Well?" he asked when he saw the women.

"It went just fine," Tamar answered. "We acted normal and natural and simply hung our 'clothes' to dry."

The sun was just rising above the horizon now, so Amon went outside and scanned the city. Though he had no idea where they had hung the signal, it took his eyes only seconds to locate and read it. Grinning, he went back inside. "It works!" he said, as if he really hadn't thought it would. "I can see them and read them easily."

Late that afternoon, reports were quietly whispered all through Jerusalem: the system worked perfectly, and the Clever One was a hero. Jotham invited Peter, Matthew, Bartholomew, Barnabas, and James the brother of Jesus to come for the evening meal where they spoke in quiet voices with the shutters tightly closed over the glass windows.

"As soon as I awoke this morning, I went outside," Barnabas said. "I looked across the city and saw the strips of cloth. After a bit of figuring, I knew to meet with my congregation at the third hour in the cistern of Jubal." He laughed as he dipped some bread in olive oil. "And at the third hour, all the congregation slipped into Jubal's courtyard from this direction or that, and we had a wonderful hour of praise together. You truly can be proud of what you've accomplished here, Amon."

The others echoed the words of Barnabas, but Amon just hung his head. "Even in my short life," he said quietly, "I have learned not to be proud, but to be thankful." He looked up at the other men. "It is not by my wit that these things have occurred, but by the grace of God, and I am thankful for whatever small part in it he has granted me."

"Well said," Peter commented, and the older men all slapped the table repeatedly in applause. "Now we must be careful," Peter said, choosing a bite of cheese, "that everyone keeps this secret."

"Yes," James agreed. "I told my congregation that a great forest can be set on fire by a small spark, and their tongues could be that spark."

Uri shrunk back. "Is there going to be a fire?"

Sitting next to him, Amon put his arm around his little brother and whispered, "No, Uri, everything is just fine."

Uri swallowed and took another olive.

"Now I must get back to the harder task," Amon said to the rest of the group.

They questioned him with their eyes. He answered, "I must find a way to bring Saul into The Way."

There was a long silence as the others ate, heads down, avoiding his gaze, and Amon could tell they didn't believe this to be possible.

"It is a particularly difficult task you have set yourself," Bartholomew said softly, still not looking at Amon.

"Amon is particularly good at difficult tasks, Father," Tamar said, "as you have seen this very day."

Bartholomew turned to his daughter. "This I know, but conveying information to the minds of a congregation is a far easier task than changing the prejudices of a single, stubborn heart."

"Do as Jehovah guides you," Peter said to Amon, "but be cautious, my young friend. Saul would not hesitate to have even you put to death in his crusade to squash The Way."

A shudder ran down Amon's spine, but he said, "I believe I know Saul well enough to remain safe."

"And I feel I must insist," Bartholomew added, "that you no longer take Tamar with you to see Saul. She may help you plan and prepare, but she is yet young, and I do not want her put in danger."

Amon's heart was saddened at this, but he understood.

Tamar clearly wanted to comment on this but knew to keep quiet.

"Or Benjamin," Amon's father said. "He is not yet a man, and I must speak for his parents. He may not make the choice to put himself in situations of danger."

Amon nodded. "It is wise advice you give, though I will miss their company."

~

Each morning a different group of women would take the signal cloths to a different place on the wall and hang them with other laundry already there. That evening they would retrieve the cloths and hand them off to a new group, along with the "code" for the next day.

After three days, the believers at the other end of Jerusalem began to complain that it was difficult for them to see the signal. The wall with the Garden Gate split the city in two, and those in the northern half of the city had to walk all the way to the gate to see the signal in the southern half. It was quickly decided to put up a set of markers in both halves of Jerusalem, and Maacah gladly donated more cloth.

Amon noticed a marked difference in Jerusalem by the end of the first week. "There are more people out in the streets shopping and visiting," he told Tamar and Benjamin as they walked.

Tamar spun around as if taking in the scene. "And they are all much happier!"

Benjamin grinned. "It's just like before Stephen was killed."

"Our meetings have filled my own heart with joy," Amon said. "It's almost as though we are free again. It seems like nothing can stop us now."

At that moment the air was filled with screams.

"What is it?" Amon spun around trying to locate the source. "What is that?"

"Over there," Benjamin pointed up the street.

The screams got louder as the three friends ran to where a crowd had gathered at an intersection with a narrower side street. They slipped through most of the mass of people, but when Amon saw what was happening, he pushed the others back toward the open street.

"What are you doing?" Tamar yelled. "What's going on?"

"Listen, both of you. You must go home right now."

"What?" Benjamin protested. "Why?"

Amon was breathing hard now and kept looking back toward the screaming. "You must go home *now*. I promised my father, Bartholomew, and Peter that I would not put you in danger."

"*What* danger?" Tamar pleaded. "What's going on, Amon?"

Amon looked back once again, then straight into Tamar's eyes. "It's Saul," he said. "Saul is arresting believers."

✦ ✦ ✦

If God can work in our lives in miraculous ways that are too impossible to be coincidences, why doesn't he *always* keep us from harm, disease, or disaster?

Why didn't he just stop Saul from hurting people, or stop the Sanhedrin from killing Stephen?

There are many answers to those questions, but all of them pretty much come down to this: God's ways are not our ways. We cannot always understand why he does or doesn't do a thing. It would be like your pet goldfish trying to understand why you wear clothes, or sing "Happy Birthday" to someone, or read your Bible.

In the last chapter, I said that God has absolutely saved my life on many occasions. But I must also tell you that I have a serious chronic disease which causes me much distress. If God can save my life, why doesn't he respond to my many prayers for healing?

I don't know. I can't understand. I'm a goldfish who can only know and understand the very limited space inside my fishbowl.

But one of the things I *can* know is that God is God—in control, knowing all, doing what he knows is best. And that's sufficient for me.

Saul is hurting people. God could stop it with a word. But he doesn't—at least not yet. Amon doesn't understand why these things happen or what he can do about them. He hasn't yet fully learned that God's ways are not our ways so we must fully depend on him in faith.

Chapter Twelve

# Fear

Tamar glared at Amon, her hands on her hips. "Who do you think you are to tell me I have to go home?"

Amon remained calm and met her angry gaze with one of apology. "What is happening around that corner is terrifying. I know you are strong and could probably help the situation, but I promised your father I would not let you anywhere near Saul again, and that is a promise I must keep."

She stared at him, then looked away and seemed to relax. "You are correct," she said softly. "We must both obey my father." She turned, grabbed Benjamin by the arm, and said, "Come, Benjamin, we must do as this old man says."

Amon headed around the corner. What he saw there sickened him.

The temple guards, led by their chief, Raphu, were dragging an entire family out of their house—a mother and father, two girls, and a boy about four years old. All were screaming, crying, and fighting. To one side, supervising, stood Saul.

A large crowd had gathered, and Saul saw an opportunity to lecture, even as the family was bound with ropes. "Pay heed!" he yelled. "This is what happens to followers of false messiahs. These people claim the dead teacher Jesus of Nazareth as their messiah. Where is he now, at their time of need? I'll tell you—*he is dead*. And so shall be any who follow him. The Sanhedrin will not tolerate heresy. Not in Jerusalem, not anywhere."

Saul led the soldiers and their prisoners away, down the street toward the temple. As they passed Amon, Saul noticed his friend and called out. "Amon! I must talk with you. Come and see me as soon as you can."

Amon managed to nod, even as his limbs grew numb. What could Saul possibly want to see him about?

It soon became obvious. As Amon walked through the streets, he realized that the time for the daily meetings—chosen at random—was approaching. He watched several people he knew to be of The Way try to appear casual as they headed toward their meeting places.

Saul had figured it out.

All the blood seemed to drain from Amon's body. His legs went weak, and he stumbled over to a low wall to sit. How could he have been so stupid? Now that he actually stopped and watched the streets, it was obvious that all these people were *trying* not to look suspicious but were really heading to secret meetings of believers. He tried to speak a warning to one of the believers, a man named Micah, but the man just ignored Amon and kept walking. A thousand thoughts scrambled together in his head, but one thing he knew for sure: he must get to Peter and put a stop to this before Saul started his slaughter.

Amon jumped up, now powered by adrenaline, and raced through the streets to his house. His parents and Bartholomew were there, along with Tamar and Benjamin "We must stop the meetings at once," he blurted without even a greeting, "and warn everyone to hide."

The others all stared at him, then his father said, "Why?"

As fast as he could, Amon told them what he'd observed and what he'd figured out.

His father looked at his mother, then Bartholomew, then back at Amon. "I think you may be blowing this out of proportion," his father said.

"You weren't *there*," Amon yelled. "It was so *obvious*."

"Amon, sit," his mother said.

Amon obeyed and began to calm down a bit.

"Think clearly now," she said, rubbing his shoulder. "You had just seen a terrifying thing in the family being arrested. Then you walked through busy streets and saw a few of The Way going this way and that. Is it possible that you were just so upset that you saw what you thought was obvious but was really just a normal day in Jerusalem?"

"I seem to remember"—his father patted Amon on the leg—"that on the day Jesus ascended to heaven, you thought the entire city was celebrating him. Your mind gave meaning to the ordinary actions of ordinary people. Is it possible you did the same today?"

*Maybe my parents are right*, Amon thought. *If so, there's no way I'm getting out of this without humiliation*. Regardless, he forced himself to say, "It is possible. Perhaps I was simply scared by what I saw."

The others, and especially Bartholomew, assured Amon there was no reason to be embarrassed, that the situation in the city was very tense, and that anyone who had the responsibilities Amon had would be nervous.

The door suddenly opened. Peter entered, closed the door behind him, then turned to those gathered. "My friends," he said, "we have a dire situation developing in Jerusalem."

~

An hour later Peter had been updated on the morning's events, and he had told the others his news. "Saul and many others have gone mad with anger. He has begun arresting people on mere suspicion. The family Amon saw arrested were quickly released when there was no real evidence against them, but soon Saul will convince enough Sanhedrin members to vote with him based solely on his word."

"But it *seems* like Saul already knows everything," Amon said, still clinging to his earlier fears. "Surely he has noticed all the believers walking through the streets, and he will soon arrest them all."

"Amon," Peter said calmly, "do you not think Saul would even now be going to all the meeting places and arresting people of The Way if he knew? This morning he arrested a family without even a hint of evidence. If he *had* a hint, or even less, he would be at all those cisterns right now, and all of us would already be in prison."

Amon leaned back and tried to make his muscles relax. "Perhaps I did overreact a little."

"However," Peter said as he stroked his beard in thought, "I do think there is some merit in your analysis. Maybe having everyone meet at the same time on a given day puts too many believers on the street going to too many meetings."

The others agreed, and it was decided to pass the word to some groups that they would meet one hour later than the cloth code indicated, and some groups two hours later.

"A good decision," Bartholomew said. "It will spread out the traffic of believers across the day."

"And then we must remind everyone, including ourselves, to be extra cautious about talking to people we do not know are of The Way."

"Speaking of which," Amon said, "I noticed today that none of the believers will even look at me—even ones who know me well and are my friends. Is everyone mad at me?"

Peter laughed. "No, no, my young friend." He turned to Bartholomew, who was also smiling, then back at Amon. "A few days ago we passed the word that no one is to acknowledge you on the street, just in case someone is watching." He put his arm around Amon's shoulders. "You are much too valuable to the cause right now, and we must protect you."

~

A few days later Amon and his two friends were walking through the city again on their way to fetch some foodstuffs for his mother. He was finally getting used to being ignored by people he'd known all his life, but it still felt strange.

Amon was silent as they walked. A thought circled around the back of his head—something he was supposed to do, or not do, or say, or not say—but he couldn't seem to drag it into the thinking part of his brain.

Tamar suggested they take a break atop the Garden Gate, since Amon's mother was in no hurry for the salt and figs she'd asked for. As the three climbed the stairs, Benjamin said, "My rabbi told me to write an acrostic. What's an acrostic?"

Amon finally gave up trying to capture his elusive thought. "It's a kind of poem. You take the letters of a common word and use them as the first letters of words to mean something else."

"Why would my rabbi want me to do that?"

"Because it makes your brain think in new ways. That's why I write oratory and play music."

"It sounds like a lot of work."

They reached the top of the stairs and walked out onto the wall. "Not at all. It's easy. Take any word you want, then make up a sentence from the first letters of that word. Let's say you chose the word 'camel.' What words could you make from those letters?"

As Benjamin tapped his chin, Tamar answered with a grin. "*Crazy, Amon, Makes, Everyone, Loony.*"

Benjamin almost fell off the wall laughing, and Amon gave Tamar a playful scowl.

"I get it!" Benjamin said. "Amon's a camel!"

With Benjamin and Tamar still giggling, they sat in the shade of an awning, dangling their legs over the side, and gazing out at the city.

When finally they had calmed down, Benjamin looked toward the holy place and said to Amon, "Why is it you hardly go to the temple anymore?"

"What do you mean?"

"Months ago, after you became a man, every time I wanted to play, all *you* wanted to do was go to the temple to pray. Sometimes twice in one day. Now you almost never go."

Amon stared into the sky. "I guess there are three reasons." He looked at Benjamin. "First, when Jesus was crucified and the earthquake damaged the temple, I came up through the floor and saw the holy of holies and the ark of the covenant. All my life I was taught that no man could see that and live, because it was the place God dwells on this earth."

"And so it was," Tamar said. "My father has told me of many times in the past when men died in-stantly simply because they accidentally saw behind the veil."

"It is so," Amon said. "But when Caiaphas and I, and many others, looked toward the holy of holies, the veil was ripped in two and we saw everything. But there was no God there."

"Why was that?" Benjamin asked.

Amon had never put these thoughts into words, so he answered slowly. "I now believe it was because once Jesus died, even before he was resurrected, God no longer needed to dwell in a building on earth in order to talk with his children." He pointed between himself and his friends. "Now his Spirit dwells in each of us instead."

Benjamin crossed his arms on his chest as if to hold in the Spirit, then Tamar said, "What's the second reason you no longer go to the temple?"

Amon sighed. "Because most of those who are supposed to be our spiritual leaders think only of themselves. They think of power and glory and money. Even if they once truly sought God, they have been blinded by human desires."

"Even Gamaliel?" Tamar asked.

At this Amon's body slumped a bit, and sadness filled his heart. "No, I do not think so. I think Gamaliel and many others are still truly seeking God and not glory, but they find it very difficult to give up the old ways of thinking." He looked up at Benjamin and then Tamar. "We are very young, and it was easy for us to see the truth of Jesus once it was obvious. But older people like Gamaliel . . ." He shook his head slowly. "It is very difficult for them to turn their backs on the traditions and rituals they have practiced all their lives."

There was silence, then Benjamin asked, "And the third reason?"

Amon sat up and smiled a crooked smile. "Because all the high priests want to kill me. They just don't know yet that it is me they want to kill."

The other two smiled and Tamar said, "Are you saying that if you walk through the snake pit, the snakes are more likely to bite you?"

"Indeed," Amon laughed. But then he saw Benjamin, who was no longer smiling and was instead staring off into space. "Benjamin, what is wrong? Did we offend you?"

Benjamin shook his head slowly and said, "No. Look."

Amon and Tamar turned to where he was looking. There, coming from the north to their left, just rounding Mount Scopus, was a frightfully long and terribly colorful caravan full of camels, horses, flags, and people in silk clothing.

"There must be five hundred camels," Benjamin whispered in awe.

"And a hundred horses," Amon added.

"It must be the caravan of a king," Tamar guessed.

They watched as the front of the long line stopped in the Kidron Valley, between the Mount of Olives on the other side and the Beautiful Gate of the temple on this side but still outside the city walls. There was much commotion as people dismounted, orders were given, camels were unloaded, and guards on horseback kept watch in every direction.

And then they saw him.

"The king," Tamar gasped.

One man, dressed in purple robes, wearing a crown, and surrounded by others taking his orders, stood with his fists on his hips and stared at the temple. Even from far away, Amon could tell that he was a man of power and a man respected by his people.

"Who are they?" Tamar asked.

"I do not know," Amon said, still staring.

Then the royal-looking man walked quickly and confidently toward the East Gate, followed by dozens of guards and advisors. People from all over Jerusalem climbed to the tops of the buildings and walls to watch the spectacle.

"We should go tell our parents," Amon said, and the other two showed their agreement by following him down the steps.

Once at the bottom, they raced through the streets, pushing past shoppers, animals, carts, and construction. It was slow going, and Amon yelled, "Come on, let's go through the upper city." He started uphill toward the large villas and Herod's palace.

Here the streets were wider and not as crowded. Finally they reached the street on which Amon lived, only to find it packed with his neighbors, many other Jews who just seemed to be gawking, and several of the newcomers in the colorful silk clothing.

"Excuse me," Amon kept repeating as he pushed through the crowd. "Excuse me." He was about to turn back and try getting to his house from a different direction when a hole suddenly opened between two silk-and-armor-clad soldiers. He dashed through it, followed by Tamar and Benjamin, then stopped short. He was standing in a clearing in front of his own house, with two soldiers standing guard on either side of his door.

Amon gulped and approached the soldiers cautiously. "Excuse me," he said, making sure to appear subservient, "this is my house."

The two soldiers stared at him without blinking, said nothing, then went back to looking straight ahead. Amon pushed the door open slowly, then stopped and stared. Standing in the middle of the room, hugging Amon's mother, and surrounded by a very old guard, Amon's father, and Bartholomew, was the king who had just arrived on the caravan.

✦ ✦ ✦

Sometimes people disappoint us. Even friends, even parents, even church leaders. No one is perfect, and sometimes even those we respect get it wrong.

That's why it's a good idea to let God be our ultimate guide. Of course we still listen to our friends, obey our parents, and respect our leaders, but in the end, we are responsible to God.

Amon is discouraged with some of the things he was taught and some of the people who taught him. Some of those things no longer seem to be true, and the teachers are ignoring facts and evidence. What seems so obviously true to him, others don't see.

The whole problem is that churches are made up of people. Remove the people from a church, and the church will be perfect.

Except that without people, a church isn't a church, right? Because a church isn't a building, it's a gathering of people.

How then can we ever have a perfect church?

It's obvious: we can't, if we mean by "perfect" that there are no disagreements and everyone believes exactly the same thing.

A great example of this is Peter. Jesus told Peter he would be the foundation stone on which he would build his new church. But Peter wasn't perfect, didn't always agree with the other apostles, and sometimes even got things wrong.

Jesus knew his church would be made up of imperfect people. That doesn't matter to him. What matters is that we all join together to support each other, share with each other, teach each other, and worship him together.

Chapter Thirteen

# The Prince

*Something is wrong here*, Amon thought. *They're all smiling and laughing and talking, as if this is a very normal thing. But this is not a very normal thing. My parents and Tamar's father are talking to and hugging some foreign king as if he's just any old friend. But no one touches a king and lives, and poor shepherds and penniless apostles do not joke with kings. Something is terribly wrong here!*

"Amon," his father called, seeing his son. "Come in and close the door. I want you to meet an old friend."

*An old friend? My father has an old friend who's a king?* Amon forced his feet to walk forward as his mother and the king embraced.

Uri and Jadon sat on the steps right above them.

His mother stepped back from the stranger. "Amon, I'd like you to meet His Excellency Ishtar, Prince of all Persia."

*A prince, not a king. But still royalty—and someone common people do not touch.*

"Amon!" Prince Ishtar said loudly. He stepped forward and reached out with both arms as if greeting a long-lost friend. He buried Amon in a bear hug that pushed Amon's cheek against the sharp corners of the prince's jewels and breastplate. "It is my very great pleasure to finally meet the son of my best of all friends."

Ishtar finally released Amon, who stepped back to look him in the eye as he'd been taught. "My house is your house, and my family your family," he said to the prince, since he was too confused to think of anything but a standard greeting.

"And this is my daughter, Tamar," Bartholomew said, stepping up next to the prince.

"Ahhh, young princess." Ishtar dropped to one knee, took her hand in his, and kissed the back of it as if he were meeting some great queen.

"I—I am not a princess," Tamar stammered.

Still on one knee, the prince looked up into her eyes. "Believe me," he said softly, "to your father you are a princess, and that is a stronger bond than any produced by the nonsense of men."

Tamar blushed and turned away.

Ishtar stood and turned toward Benjamin. "And who is this fine young man?"

Benjamin's mouth moved a few times, but no sound came out.

Amon glanced at his father, who urged him on with a nod. "This is my friend, Benjamin, son of Enoch."

The prince stepped forward and shook Benjamin's hand. "A friend of Amon's is a friend of mine. Greetings, young Benjamin, son of Enoch."

Benjamin's mouth moved, but the only words that came out were, "Amon's a camel!"

The prince looked at him in surprise, then at Amon, who had plastered his hand over his face and was shaking his head slowly.

Amon finally faced the prince. "It's an acrostic—a kind of—kind of joke."

The prince still stared at him and said, "So, Amon, *are* you a camel?"

Amon smiled and answered, "Yes, I probably am."

Everyone laughed, even though they had no idea what was going on.

"Ishtar my friend," Jotham bellowed. "Come. Sit. Tell us what brings you back to Jerusalem."

*Back?* Amon thought. *He's been here before?*

Jotham sat on the rough and worn bench on one side of the wooden table, Ishtar and Bartholomew on the other side.

As Amon, Tamar, and Benjamin pulled stools up to the end of the table, Benjamin whispered to his friends, "I can't believe I told the prince you're a camel."

Amon and Tamar grinned, and Amon patted his friend on the back to comfort him.

Amon's mother filled a cup with water from the pipe in the wall.

Ishtar gasped. "What is this thing I see? Water that comes from the wall on demand? Is this sorcery?"

Jotham chuckled. "No, my friend, it is my son. He invented this device to make his mother's work easier."

Ishtar spun around toward Amon. "The truth you tell! Well, perhaps I will have to kidnap this boy and take him back to Persia to build one for me."

Everyone laughed at this except Amon, who was busy trying to decide if Ishtar was serious.

Tabitha started to hand the cup of water to Ishtar, but the very old guard jumped forward and intercepted her.

"It is alright, Kazeem." Ishtar held out his arm. "There is no danger in this house and no poison in the water."

Jotham's face snapped up to look at the old man. "Kazeem? Is that really you?" He jumped up and embraced the guard. "I did not recognize you! I am so glad you are still alive."

Amon's head was spinning now—he didn't understand anything at all that was happening.

Jotham sat back down, still smiling. "Apologies, my friend, but you may not whisk my son away to Persia. He is needed here for more important work than plumbing. And, just so you know, by our tradition and his training, Amon is now a man, not a boy."

Ishtar bowed his head toward Amon. "*My* apologies, Amon. I did not realize you had already passed your exams."

"No trespass," Amon said, bowing slightly. "How do you know of our customs?"

The four adults looked at each other as if they had a secret, then Jotham spoke to his son. "It is a very long story," he said, "but I will say this for now, that the four of us had many adventures together as children, and we were all in Bethlehem when Jesus was born."

Amon lowered his gaze to the table. "Were these some of the stories you tried to tell me, but I didn't believe?" he asked softly.

Jotham took a deep breath. "Yes, my son. But now, I think I would like to tell them all to you again sometime soon."

Amon looked straight at Ishtar. "You saw Jesus when he was a baby?"

Ishtar nodded. "Yes, indeed. But more than that, I held him in my arms just minutes after he was born. In fact, that is why I have come to Jerusalem. I would like to meet the *man* that baby became and hear the story he has to tell."

There was an awkward silence as the others looked at each other.

Amon's father cleared his throat. "Then you have not heard the news."

"What news? We have been traveling for many months."

And so Jotham told the prince of the death and resurrection of Jesus, and the news of his Holy Spirit descending on believers. When he was finished, Ishtar leaned back against the wall and stared off into space. "I have always believed in your one God," he said in a low voice, "though my father disapproved. But now, to hear this tale of sacrifice and rebirth . . ." He returned from his thinking and looked at Amon's father. "I must hear more of this, but I want my children to hear as well."

"You have children?" Amon's mother asked.

"Yes, I have ten. But only my two eldest are with me."

"Ten children," Bartholomew gasped. "And how many wives?"

Ishtar sat a little straighter. "Only one, like my father. Her name is Anahita, and she is home with the rest of them. We do not believe in having servants raise our children." He turned to one of the guards at the door and spoke in Persian, and the man left.

Happy to hear a language he rarely got to speak, Amon asked in Persian, "How is it you knew how to find our house if you haven't been to Jerusalem since you were a child?"

"You honor me by speaking in my language. When I was here before, I visited your King Herod with my father. His palace is just a short distance away, and your father once told me in a letter that he had built the only sheep pens between the palace and the Gate of the Essenes."

Amon was so shocked he blurted out in Aramaic, "You met King Herod?"

Ishtar grinned and also replied in Amon's native tongue. "Yes, and I can tell you it was no great pleasure. Now tell me more about this water that comes from the wall."

Amon explained how the system worked, and about the glass windows. He was just finishing as the guard returned with two young people about Amon's age—a boy dressed in colorful silk pants and shirt, a girl in a colorful silk gown, all of it lined in gold.

"Ah, my daughter Yasmin and my son Zana," Ishtar said proudly.

The two seemed identical except for their clothes and hair.

"Twins?" Amon's mother exclaimed and jumped up to greet them.

"Indeed," Ishtar said, looking very proud.

While his mother greeted the children, Amon analyzed them. The boy was a bit shy, but the girl was very outgoing. They struggled to speak in Aramaic yet could still make themselves understood. They also stared curiously at the house and furnishings, probably because they were used to life in a palace.

"I shall make dinner for us all," Tabitha announced, and Ishtar seemed pleased. Tamar and Jadon helped, and Benjamin went to his house to borrow more olive oil from his mother. Jotham, Bartholomew, and Ishtar then talked of their lives since they'd last been together.

Soon the smell of roasting sheep filled the house and Amon's stomach rumbled. He kept looking at the Persian twins, and they kept looking at him, but none of them knew what to say.

After a time, Tabitha announced that dinner was ready, and everyone pulled up to the table. She set a large bowl in front of Ishtar, then stood back and watched.

Ishtar stared at the bowl in surprise, then he and all the adults started laughing until they cried. "Millet?" Ishtar exclaimed. "What a wonderful surprise!"

The young people were all confused by the behavior of their elders, but Ishtar wiped his eyes and explained. "Your mother remembers well the story of my youth, Amon. I grew up with only servants as a mother. My father was a wonderful man but very busy. I only ever knew the finest of foods the world has to offer, and always had at least three desserts at every meal. Until, that is, my father made me go on a caravan to this very city. For months I had nothing but millet to eat three times a day. I thought I would die and hardly ate anything the first few days."

The adults all broke into laughter again, though the young people still didn't see what was so funny.

Ishtar finished his story. "But eventually I learned to appreciate having any meal at all."

"Is this why we eat simple meals at home?" Yasmin asked.

"Yes indeed," Ishtar answered. "Your mother and I didn't want you to be spoiled the way I was."

"Enough talk, Ishtar!" Kazeem spoke for the first time. In the same gruff voice he barked, "Now eat your millet."

For a moment everyone was shocked at the rebuke the elderly man gave the prince, then Kazeem grinned. "I haven't got to say that to you in over thirty years!"

They all laughed again.

Tabitha tried to take the millet away, saying it was just a joke, but Ishtar insisted on eating it. Then the roast and the rest of a fine meal were served.

As the sun began to set, the crowds outside headed home for their own dinners. With the travelers' bellies warm and full, Ishtar leaned back once again and said to Jotham, "Now, tell me about this messiah."

Amon's father looked a bit nervous and searched outside the open windows to see who might be listening. "I think that is a story best told in your own language." He turned to Amon, the only one of them who could speak Persian.

Still not believing he was sitting in his own house speaking to Persian royalty, Amon told the story of Jesus in a language in which it had probably never before been given.

And as Amon spoke, the eyes of Ishtar, his children, and even Kazeem, grew wider and wider in amazement.

✦ ✦ ✦

I've been to many countries in my lifetime and have heard the good news of Jesus preached in many languages—French, German, Russian, Chinese, Spanish, and more. I also spent many years reading the Bible in Greek. What I've found is that in every new language, I hear new meaning in the gospel. Whether from individual words that translate into a different thought or the cultural background that carries the words, the story of Jesus is new and fresh in each new language it encounters.

The Bible, or portions of it, has only been translated into about a third of the languages in the world, so there's still a lot of work to be done. Imagine being someone who speaks one of the other two-thirds of languages. Imagine hearing about the miraculous birth, sacrifice, and resurrection of Jesus for the very first time. What would you think? How would you feel?

Amon has just spoken the gospel in the language of the Persians for the very first time, and his audience was amazed and excited. Maybe next time you hear the gospel in *your* language, you could imagine you've never heard it before and allow God to once again fill you with wonder.

Chapter Fourteen

# Swim Lessons

Amon couldn't get to sleep. He'd never before slept next to a statue—certainly not a statue on the roof of his own house—and it was a strange experience. Most strange, because this statue was alive. It was standing only a few feet from him, wearing the leather armor of a Persian soldier, holding a giant curved sword in one hand at the end of its crossed arms, and was staring directly at Amon.

How could anyone sleep like this?

Of course, the statue wasn't really staring at *him*. It was staring at Zana, lying on a gold-embroidered sleeping mat between Benjamin and him. Zana was sound asleep. Apparently he was used to having statues watch him all night.

Amon looked again at the statue—a Persian special guard. He was still amazed, and annoyed, that the man never moved, didn't seem to breath, and hardly ever blinked as he watched over Zana. There were four such statues stationed around the small roof, two watching over Ishtar's son, and two watching over his daughter, who slept next to Tamar on the other side of the roof.

Strange.

After the long supper the night before, Amon's father had invited the twins to stay the night. Zana didn't seem too happy about that, but Yasmin was excited. Ishtar allowed it—as long as four special guards accompanied them—and had sent for their sleeping mats from the caravan. So here they were, statues and all.

A moment later Amon decided he must have fallen asleep because he was suddenly alone on the roof, the heat of the sun roasting him under his blanket, and laughter came from below him.

"Shalom, Amon," his father said as he descended the steps. Everyone was there—his parents, his brothers, Ishtar and the twins, Kazeem, Benjamin, and Tamar—and they were all still laughing as if someone had just said something funny. On the table sat an almost-empty plate of bread and an almost-empty pitcher of milk.

"We saved you some breakfast," his mother said, placing another plate of cheese on the table. Half the cheese was gone in seconds, and Amon grabbed some while he still could.

"Thank you," Amon said as he sat on the last stool.

"Prince Ishtar was just telling us about driving a herd of chairs across the desert to get here," Amon's father said. "It was very interesting."

Amon thought that perhaps he was still asleep until Ishtar explained simply, "A dream."

Amon smiled as he filled a cup with goat's milk.

"So, what do you have planned for today?" Jotham asked.

Amon chewed and swallowed before speaking. "I thought we could take Yasmin and Zana swimming. If they like to swim, that is."

Ishtar laughed, and Amon didn't think it was a particularly princely laugh. "They've been swimming almost every day of their lives. I'm sure they'd love it."

Once again Zana was silent, but Yasmin said, "Yes, we'd love to!"

"And so would your brothers," Amon's mother said.

An hour later the seven young people, with four Persian Special Guards watching from the side, were splashing in the middle of the Pool of Serpents. Amon had assured the two guests he'd never in his life seen a serpent in or near the pool, which seemed as big as the temple and as deep as the Arabian Sea Yasmin had described to them.

Though the pool was really for storing water and not swimming, it had two areas where people could swim—one for boys and one for girls. Amon kept watch on Jadon and Uri as they played near the shore, while he and the other two boys floated and relaxed. He decided to get Zana to talk. "Since your father is a prince," he said in Persian, "is his father the king? And are *you* a prince?"

Zana seemed embarrassed to be asked a question but forced himself to answer. "It does not work that way in my country. Someday I may become a prince, but I also may not. My father is a prince but may or may not be king if our king dies. It all depends on many things."

Amon relayed the question and answer to Benjamin in Aramaic out of courtesy, then switched back to Persian to ask Zana, "Can you tell me about the place where you live?"

Zana grinned for the first time. "I would *love* to. Amaranth is a most beautiful city, sitting on a hill overlooking the Arabian Sea. It is full of the most wonderful people and marvelous food and fearless soldiers."

Amon translated under his breath to Benjamin but had trouble keeping up with Zana's excitement. For several minutes Zana gave details of the palace they lived in—with a swimming pool right in their apartments—and all the buildings and people of the great city. He was just starting in on the foods they eat when three men on horseback rode fast out of the Essene Gate.

"Uh-oh," Amon said as he stopped translating.

Benjamin looked up. "Men riding fast on horses is never good news."

For a moment it seemed as though the men were riding directly at them, then Amon realized they *were!* As they got closer, he identified them as temple soldiers.

The four Persian Special Guards all drew swords at the sight of the riders. Two of them jumped into the shallow water and stood directly in front of Zana and Yasmin.

The riders reined their horses to a stop, then the front one dismounted, holding his bare hands up for the guards to see he meant no harm. The soldier walked up to the edge of the water and scanned the three boys, his eyes stopping on Benjamin. "Amon, son of Jotham, I require you."

Benjamin looked terrified and turned toward Amon.

"I am Amon, son of Jotham," Amon said. "What is it you require?"

The soldier shifted his gaze to Amon, sized him up, then said, "Saul of Tarsus demands your presence at your convenience, even if it is not convenient."

Amon threw his head back. "Argh," he cried. "I totally forgot!"

"Forgot what?" Benjamin asked.

"I forgot that Saul asked me to come and see him a few days ago." To the soldier he said, "How did you know where to find me?"

The soldier smirked. "Saul has ways of knowing what he wants to know."

Amon swallowed hard. "Please tell Saul I will come immediately, as soon as I get dried off and dressed."

The soldier mounted, kicked his horse into action, and rode back into the city without acknowledging Amon's request.

Amon turned to Zana. "I am so sorry," he said in Persian, "but I must go." He switched to Aramaic. "Benjamin will stay with you, right, Benjamin?"

Benjamin's mouth dropped open, and he looked back and forth between Amon and Zana. "Oh, right."

Amon yelled a quick explanation to the girls, then ran home to change into dry clothes. His father and Ishtar weren't home, but he told his mother what was happening.

She grew worried. "He sent three soldiers to get you? That doesn't sound like a simple meeting between friends," she said. "Since when does Saul command soldiers?"

Amon shivered. "I do not know, but I soon shall." He gave her a kiss and ran out the door.

The sun had hardly moved before Amon arrived at Saul's house, winded and thirsty. He knocked on the door, which opened instantly.

"Finally!" Saul barked, turning away from the open door and pacing. "I asked you to come days ago."

"Forgive me, my friend," Amon said as he closed the door. "Friends of my father arrived from Persia unexpectedly, and I have been entertaining. Your request slid from my mind."

Saul stopped and stared at Amon. "The Persians? They are friends of your father?"

Amon froze as a sense of danger ran up his spine. "Yes," he said slowly. "The Persians."

Saul started pacing again and speaking things that didn't make sense. "The Persians . . . Persians . . . there is a breech. An act of irony. Long ago, in Bethlehem. Traitorous murder, lies of citizenship . . ."

Amon listened for several minutes, having no idea what his older friend was babbling about. Saul paced and ranted until Amon finally broke in. "You wanted to see me about something, my friend?"

Saul stopped in a shaft of light from a window. *A ghost*, Amon thought, seeing Saul's appearance. He'd lost weight and his eyes were sunken into black pits. His hands were folded in front of him, and the hood of his robe covered his head. *A dead man from the grave, only not quite dead.*

"See you?" Saul asked. "Ah, yes, I remember now." He returned to his pacing.

Amon watched, eyes wide, the sense of danger he'd felt erupting into a terrible fear that clawed at his insides.

"I have a most urgent matter, and need your help, my young friend," Saul said without looking at him.

"With what?"

"We know, that is, I have heard rumors, that there is a man among the believers who has devised some sort of system to signal the Jesus followers when and where to meet."

Amon sucked in his breath and stared, wide-eyed. He was silent until Saul stopped and turned to him again. "Oh, really?" Amon squeaked.

Saul also stared, as if evaluating Amon. "Yes. He is a most dangerous man, with vile evil in his heart. He is helping to mislead proper Jews into a sinful life of idol worship. He must be stopped."

He returned to pacing and Amon's mind swam in circles as he tried to decide what to say. "And what is it you wish of me?"

Saul responded as if this was a stupid question. "I want you to find him, of course. I want you to track him down. You are much better than I at investigations and such. I have no doubt you can identify this man."

Amon gulped. "And after I identify him?"

Saul spun around, his face inches from Amon's, and whispered coldly, "He will be taken before the Sanhedrin and properly dealt with."

Amon met Saul's gaze. "You mean . . . killed."

"If Jehovah, through the Sanhedrin, decides that is his fate, yes."

Amon leaned back on his feet a bit to put some distance between them. "And what of this system of signaling?"

"Once you discover it, we will use it to track down the Jesus followers and . . . bring them back to Jehovah."

A tremble went through Amon. "You know, Jerusalem is not such a large place. It is quite likely that some of the Jesus followers are people you know. Possibly even your friends."

Saul turned away, seeming weary now. He slumped down on a chair as if carrying a heavy load. When he spoke, his voice was distant, hollow. "Anyone I find who follows this false messiah, will no longer be my friend. They will be my enemy."

A long silence followed as Amon tried to corral the thousands of thoughts slithering around inside his head. Finally he asked, "And how will I know this evil one?"

Saul spat on the floor, then looked up at his friend. "No doubt he has the appearance of a demon, and you will probably know him the moment you see him. But he is also known by a nickname. That's why I thought of you. You are the cleverest person I know in all of Jerusalem. Surely, if anyone can find the Clever One, it is you."

✦ ✦ ✦

Many people who have heard the name of Jesus, and even know his story, still do not believe he is the Son of God or the Messiah. Most often, in my experience, that's because they've already decided what they believe and have no desire to change their minds. Think about it—if someone came up to you and told you that following a fuzzy blue bear into the woods would bring you salvation, would you drop all your beliefs about Jesus and look for the trail of blue fuzz?

I hope not.

But to someone who already has a firm set of beliefs, that's exactly how we sound when we tell them they should follow Jesus. The story isn't enough. It sounds ridiculous. Especially to someone like Saul, who has studied the Old Testament Scriptures faithfully.

What they really need is to meet Jesus in person, face-to-face, and live with him for a while.

Hmm, how could we make that happen, since Jesus is no longer on earth now?

I know! What if you and I were Jesus to others? What if you and I learned how to be patient, loving, forgiving, accepting, inclusive, and selfless, like Jesus? Then, instead of just hearing words *about* Jesus, others can actually *see* Jesus in action for themselves, and understand the truth of him.

My goal is to be more like Jesus in the things I think, do, and say. Will you join me?

Chapter Fifteen

# The Clever One

The moment Amon was out of sight of Saul's house he took off at a dead run. As fast as his legs would pump, he climbed the hill to the upper city, dodging mules, carts, people, and children. On one turn, his right sandal flew off. He skidded to a stop, retrieved it from a basket maker, thanked her, and took off again. He passed the twins, headed back to their caravan to change, and saw Benjamin just entering his house. All the while he was wondering how Saul found out about the "Clever One," and who had revealed the secret.

When he arrived home, Amon slammed through the door, breathless. "Where is Father?"

"Here, son," came his father's deep voice. Jotham was sitting just to Amon's right, next to the door.

Amon instantly dropped to one knee and whispered in his father's ear.

Jotham sat up, staring straight ahead. "What's the closest cistern that isn't being used today?"

"The well of Boaz."

Jotham looked at Tamar. "Quickly and quietly, go find your father, James, and Peter. Have them meet us at once at the house of Boaz."

Tamar asked no questions but simply obeyed and ran out the door.

"What is it, Jotham?" Amon's mother asked.

Jotham went to her and whispered in her ear, then he said to Amon, "Come!"

Even though he was a man, Amon knew better than to not obey his father. He followed, understanding that his mother had to stay and take care of Jadon and Uri.

Amon trailed his father, who was walking quickly down the street. They passed the street of Benjamin's house, and he saw his friend playing with his younger siblings. "Benjamin, come with us," Amon yelled.

Benjamin ran for a ball his brother had tossed, and almost tripped. He caught himself and called back, "I cannot. I'm watching the children while my mother is away."

They arrived at the house of Boaz, and Jotham slowed, trying to look casual while still watching for anyone suspicious. Neither he nor Amon saw anyone that seemed to care who went where, so they slipped into the garden behind the house.

Once inside, Jotham explained to the owner their need for using his cistern, and he quickly agreed. They took no torch down into the rock chamber, so the only light came from the entrance hole above. They sat and waited in silence for a few minutes, then James the brother of Jesus arrived.

"We have a most urgent situation," Amon's father whispered to the leader of the believers. "I've sent for Peter and Bartholomew as well."

James nodded his understanding, then they continued to wait.

Amon was just starting to think something had gone wrong, when Tamar descended into the cistern, followed by Peter and Bartholomew. Quick greetings were exchanged, then Jotham explained that Saul knew about the Clever One.

"Now," he concluded a few minutes later, "you must decide what to do."

The three apostles discussed the matter for almost an hour, occasionally questioning Amon. It was eerie, sitting in the dark cistern with only the daylight that shone through the one opening above. In the dim light Amon could only see shadows of the men before him, could only hear the voices coming from blackness.

"And you are sure he doesn't know you are the Clever One?" Peter asked.

Before Amon could answer, Bartholomew said, "Saul isn't clever enough himself to play such games. If he knew, Amon would already be condemned and stoned."

Amon shuddered at the thought of that.

There was much talk of getting Amon out of Jerusalem, of hiding him in Hebron or Jericho, or even taking him to Damascus to live with some believers there.

"As much as I would hate to see it," Jotham said when the apostles seemed to be unsure of what to do, "I have a friend visiting here from Persia. A prince of Persia, in fact. I'm sure he would be happy to take Amon back to Arabia with him. There are no temple soldiers who could defeat the Persian army. Not even the Romans can do that very often."

This launched the discussion in an entirely new direction, and there was much debate. But still no firm conclusion. Through it all, Tamar sat alone, to the side, in the darkness.

After all the discussion seemed to lead nowhere, it was James who finally addressed Amon. "You are a man now," he said. "What do *you* want to do?"

Amon had been wondering this himself the entire time. There were really only two options. The first was the one the others had been considering most closely: run away and hide somewhere. The second one, the one he felt he must choose, he now spoke.

"If I am truly a believer in Jesus as the Messiah," he said, "I must put my safety and even my entire life into his hands. And if his Holy Spirit lives inside me, then he will make his will known." There was silence as Amon paused to think through the next part one last time before he brought it into the light. "Nothing inside me is telling me to run and hide. Everything inside me is telling me to trust in Jehovah and do his will. Just the way Jesus did, and Stephen did, and the way each of you does every day."

James took a deep breath. "Then so be it. If his father has no objections"—he glanced at Jotham, who shook his head—"Amon will continue his work here in Jerusalem. Obviously he will *not* tell Saul who the Clever One is, but he must not lie either."

The others mumbled agreement with this. "You will indeed need to be clever," Peter said, "to answer Saul's questions without lying, but without telling the truth either."

When all the words that needed to be spoken seemed to have been spoken, everyone laid a hand on Amon's shoulders and prayed for wisdom and protection for him.

The next day at their regular afternoon meeting in the cistern of Jabal, Amon spoke to the thirty people gathered and explained his task. Prince Ishtar and the twins were there as well, along with their guards, all wearing ordinary clothes loaned to them from believers. "And so now," he said slowly and carefully, trying to look each person in the eye under the light of a dozen torches, "I must ask each of you. Can you describe to me a man who is not here among us, but whom you might call clever?"

The group was quiet and seemed confused by the question. But one young woman, two years older than Tamar, said, "I believe I know such a man. He is quite old, with white hair and a white beard." She raised an eyebrow at Amon, who knew she was describing her grandfather.

A moment later it was as if the entire crowd understood. "No, no," said a man, a father of six children. "I'm quite certain I know of a clever man, and he has a long brown beard and no hair."

Suddenly everyone was trying to talk at once. "I know the man! He is tall and thin," said one. "No, he is short and quite plump," said another.

"The cleverest person I know," Zana said, "is as old as dirt and is Persian."

Everyone laughed, and Amon was surprised his friend spoke up in front of a crowd, especially while speaking Aramaic.

"I believe you all have it wrong," came a girl's voice. It was Tamar, and everyone stopped to look at her. "The cleverest one I know," she said, "has long white hair, sparkling brown eyes, and is a woman!"

"Of course," Amon shouted, then shushed himself. "Who said the Clever One has to be a man?"

This took the conversation in a whole new direction that lasted the rest of the meeting.

As they walked home afterward, Amon moved over next to Tamar and whispered, "Which woman were you describing?"

Tamar looked at him with a smile in her eyes. "My mother," she said softly. "If she had lived, I could prove it, but I'm quite sure she was the cleverest person in all of Judea."

"Oh? And what made her so clever?"

Tamar grinned. "She gave birth to *me*."

As they walked home, Jotham put an arm around his son. "I know you've been given much to think about today, but I need to ask you to take the sheep to market this afternoon. I have some important business I must attend to."

Amon looked at his father curiously. "What 'business' is that?"

Jotham raised his eyebrows. "Even though you are a man now, I am still your father, and I still carry some of the secrets of a father."

Amon smiled and bowed as if his father was royalty.

"I'll help you," Tamar said to Amon, and together they wound their way home to gather the sheep.

Zana and Yasmin also offered to help.

Amon and Tamar looked at the two and hesitated. "It is a very messy job," Tamar said.

Zana shrugged. "We don't mind."

"Will your father?" Amon asked.

"No. Our parents raised us to help others whenever we can and to not think too highly of our positions in life. We often helped pull camels and load cargo on our trip here."

Amon tried to picture Zana pulling a camel. "Well, I have an extra tunic you can borrow if you'd like." Soon the four were herding a half dozen sheep through the streets of Jerusalem while Persian guards followed and watched.

They reached the sheep market on the far side of the temple and herded the sheep into the family pens. For much of the afternoon, they sold and bartered the animals. Zana was particularly good at selling, often getting four days' wages instead of three for a sheep.

"Why are you so friendly and outgoing with buyers," Amon asked, "and so shy with the rest of us?"

Zana seemed embarrassed. "My father is a politician. I guess I have learned from him the tricks of getting people to do what you want them to do."

All the sheep had been sold, so the four headed back to Amon's house, followed by the guards. They walked up the other side of the Tyropoeon Valley, directly away from the temple. When they were far enough up the hills, Amon looked back over the roofs of the houses they'd just passed. The Mount of Olives rose against the sky on the other side of the city wall, and Ishtar's caravan still filled the valley between them. Some movement to the right of the city caught his attention. When he looked, what he saw made him stop.

"Romans," he said loud enough for the other three to hear. They also stopped and looked. A long line of Roman soldiers on horseback escorted someone in a fancy cart covered with a canopy and headed toward the city.

"That's Pontius Pilate," Tamar said. "What's he doing here? There's no festival happening any time soon."

Yasmin asked, "Who is Pont-eeus . . .?"

"Pilate," Tamar finished the question. "He's the Roman governor of Judea, but he usually only comes here during special holidays."

"Oh nooo," Amon groaned. "I am in so much trouble."

The others turned to him, and Tamar asked what was wrong.

"I was supposed to finish putting glass in Pilate's windows before he returned, but with everything that's been going on, I completely forgot." *That was the thing I couldn't remember!* he thought.

"Go. Do it now," Tamar prodded.

"There's not enough time," Amon answered. "They'll be in the city in just minutes."

"Let us take care of this," Zana said. "You go do the thing you must do. Yasmin and I will delay this Roman."

Amon looked from one to the other and almost asked how but realized there was no time. "Thank you," he said.

Then Zana and Yasmin and their statues took off running down the hill toward their caravan, while Amon took off running toward the governor's palace. He raced up to a back entrance where guards who knew him were on duty. They let him pass and he ran up several stairways to Pilate's throne room. Amon's ladders and supplies were still in the small chamber next to the hall, and he quickly brought them out. He had seven more windows to fill with glass out of the original forty. But all the panes had been formed already, so all he needed to do was put tar on the edges of a pane, carry it up the ladder, and place it in its window.

*This will take at least an hour,* he thought, *but Pilate will be here in a tenth of that.*

He worked as fast as he could, while still being careful not to break the glass. It had been almost an hour when he climbed the ladder to install the last pane in the last window, which was behind a curtain behind Pilate's throne.

That's when the huge door to the hall opened, and Pilate walked in, followed by the chief priest, Caiaphas.

"What is it you think is so important that it can't wait until tomorrow?" Pilate said loudly, his voice echoing off the stone walls. "I want to soak in a pool."

"A matter of most urgency, Your Excellency. It involves the security of the entire city."

From high up on the ladder, Amon could see over the top of the curtain to the throne below.

Pilate plopped down on the throne with one leg slung over an arm of the chair. "Caiaphas, your 'urgent matters' are never very urgent to Rome. I've been traveling all day, I'm tired, and everything I'm wearing is full of dust. So tell me this news quickly and then get out."

Caiaphas was standing directly in front of the Roman governor and didn't seem bothered at all by his manner. "There is a devil among us," he said. "A devil among the Jews, and he must be eliminated. For this I need your help."

"I crucified the last devil you came to me with, and now you have another? What's the name of *this* one?"

Caiaphas stood a bit straighter, pulled his shoulders back, and said, "I do not know his real name, but he goes by the title of 'Clever One.'"

✦ ✦ ✦

Will God protect his followers, or should they run and hide?

This is a question that many people have faced over the centuries. Sometimes it seems God's answer is, indeed, to hide from the forces of evil. It can be his answer to their prayers, just like David hiding from King Saul (not the Saul of this story).

Other times, as with Stephen, and later with many of the apostles, God's answer seems to be to stay and face the enemy. Even if it means the death of the body, God promises to take care of our souls in an eternal paradise.

What should Amon do? He would surely be safe with Prince Ishtar and his caravan, and that would look to be the smart move.

But Amon feels strongly that God is telling him to remain in Jerusalem and trust in him.

There are still Christians in danger because of their beliefs today. But most of us are free to worship and express our faith freely. That's why I can write this book and a company can publish it without being afraid of the government.

Are we taking full advantage of our freedom to preach Jesus?

## Chapter Sixteen

# Romans

Whatever 'Clever One' you search for is your own business," Pilate said to Caiaphas. "It is no concern of Rome's. Now leave me be and do your own dirty work."

Amon was still on the ladder, looking down at the two officials from high above.

"I was sure that would be your answer," Caiaphas said slowly, as if he was enjoying this, "but it is not me making this request, it is another. And when I realized who he is, well, I just knew you'd want to handle this personally."

Pilate leaned back in disgust. "Stop your foolish games and tell me—who is it that wants to find this Clever One?"

"Saul, of Tarsus. A citizen of Rome."

~

An hour later Amon was back at home. "Pilate told him he'd assign his best centurion to track down the Clever One," Amon said, his voice shaking almost as much as his body. It was a warm night, but he shivered as if it were bitter cold. He was standing in the dark outside his house, in the middle of the sheep pens, talking with his father and Bartholomew. The others of their families, plus Ishtar and his children and all his guards, were crowded into the small house, eating dinner and laughing.

"This is serious news indeed," Jotham said. "It's one thing to have Saul searching for you, quite another to be hunted by . . . by . . ."

"The entire Roman legion?" Amon finished the thought his father did not want to speak.

Jotham frowned. "Yes, the entire Roman legion."

Faint music drifted up the street, and Amon realized there were still people in the world who didn't carry the worries he did.

Bartholomew spat into the mud. "In one very real sense, this changes nothing."

Amon and his father looked at him.

"We have been trusting all along that Jehovah, in his spirit, will watch over and protect Amon. That has not changed. Whether it is Saul or the Roman legion or the Evil One himself—which it probably is—Jehovah is stronger and more powerful than the forces that oppose us."

"Then we do nothing other than pray and trust?" Jotham asked his old friend.

"There is nothing better we *can* do."

Amon could tell from the look on his father's face that he wanted to believe this but was struggling. "Or we could send Amon away to Persia with Ishtar."

There was a long pause, then Amon said, "As much as I would enjoy that, and as much as I would love to get away from Saul and Pilate, I believe I must stay here and continue my work."

Jotham put an arm around his son's shoulders. "I know, Amon. I know."

They went back inside the house and joined the raucous dinner.

"Amon," Ishtar yelled from the far side of the table, where he sat eating. "Yasmin and Zana have had a wonderful idea. You should return with us to Persia and learn of our ways."

Amon looked at his father as if to say, "Maybe this is a sign from God?"

Jotham shrugged as if to say, "Perhaps, but perhaps not."

Then Amon remembered a question that had bothered his mind all evening. "How was it that it took Pilate over an hour to get from the Kidron Valley to the palace? It's only a tenth of an hour walk."

Everyone looked at Ishtar, but it was Yasmin who finally told the story. "While I went ahead and told Father about your predicament, Zana intercepted Pilate and invited him into Father's tent for some refreshment."

Zana was grinning and butted in. "The Romans hate us Persians, but they know we can beat them any time we want, so he didn't dare refuse the invitation."

"That's not *exactly* true," Ishtar corrected, "but close."

"Father just kept him talking and eating baklava as long as he could." Yasmin finished the story.

The others laughed.

"So *that's* why Pilate was in such a bad mood when he got to the palace," Amon said. He then thanked the Persians for their help. "Zana, you're so shy. How did you ever make yourself go up and confront the governor of Judea?"

Zana stared at the ground. "I guess I decided that helping you was more important than hiding in the background."

Yasmin placed a package wrapped in cloth on the table and started untying it. "Of course," she said, "we didn't give Pilate *all* the baklava." There were oohs and aahs at the sight of the sweet pastry, and Amon drowned his fear in three of the treats.

Over the next few days, Bartholomew quietly told the other apostles of Pilate's plan to hunt down the Clever One. They each passed the word to their groups to be very, very careful to not talk of these things outside the safety of the cisterns. In a very short time, believers started reporting that they had been interrogated about the Clever One by a Roman.

"It wasn't at all unpleasant," one man explained. "He was dressed like an ordinary citizen and just asked casual questions as he shopped at my stand. But his tattoos and the size of his arms marked him as a Roman soldier."

Reports continued to come in over the next several days, and Amon felt like the city walls were closing in, snaring him in a Roman trap. Everyone reported the same thing—a large Roman soldier had questioned them about the Clever One, but they had given him no useful information.

Later, Peter, James, Jotham, and Amon discussed the fact that it would be much harder for the people to continue to resist the questioning of a Roman than it had been the questioning of their neighbors but could think of no new action to take.

Saul would be expecting a report soon, Amon knew, so he decided he needed to make a show of investigating. Each morning and afternoon he walked through a different part of the city, quietly asking people if they'd heard of the Clever One. But not too quietly. He would ask just loud enough that any temple guards, priests, or spies who happened to be nearby would hear.

Late one afternoon he saw Raphu, the captain of the temple guard, eating his dinner at an open-air inn. He also saw one of the believers at a table near Raphu—a believer named Nabal, whom Amon was sure he could trust. He went to Nabal's table and sat down.

The believer looked up, surprised.

Amon knew the man was supposed to pretend he didn't even know him. "Excuse me, sir," Amon whispered, but a little bit loudly. He looked Nabal in the eyes intently, trying to communicate that he should go along with Amon's game. "I am trying to find a man they call the Clever One. From what I've heard, he is an elder, probably with white hair and a white beard. Do you know of such a man?"

Nabal paused exactly long enough to make it seem as if he was thinking about the question but not so long that it looked as though he was trying to make up an answer. "No, I don't believe I do," he said as he stirred his bowl of stew. "Why is it you search for him?"

Amon scoffed. "Oh, nothing important. I'd just like to find out why he's so clever."

Nabal took another bite of his stew. "Sorry. I've never heard of such a man."

"Thank you, and forgive me for disturbing your meal." Amon left the inn, making sure he didn't look at Raphu.

~

The next afternoon Amon went to Saul's house and knocked.

When Saul opened the door, it was as if a demon himself had come to let Amon enter. Saul looked as though he hadn't bathed or groomed in days. His hair stuck out in all directions, there were dark rings under his eyes, and his beard was spotted with bits of bread and streaks of olive oil. "What is it?" he demanded, and Amon took a step back.

"I—I just came to report," he said, wide-eyed.

"Report? Report what?" Saul growled. Then answering his own question said, "Oh! Amon. The Clever One. Come in."

Amon entered the dark house. All the windows were covered with blankets, the table was covered in scrolls and parchments, and the floor was covered in stacks of small stones. Saul closed the door and latched it, and in the dark Amon accidentally kicked over one of the stone stacks.

"Be careful," Saul yelled, and dropped down to his knees to restack the rocks. "These are the only things keeping the evil spirits from entering."

That job finished, he stood straight up into Amon's face, so close it made Amon terribly uncomfortable.

"Now," Saul hissed, "tell me what you have found."

Amon gulped. "Uh, I am not yet able to give you a name," he said, Saul's eyes inches from his own, "but many people have described him to me. However, the descriptions are all different. Some say old, some say young. Some even say it is a woman, not a man."

Saul jumped back and yelled, "Conspirators! Conspirators!" He paced wildly. "They are all in on it, and they all lie to protect the real devil," he screamed.

Amon shuddered in fear, partly because of the screaming, but partly because Saul was exactly right—the people he had talked to *were* all in on it, and they *were* trying to protect the Clever One.

Saul shook with rage, then calmed a little and moved close to Amon's face again. "You must continue your quest," he hissed. "You must root out this evil one, and when you do, we will crush him together!"

Amon nodded, and whispered, "I will continue to ask." Then the first moment he could, he slipped out the door and left Saul pacing and ranting.

Ishtar and his family attended two more worship gatherings with Jotham and his family. Their meetings were always led by Bartholomew and always in one cistern or another. Amon, Benjamin, and Tamar became good friends with the twins.

But always, Amon remained very aware of his surroundings and watched carefully to see if anyone—especially any Romans—watched him.

~

Three days after the Sabbath, late in the afternoon, Amon was repairing part of the fencing in the sheep pens. He had just returned with his father from buying several animals from a passing shepherd, and one of the larger rams had kicked at the gate. As he worked, he was deep in thought about Saul, Pilate, and the danger he was in, when suddenly a shadow of a man blocked his light. Amon jumped, spun around, and yelled in fright.

"Peace, my friend," the man said, backlit by the sun.

Amon finally recognized him as James, the brother of Jesus. Over the last several weeks, it had become clear that James was the leader of all the believers, though it was not a formal office or official title.

"My apologies. I did not mean to startle you."

Amon both slumped against the fence from the momentary fright and chastised himself for letting his guard down. "No trespass," he said, breathless. "I should be more aware of my surroundings these days."

"That may be wise, considering all that is happening. Did you hear the news of this morning?"

Amon shook his head, now looking intently into the apostle's eyes.

"Saul dragged two more men of our number out of their houses and had them arrested."

Amon felt his body go weak, and he leaned harder against the fence. "Who?"

James shook his head. "I don't yet know. But I do know we now have two more families to take care of. And I know that the persecutions of Saul are only going to get worse. He has become a madman."

Amon nodded. "Are you here to see my father?"

James shook his head. "No, my friend. I am here to see *you*. I have another task for you, Clever One." He whispered that name so softly that even Amon could barely hear it.

"I believe my task right now is to stay alive," he said glumly.

James put a hand on his shoulder. "Perhaps you should leave that for Jehovah to worry about and concern yourself with doing his will."

Amon wanted to argue but was far too tired. "Very well. What is this new task?"

"Many of the believers have asked for some way to identify each other. When meeting someone they do not know or have not seen in the meetings, they are afraid to talk of Jesus for fear of Saul and his persecutions."

"So they would like a device or something so they can know if the other person is a believer?"

"Exactly."

Though Amon's mind and body both still carried the weight of being hunted, he said, "Very well. I will work on it."

"Thank you, my friend, and know that all the believers in Jerusalem are praying for you." James turned and walked away.

Amon picked up a hammer and went back to work. *Now I have yet another task*, he thought. *At least the believers are praying for me*.

Suddenly another man stood right next to him.

Amon jumped, spun around, and yelled in fright.

The man, whom Amon did not know, took a step back. He was dressed in the clothes of a shepherd, but he had the look of a temple guard about him. "My apologies, young man. It was not my intent to scare you."

Embarrassed now, and again chastising himself for letting his guard down, Amon said, "No, no, I was not scared. Just momentarily startled. Are you wanting to buy some sheep? My father is not here, but I can sell you one if you'd like."

"I am not here for sheep or for your father. I am here for you, Amon. I bring a message from Saul of Tarsus. He will see you at once."

Amon's insides seemed to turn to stone. The man's voice had a bite to it that said, "or else." But Amon quickly put his thoughts straight. "I will go to his house immediately," he said and started gathering his tools.

"No, not to his house," the man said. "Saul will meet you at the temple. In the Chamber of Hewn Rock."

✦ ✦ ✦

What next? First Amon has the temple guards searching for him, and now the Roman legion's best centurion.

How much pressure can a young man take?

Maybe he really *should* escape to Persia with Ishtar.

But 2 Corinthians reminds us that, "We are hard pressed on every side, but not crushed; perplexed, but not in despair; persecuted, but not abandoned; struck down, but not destroyed" (4:8–9).

In other words, no matter how hard that thing we're going through seems, God is promising that it will not destroy us. We can survive it, either in this life or the next.

There have been many times when I didn't think I could survive a given situation, times when burdens seemed to be crushing me like a boulder. In those times I tried to realize that most likely the thing I was going through was an attack of Satan and remembered a familiar phrase from Psalms: “God is our refuge and strength, an ever-present help in trouble. Therefore we will not fear” (46:1–2a).

When life gets tough, remember these words and exercise some faith. They’re a promise from your Creator.

Chapter Seventeen

# The Lion

As Amon walked toward the temple, all he could think of was Daniel being thrown into the lions' den. He was Daniel, the Chamber of Hewn Stone was the den, and Saul was the lions.

Only this time, the lions wouldn't be so nice.

By God's direct command, the entire temple had been built out of stone that had never been cut with iron—rock that had not been "hewn." But the chamber where the Sanhedrin met was not technically part of the temple. It was an add-on, a separate meeting room, so it was built of hewn stone. And for longer than anyone could remember, it was the lions' den men had been thrown into for violating this or that of the Jewish laws. And the lions always won.

Amon had never been inside the chamber. He had seen it through the open doors a few times—large, with a domed ceiling, almost an oval, with the high priest sitting on a throne-like chair at the far end, thirty-five members seated to his left and thirty-five to his right. Scribes, students, and other non-members occupying the near end. The accused always stood directly in the center, facing the high priest.

Amon went through the ritual baths at the south entrance to the Temple Mount to cleanse his soul—a process he was beginning to feel might be unnecessary with the sacrifice of Jesus—then made his way through the Court of the Gentiles, through the Court of Women, to the Court of Israel. There, to the left of the temple itself, stood the two huge, tall doors to the Chamber of Hewn Stone.

On either side of the doors stood a temple guard wearing armor and holding a long spear. The doors to the chamber were closed.

Amon walked toward them, wondering how he would get in. But as he approached, the guards opened the doors without a word.

*Uh-oh. They know who I am and are expecting me.* Amon entered the chamber, shaking just a bit. *If the temple is the holy place of God, he thought, this feels like the UNholy place.*

Any other time in his life, Amon would have been thrilled to be in this room. He had grown up learning and living the laws of God and the teachings of the rabbis as recorded through all history. But ever since he'd started hearing the words of Jesus and had lived through his sacrifice and victory, Amon had a nagging feeling that there was more to the law now—that it had somehow changed. Jesus had said he didn't come to abolish the law but to fulfill it.

The law had been fulfilled in Jesus.

Amon was still trying to figure out exactly what that meant.

And now, here he was, in the "lions' den" where, for centuries, those accused of breaking the law had been called to account for their actions.

The room was empty except for furnishings. Torches around the sides and high windows on the walls provided light, but it was still dimly lit with dark shadows hiding the spaces around the edge. A hint of incense filled the air.

Amon gawked as he walked toward the center of the room. Here, on this very pavement, many men had made their defense. Most had been found guilty and heard their punishment in this place. More than a few had been condemned to death.

"Amon!"

His name, flying in from the dark shadows, cut through the air like a hard-thrown spear. Amon spun around to face the sound.

Saul, still looking like some hideous recluse who had been living alone in a cave all his life, seemed to float in from one side of the chamber. "I am glad you are here," Saul said in a hoarse whisper that sounded like evil.

Out in the light now, Saul looked as if he hadn't slept in a week. His face was pale, thin, and gouged with wrinkles, his clothes stained and foul.

He glided over in front of Amon and stared at him, seemed to be measuring the younger man's character, integrity, and soul.

Apparently Amon passed the examination, because Saul smiled. It was a weak smile, without humor, tinged with pity. "I have heard reports." Unlike the last few times Amon had seen him, Saul was speaking softly, almost calmly, almost rationally. "Very good reports of your investigation. But now," he said, the old agitation beginning to peek out, "I need to hear from you the progress you've made. Are you close to finding the Clever One and exposing this nest of vipers, this, this cult of Jesus followers?"

Amon fought his fear, fought to remain calm and rational. "One cannot know if he is close to a discovery until he discovers it."

Saul started pacing. "Yes, of course. You are correct. But have you any feeling, any intuition, that you are close to that discovery?"

Amon wasn't sure what to say, was terrified of saying the wrong thing. He decided to go with the truth. "Not really. I'm not sure how this investigation will end, or when."

Evidently that was the wrong thing to say. "Not sure?" Saul screamed. "Not sure? How can you be 'not sure' when the end is so obvious? It will end with every believer in this false messiah being stoned to *death*. It will end when we have rid ourselves of this infestation, this foul and evil stench, that hangs over our people. It will *end*, my friend"—he put his face right in Amon's and screamed—"when *you* lead us to the devil who is *protecting* this vile mob!"

Amon stood absolutely still, eyes wide, heart pounding, breathing shallow, as the echoes of Saul's ranting faded into the walls. Oddly, he noticed for the first time the sound of water dripping somewhere in the chamber. "I was merely saying," Amon whispered in short stabs, "that I do not yet know exactly when this investigation will be complete."

Saul stared Amon in the eye. Then, through lips barely parted and with words barely audible he whispered, "You *are* on my side, aren't you, Amon? You *do* want to see me victorious in this fight?"

Amon swallowed and returned the stare. "With all my heart, Saul, and with all the love I have in my heart, the thing I most want to see is you, victorious, carrying out the will of God."

Another long stare, then another smile. A real one this time. "You are a good friend, Amon. I know I can count on you to support me and walk by my side. I predict you and I shall indeed do much together to carry out the will of God." Saul spun around and glided out of the room through some door Amon still could not see in the shadows.

Trembling, Amon walked to the doors he'd entered—this time pulling one open himself with great effort—and walked out into the evening.

It used to be that Amon would stare at the temple from wherever he was in the city. Today he just turned his back on it and walked away. He was out to the Court of Women and almost to the Court of Gentiles when he heard a shout.

"Amon," the voice called. "Amon, wait, please."

He saw Peter walking quickly up behind him.

"My friend," Peter said, huffing, "I have a request to make of you."

Amon bowed slightly, though he really just wanted to go home. "Whatever I can do to assist you."

"We all appreciate that you made it possible for us to meet in small groups," Peter said, and Amon knew there was a "but" coming. "But many of the people are begging for a chance to meet all together once in a while. I know this is a very large problem, but I also know that if anyone can solve it, you can."

Amon said, "Of course," and pledged to have a solution as soon as possible.

When he arrived home the house was once again packed with his family, Ishtar's family, and Bartholomew and Tamar, all talking and joking. Jotham saw him enter and said, "Amon! Where have you been?"

"Taking care of a problem."

"Well, we have another, and need someone clever to solve it," his father said.

Amon gritted his teeth. *I can't take any more problems.*

Even though Amon hadn't asked, his father explained further. "Ishtar, Yasmin, and Zana have asked to be baptized into The Way," he said, "along with Kazeem and three of the guards."

A grin broke out on Amon's face, and all the tension of the day evaporated. "That's just about the best news I could have heard today."

The problem, of course, was exactly how to accomplish this. Many people had been baptized in the last weeks, but they were all Jews, living in Jerusalem, looking like all the other Jews. It wasn't at all suspicious to see them in a pool of water bathing or playing and, oh by the way, being baptized into Jesus.

But Ishtar was Persian royalty. The colorful silk clothes they wore, their demeanor and speech—everything about them screamed for attention. Everywhere they went, people—as well as Roman soldiers and temple guards—were always watching. So, how to baptize them as followers of Jesus without being noticed?

"I know not of what problem you speak, Father," Amon said, having instantly solved it, "but I was thinking it would be fun, before they leave for home, if we took Ishtar and his family up to the Pool of Serpents for a nice lunch outdoors. And, perhaps, if it is a hot day and we all need some refreshing, we could go swimming in the pool."

"Amon, that's a very nice idea," his father answered, "but what I'm saying is that we need a way to secretly get Ishtar and all his fam—" The look on Jotham's face told everyone he finally understood what everyone else had already figured out. Then his face blushed and the others started laughing. "Uh, yes, I see," he stammered as they enjoyed his embarrassment. "A very good solution indeed, Amon."

And so it was that after a fine lunch the next day at the edge of the Pool of Serpents (at which Amon had never in all his life seen a serpent), everyone, including Amon's mother, went swimming and, without anyone on shore seeming to notice or care, Bartholomew quietly baptized Ishtar, prince of Persia, and all his clan.

That night Amon and Benjamin stayed in the tent of Zana at the caravan, and Tamar stayed with Yasmin. Both Persian teenagers were excited about their new faith. Zana talked through most of the hours of darkness, and Amon grinned at the difference in his friend since their arrival. In the morning Amon's parents and many of the believers Ishtar had made friends with came down to the Kidron Valley as the camels were loaded and all preparations made for their trip. After many hugs and amidst many waves, the long Persian caravan moved forward and began the journey home.

As his family started their own very short trip home, Amon pondered the next problem on his seemingly ever-growing list of problems to solve: a way for believers to identify themselves to each other.

As they were passing through the market, with its bread and cheese and fish and meat, the answer seemed to jump out at him. And though his heart was sad at the departure of his new Persian friends, he grinned so big that his father asked him what in the world he was thinking about.

✦ ✦ ✦

I find it hard, sometimes, to think about the grace God has shown us humans. He started by creating us as perfect beings in a perfect place—a paradise, a beautiful garden full of everything we could possibly need. Then we humans turned selfish and decided we wanted to be our own gods (and we can't really blame Adam and Eve for this, because you and I would have done the same thing).

So God allowed us to be in control of our lives but said if we wanted to come back to him and his paradise, we would have to perfectly follow a set of rules, a set of laws.

But God knew we could never do that. He knew we were too weak and still way too self-centered to ever be able to reach his paradise by following his law. That meant the only option was for us to pay the price for our selfishness (sin) and be punished for eternity.

Fortunately for us—*very* fortunately for us—God didn't want that. Instead, he sent his son down as a substitute, to be punished in our place. He was perfect and sinless himself but offered to take the punishment we deserved, so that we could be made pure in the eyes of God and live with him forever.

Amon is still trying to figure all this out. Less than a year earlier he had been living under the law, with all its rules and punishments. Then Jesus was killed and raised up again, and suddenly everything was different—the law had been fulfilled, and all Amon had to do to be welcomed into paradise was accept Jesus as his savior.

It's kind of confusing, and sometimes I just can't figure out why God would save us from our own selfishness like that.

But he did. And I accept it, even if I don't always understand it.

Chapter Eighteen

# Signs

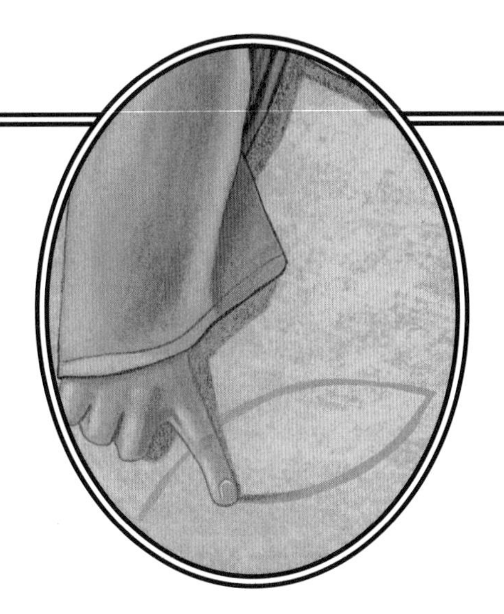

I don't think I like this," Benjamin said, pulling on the sleeve of Amon's tunic. "Can't we go a different way?"

"What are you so afraid of?"

"Uh, drunk Roman soldiers of Greek Syrian descent."

Amon clucked his tongue. "It's the middle of the day, and there are hundreds of people along here. No one's going to bother us."

"And if they do," Tamar said, walking beside her two friends, "I'll take care of them for you."

Benjamin gave her a sarcastic smile. "I don't need anyone to take care of them for me. I just don't want to meet up with them in the first place."

The three were walking through the Tyropoeon Valley, headed toward the bridge where Amon and Benjamin had been confronted by the two Greek soldiers.

"Okay, stop here." Amon said, standing directly under the bridge. "Look up."

Tamar and Benjamin craned their necks and looked straight up at the bottom of the bridge. "What are we looking for?" Tamar asked.

"Any kind of writing or drawing," Amon answered.

As their eyes adjusted, it was Benjamin who first spotted it. "There," he yelled and pointed.

Several people passing by stopped and looked up to see what he was pointing at. Amon just waved them on.

"Perhaps you could be a little less obvious?" Amon suggested. Then he, too, looked to where his friend had pointed. "Yes! That's it. I knew it. Let's climb up there but make it seem as if we're playing."

Tamar and Benjamin looked at each other and shrugged, then followed Amon up the inclined bank under the bridge. Garbage covered the ground, and it was obvious that many people had been up here over the years, probably to hide or get out of the rain or sun. At the top, they sat and stared straight out at the bottoms of the beams.

"Just as I thought," Amon said. "Those soldiers weren't just drinking up here. They were making their mark."

On the bottom of one of the beams, barely visible from the ground but clear at this distance, was a drawing of a fish.

"It looks like a biny," Tamar said, naming a common white fish.

"No, I think it's a musht," Benjamin countered. "Why were you looking for this," he asked Amon, "and how did you know it would be here?"

"When the soldiers were harassing us, I noticed some white dust on the tips of their fingers. I figured they must have been writing with chalk."

They all looked at the symbol again. "It looks kind of crude," Tamar said.

"True, it's not a very good drawing," Amon said, "but you can see the scales and gills and fins okay."

They slid back down the hill, almost falling into a man carrying a large bundle, then Benjamin asked his question again. "So *why* were you looking for this?"

Once again Amon did not answer, and instead said, "Come on." He headed down the street, scanning all the buildings. "Help me find any other symbols like that, if there are any."

It wasn't long before Tamar said, "There," and pointed at the bottom corner of a building.

Amon looked, and sure enough, there was an almost identical drawing of a fish near the ground.

In the next half hour, they found seven more instances of the fish symbol. One of them had been carved into a stone wall many years before even their parents were born, by the look of it.

They reached a public well in the center of the street and each took a drink.

"Will you now tell us?" Tamar asked.

Amon slurped up his water. "Not quite. We need to get somewhere more private."

"Somewhere" ended up being in the shade of the entrance to Herod's theater. It was a covered area where people paid to enter the theater, but since there was no play being performed at the time, the area was deserted. The streets on either side of the entrance were busy, but much too noisy for anyone to hear the three talking.

"James asked me to invent some way for us believers to identify ourselves to each other," Amon said as they sat in the shade. "A way that would not be obvious to anyone watching."

Tamar and Benjamin already knew this, so they gave impatient nods to Amon.

"I thought of creating some kind of handshake but decided that is far too obvious. Then I noticed that everywhere I went, people had drawn pictures and symbols and cartoons on the outside walls of buildings."

Tamar sat back. "You want us to draw fish on buildings to identify ourselves as being of The Way?"

"Almost," Amon said. Then he told them his entire plan, which is when they finally got excited.

"The soldiers drew a certain kind of fish to do what exactly?" Tamar asked.

Amon shrugged. "Who knows. Maybe it has something to do with their gods, or a secret society they belong to. I don't know. But the important thing is that lots of groups use some kind of fish symbol to communicate, so it's not unusual."

The next afternoon Amon had once again arranged for a special meeting of all the congregation leaders. This time they met in the cistern of Jesse, and there were several new faces among the leaders. Amon explained the problem just as he had to his friends the day before. "I had also thought of using a simple cross, to represent the crucifixion of Jesus," he told the group under the light of several torches. "But I decided that would be too easy for outsiders to decipher. Then, when walking home through the market one day, I saw tables and tables full of fish, and it struck me."

He waited a moment to see if anyone would laugh at the mental image of him being struck by a fish, but no one did, so he continued. "Fish. Jesus was always talking about, multiplying, eating, or telling stories about fish. It's a perfect symbol to represent his ministry."

Many heads in the crowd nodded.

"I like it," Peter said, and Amon figured he was thinking about the time Jesus cooked him some fish for breakfast.

"So I started looking around the city, with the help of Tamar and Benjamin, and discovered that not only are there symbols and writings all over the walls of Jerusalem, but some of them are actually fish."

"Oh no," Bartholomew said softly. "That's a shame. A fish would have been the perfect sign for us."

"It still *will* be," Amon said. "The fish symbols we saw were for a pagan goddess or secret society and were realistic drawings of fish. What I propose instead, is this." With his foot, Amon drew two simple intersecting arcs in the dust of the floor.

"A fish!" James said.

"A fish *symbol*," Amon corrected. "It's simple, it's fast, and anyone at all can draw it. But best of all, we can use it as a perfectly safe way to ask someone if they are a believer." He stood and walked to one end of the chamber, and, as preplanned back at Amon's house, Benjamin stood at the other end. They slowly walked to the center and played out a scene they had practiced several times.

"Good afternoon, friend," Amon said. "How is your wife and family?" While he was speaking, Amon used his foot to draw a small arc on the ground.

"Very well, friend," Benjamin replied. "And yours?" During his reply, Benjamin drew a second arc intersecting the first. As soon as the fish symbol was complete, several people jumped to their feet. "They drew the fish together!"

Amon's plan needed no more explanation, nor could he have given any, since everyone was talking excitedly. Many even practiced drawing the symbol with the person sitting next to them.

When all was quiet again, Amon looked at each person in turn. "In this way, you can know if the person you are talking to is of The Way." He took a deep breath, then spoke softly. "But there is also another use for the fish. If you want to mark your place of business as being run by a believer, or if you want to mark a building as being a meeting place, you can draw the fish symbol on the wall. There are so many markings on the buildings to begin with, and a fish symbol is not at all unusual, so no one will ever notice or wonder what it means."

Again an agreeable murmur drifted through the group.

"Finally," Amon said, "if you want to actually carve it into the stone to make it permanent, and if you have the skill, you can add this in the center of the symbol."

He took a piece of chalk he'd brought and wrote five Greek letters on the wall, speaking them as he wrote. "*Iota*, *chi*, *theta*, *upsilon*, *sigma*." He drew the simple fish symbol around the letters, then turned back to the group. "I know most of you don't know Greek, but these are the letters that spell 'fish' in Greek. The word is pronounced 'ichthus.' But I'm using the letters as an acrostic to spell out in our language, '*Jesus*, *Anointed*, *God's*, *Son*, *Savior*.' It's yet another way we can keep the message of Jesus alive for centuries."

Not only was there a great round of applause at this, but several people actually had tears running down their cheeks.

The meeting broke up and people left one or two at a time to avoid attracting attention. As he waited for his turn to climb the stairs out of the cistern, Amon was approached by James and another man.

"Amon, if you have a moment," James said, "Terah has something to say to you."

"Of course," Amon said to the man. "I am at your service."

Terah looked sick, as if he might vomit, and kept his eyes staring at the floor. "I must give you my apology, young man, and I must beg your forgiveness." Then he looked up at Amon. "Not that I deserve it or expect you to grant it."

Amon scrunched up his eyebrows. "What trespass could you possibly have made that I would not forgive?"

Terah hesitated and lowered his gaze to the floor again. "I was not in Jerusalem when Jesus departed this earth," he said softly. "I was traveling on business and did not know of this great thing, though I had already committed myself to him."

"That is a wonderful thing," Amon said, confused. "Surely I need not forgive you for that."

"No, no, of course not," Terah said. "But when I came back to Jerusalem, I heard that a man they call the Clever One was working to keep us all safe and hidden from the Sanhedrin." He looked up again. "It made me very happy, and it felt good to know someone was organizing all this." He waved his hand around at the people still talking and at the cistern itself. "But the next day, Saul came to me to purchase some chain—I have no idea for what. I had not heard of his views of The Way, and just assumed he was a follower of Jesus." He looked quickly from James to Amon. "And why would he *not* be? He is a man of God, and Jesus *is* God."

Amon couldn't argue the point and began to see where the story was going.

Lowering his gaze once more, Terah said in almost a whisper, "Then I commented to him how the Clever One would surely keep the people of The Way safe."

"So that's how he found out." Amon let out a sigh. "Now, that is a relief."

Terah's head snapped up. "A relief? To know that I put your life in danger?"

Amon shook his head. "I always wondered how Saul had found out. I was afraid there was a spy among us who was feeding him information. I am quite relieved," he said, putting a hand on Terah's shoulder, "to know it was simply a mistake. Of course I forgive you, Terah. You did not intend to put me in danger, and even so, you are my elder. That, if nothing else, tells me I have no right to hold a confessed trespass against you."

A short time later it was Amon's turn to slip out of the cistern and into the street. As he headed toward home, he noticed a stone, quite insignificant in size, shape, or color, close enough to be associated with the house of Jesse but far enough away that it could easily be seen as just a random stone connected to nothing. And on the stone, he saw already the symbol of a fish with five Greek letters filling its center.

✦ ✦ ✦

I've seen it thousands of times: a little sticker on the back window or bumper of a car displaying a simple drawing using two curved lines to form a fish.

We use it today to tell others that we, too, are believers. We use it today the same way Christians used the symbol two thousand years ago.

But not really.

Because our lives (at least in the West) are not in danger. We have no fear that we'll be jailed or killed simply because we love Jesus. When *we* use the symbol of the fish, it's like waving to people and yelling, "Hey! Over here! I'm a Christian too!"

For Christians in the early days of the church, it was more of a secret code. If the religious leaders had ever broken that code, it could have meant death to many.

So use the symbol of the fish all you want, and use it to let others know you love Jesus. But as you use it, let it also be a reminder that the faith we sometimes take for granted is a precious gift, bought with the pain and suffering of Christ and championed by the early church.

Chapter Nineteen

# The Search

Amon!" Benjamin yelled, "Look out—chariot coming!"

The two-wheeled Roman weapon wheeled around the corner, thundering toward Amon. It was pulled by two powerful, white Berber horses, specially bred for pulling, and driven by one Roman soldier holding the reins while a second aimed his spear directly at Amon's heart. Amon had only seconds to react.

"Oh no," Amon cried in a fake sort of way. "I'm so scared. Help me someone."

"Do not fear," Tamar yelled, running toward Amon. "I shall defeat your foes and send them back to Rome."

At this they all started laughing, and the scene they had been imagining in their minds evaporated.

They were standing in the middle of the great Hippodrome, built by King Herod for chariot races and other sports. The large, oval arena had steps where spectators could sit rising all around from the center, a dirt track on which the three friends stood, and a wall running straight down the middle of the track. The chariots raced around the wall at great speeds running over anything in their paths.

"Well, this is fun," Amon said, "but it will never work." With the help of Tamar and Benjamin, he was searching for a place where all the congregations of the church could meet together. "Obviously it's far too open. Anyone walking by can see in here, so even if we were very quiet, our secret would only last a few moments."

The three had already searched the upper city, including Herod's theater, and found no suitable place to meet.

"But if we ever get a chariot and want to race it," Benjamin said, "we know where to come."

"You boys!" Tamar said. "All you ever think of is swords and chariots and fast horses."

"If that's all we do," Amon said, "then that must be how Jehovah created us." He flicked his eyebrows twice at her.

"Oh," Tamar cried, "you and your quick wit are so annoying, you camel."

She chased him out into the street, Benjamin following, until they got caught up in the crowd.

For the rest of the afternoon, the three friends searched all of Jerusalem. Amon already knew they'd find nothing—he'd been exploring the city since he was five and knew every crack in the walls and bump in the roads. "But we'd still better look," he told his friends as they walked through the Tyropoeon Valley, "in case I've missed something."

"What's this?" Tamar teased. "Is Amon admitting there might be something he does not know?"

"I believe the only thing I do not know," he answered, "is why Jehovah thought it necessary to create women with no sense of what's truly important—like swords and chariots and fast horses."

That earned him a punch on the arm, which earned Tamar a scowl from a passing rabbi.

They spent the rest of the day searching but found no place suitable for a large, secret meeting. At Amon's house that evening, they reported their results to his parents.

"Then perhaps you should search *outside* the city," his father suggested.

Amon nodded. "That may be our only choice."

"You should take your brothers with you," his mother said. "You haven't spent much time with them since this all began."

Jadon and Uri both looked up from their stewed veal and grinned at Amon.

Amon sighed and glanced at his little brothers. He loved them, but they were always difficult to control when his parents weren't around. "If you think it wise," he answered, making sure his mother knew he thought it anything but.

~

The next morning, they all set out early—Amon, Benjamin, Tamar, Jadon, and Uri. Amon wasn't exactly sure what they were looking for, so just watched for any kind of canyon, building, cave, or other enclosure where the believers could meet in secret.

Since it was closest, the group headed south, out the Essene Gate, and turned left. The hill dropped off sharply here, into the Hinnom Valley. A well-worn trail meandered through the narrow canyon. Amon hoped to find an undiscovered cave or cleft in the rock or wall to his left.

"I'd forgotten how steep it is," Amon said as he looked up the incline to the city wall high above. "Even if we found a place, there would be no way for hundreds of people to get to it without being seen."

They followed Hinnom to the east side of the city, where it met with the Kidron Valley. This side was not nearly as steep but was well traveled and busy. They turned left up the Kidron, with the Mount of Olives to their right, where Amon hoped there might be a large tomb or something. "Father told me he and Ishtar came to Jerusalem through a large catacomb here."

They climbed a steep, rocky path and found the entrance high on the Mount of Olives.

Several men were working around the opening.

Amon asked if they could enter. The men stopped and looked at the five young people. One of them said, "Why would you want to go inside a catacomb?"

"Just to see what it's like inside," Amon answered.

Some of the men laughed, but the one who had spoken bowed, pointed to the tomb with his arm, and said, "If you'd like, go ahead."

They weren't even all the way through the doorway before they knew it would never work. "It *stinks* in here!" Uri said. Jadon, Benjamin, and Tamar all expressed their agreement with Uri's assessment.

"Well, I guess we should have expected this," Amon said, and quickly led the way back out.

As the group ran from the tunnel, the workers all laughed again. "You are welcome to come back anytime," one of them yelled.

"My father told me it was a very large cave," Amon said as they walked back down into the valley, "but he never said it had a large smell to go with it."

By the time they reached the north end of the Kidron, Jadon and Uri complained of being tired and thirsty. They stopped in the shade of the garden of Gethsemane for a drink of water, a few figs, and a rest. For Amon, the setting brought back frightening memories of the night Jesus was arrested.

"I don't think we're going to find anything out here," Benjamin said. "There are too many people. Even if there was a good place to meet, everyone in the city would already know about it."

"You're probably right," Amon said, "but we'll keep looking on the other two sides of the city on the way home."

They crossed back over the Kidron, then up the north side of the city along the Valley of Jehoshaphat. It wasn't as steep or as high here as the south end of the city, though it was much more rugged-looking. Hills, short and tall, pushed their way up, and mounds of jagged rock had piled up at the bottom of the city wall. The sun was straight overhead now, and Jadon complained constantly about heat and thirst.

"We'll stop in that shade over there." Amon pointed to a small stand of palm trees. Another family was already spending their afternoon in the same shade but shared it without comment. They had a boy about Uri's age, so the two went off, climbing among the rocks.

"I think this is hopeless," Benjamin said. "There couldn't possibly be a place here big enough for us to meet that wouldn't be seen by everyone passing by."

Amon lay back in the shade. "I think you're right. The west side is still a possibility, but we'll probably have to go into the hills to find something big enough and private enough."

"If we have to go very far from the city," Tamar added, "it will take more time to get there than many people have. It will also be more obvious to anyone watching from the city wall, and many of the elders won't be able to climb."

"Alright, let's search the west side, then go home and talk to my father. Maybe he'll have a better idea." He yelled up the hill for Uri, but the boy didn't answer. Amon called several more times, becoming more impatient with each yell. He was about to send Jadon to go retrieve their brother when Uri's head popped up over the top of a rock.

"Did you say something?" Uri asked.

"I said to come. We're leaving."

"Yes, Amon," the boy said, and trotted down the hill.

The group thanked the other family for sharing their shade, then headed west again, the city wall still to their left.

"You should have come with us," Uri said as he took ahold of Amon's hand. "It was fun. We played Princes and Thieves. I was the thief."

"It sounds fun, Uri," Amon mumbled. To the others he said, "We should look carefully in the tomb area ahead. There are several natural caves. I've only ever seen small ones, but maybe there's something bigger."

"Maybe there's another catacomb under that hill," Tamar said with a smirk.

Benjamin grinned. "If it stinks like the last one, no thank you."

"It was a lot cooler in there too," Uri said.

Amon smiled. "Yes, but cooler isn't better if it smells like that, Uri."

Uri was still holding Amon's hand. "It didn't smell," he said.

"What didn't smell?" Amon asked.

"The cave."

"You mean the catacomb, where the bodies were buried."

"No, not the stinky place, the *cave*."

"*What* cave?"

"The cave Reuben and I played in."

"Who's Reuben?"

"My new friend back at the palm trees, where we stopped to rest."

Amon stopped walking and got down on one knee in front of his little brother. "Uri, what are you talking about?"

Uri let out a loud sigh as if Amon were as dumb as the Romans. "When we stopped to rest, I met Reuben. And him and me found a cave, and it was cooler inside."

Amon looked from Uri to the wall behind them and back again. "Show me."

Uri grabbed Amon's hand and pulled him along. When they got to the palm trees, the other family was gone. Uri let go of Amon and ran ahead up and over the piles of rocks and boulders. A moment later, he disappeared.

✦ ✦ ✦

Amon is a very smart kid. So smart that he learned very early to respect and obey his parents in all things. When his mother suggested he take his little brothers with him, even though he didn't want to, he obeyed.

Trust and obey. There's no other way, really. If we believe God exists and believe he really is in control of all things, what good does it do us to go our own way and do our own thing?

The times in my life when I've trusted and obeyed God have led to wondrous, life-changing things. Miracles, really. Circumstances I couldn't have predicted and did not deserve.

The times when I've gone my own way—well, let's just say it's been disastrous.

Obedience is difficult for just about everyone. But just about everyone eventually learns, sooner or later, that there really is no other way to be happy.

Chapter Twenty

# Discovery

"Uri! Where are you?"

"I'm in here," came the muffled reply.

Amon followed the voice around a jagged boulder. A large section of slate about the length of a house hung out over the huge rock, creating a sort of roof. And then he saw it. Right where the line of the rock should have run into the city wall, it cut away from it, creating a triangular opening between the two. Other piles of rocks around hid it from view, and the whole area was hidden from the path below by the stand of palm trees.

"You have to be right on top of it to even know it exists," Tamar said.

Amon ducked down and entered the shoulder-high opening.

It was dark inside.

"It's dark in there," Benjamin said.

"Very observant," Amon sassed. He moved forward, reaching into the dark with his hands and stepping carefully, so as not to run into a rock wall. "Uri, where are you?"

"Right here."

The voice had been only inches away and Amon jumped and gave a little yell, at which Tamar and Benjamin laughed. "Don't do that!" Amon said, still trying to see the boy. "Hold out your hand."

Uri did, and Amon grabbed it and held tight. "How deep is this cave?"

"I don't know," Uri said. "I've only been this far."

Still holding onto Uri with his right hand, Amon reached out with his left and moved slowly forward.

"What do you see?" Tamar asked, "or rather, feel?"

"Nothing," Amon's voice went out into the darkness. "Nothing at all." He stepped into the light next to his friends. "I went about twenty paces and didn't find a wall opposite. I think we need some help."

After a quick discussion it was decided that Tamar would stay with the younger boys while Benjamin and Amon went up to the city for torches. They returned before the boys had finished an impromptu game of King's Ransom. Amon also brought a long rope coiled over his shoulder. Once the torches were lit, they all stepped back inside the stone doorway.

The cave seemed to stretch a long ways, far beyond where the torchlight could reach. Dust and pebbles covered the floor. The distance between the side walls started out about the width of Amon's house, but quickly widened. The ceiling was the height of a tall man reaching as high as he can over his head. The floor sloped downward at a sharp angle taking the ceiling with it, which created a long, wide tunnel with a fairly low ceiling.

"I don't believe this," Amon whispered. "How could a cave have been under our feet all this time and remain hidden from our knowledge?"

They slowly walked down the incline, Amon continually looking to the edge of the light ahead. As they walked, he surveyed. "See how the yellow light of our torches makes the walls seem yellow? That means the stone here must be almost white. Otherwise the stone would look some other color."

"That's very nice," Tamar said, "but what I really like is that it's so cool in here." As they descended farther, she added, "This cave seems to be very . . . square."

Amon stopped suddenly and turned his head left, right, forward. "You're right. This is not a cave. This is a rock quarry. See how straight the walls are? And look at the marks." He went to the sidewall and felt it with his hand. "These were made by the tools of men, not the hand of God."

Benjamin walked over to another wall. "Do you think this cave was created by men cutting out the rock to build buildings?" He rubbed his hand along the cut marks.

"I believe so," Amon said. "Obviously it's not all square, but there are just too many straight lines for this to be natural."

They moved on past two large pillars of rock that seemed to be holding up the ceiling. The pillars weren't straight, but still looked as if they'd been carved from the rock rather than formed by God.

"Is it safe here, Amon?" Uri asked. They had come a great distance and could no longer see the light of the entrance behind them.

"Yes, it is safe, brother."

"What if there's a lion? Or a bear? Or Romans?"

"No lion or bear would want to come in here, and no Roman would be smart enough."

The walls spread apart and the group found themselves in a large cavern. It seemed as wide as Herod's theater and as tall as three men standing on each other's shoulders. The chamber was more or less round, and tunnels ran off from it in other directions.

Tamar gasped. "This would make a perfect meeting place!"

Amon looked slowly around the chamber, then scanned the ceiling. "You're right. But we have to make sure it is truly hidden," he said. "We know no one has been here in many, many years, but there might be an air shaft or other opening that others might find, or through which the sounds of worship could escape."

"How do we know no one has been here?" Jadon asked.

"Look at the floor behind us," Amon said. "Our footprints show clearly in the dust and dirt. But ahead of us the dust and dirt are smooth and undisturbed. There is no wind here, so we know this dust has been waiting here for a very long time."

"What now? We search every tunnel and alcove?" Benjamin asked, guessing their next move.

Amon nodded. "Yes. We must all look carefully for any other opening."

For the rest of the afternoon, the group of five walked every inch of the tunnels, searching walls, ceiling, and floor for any openings. Sometimes a tunnel went around in a circle and ended up back at the same place, other times a side tunnel would dead-end. But when they had walked every possible path—as indicated by their footprints on the floor—Amon made an announcement. "Not a single opening," he said. "So no sound can reach up to the surface, and no people can climb down."

"Then we can use it for meetings?" Tamar asked.

Amon shook his head. "Not quite. First we must see how far under the city this goes, and we must make sure no sound will reach out to the entrance. Jadon," he said, pulling the coil of rope from his shoulder, "take the end of this to the farthest point in the long tunnel."

Jadon looked at his older brother with wide eyes. "Me? You want *me* to go back there alone?"

"Certainly. It's perfectly safe. We were just there."

Jadon gulped, then with an end of the rope and a torch drifted into the depths of the tunnel, looking back every two steps. Amon took the other end of the rope and walked back toward the entrance. Once the rope was pulled tight, he had Jadon come up to where he was, then Amon again walked toward the entrance until the rope was tight. He counted as they repeated this, and soon they had found that the tunnel was just under seven rope-lengths long.

"Almost seven hundred feet," Amon announced when they returned to the group. "Now, one last thing. Tamar, start counting slowly with me, and when you reach one hundred, all of you scream and yell as loudly as you can for the length of one verse of a song. Then come out to the mouth of the cave."

Tamar gave him a questioning look, but when he started counting, she did too. "One . . . two . . . three . . ."

As they counted, Amon walked quickly toward the entrance. Halfway there he could no longer hear Tamar but kept counting at the same pace. As he reached the entrance and stepped outside, he was just passing eighty-five. He stood between the cave and the boulder, counting under his breath. When he reached a hundred, he listened carefully.

Nothing.

He stuck his head inside the cave.

Still nothing.

Then, for the first time since they'd entered the cave, he let out a deep sigh and grinned.

~

Amon found Peter at the northwest corner of the fortress of Antonia, where the Roman garrison was housed. James was with Peter, so both of them looked as Amon ran up, excited.

"Peter!" he shouted. "I found it."

Peter looked around, just a bit nervous. "Hush, boy, do you want to attract all the priests in Israel? You found *what*?"

Amon lowered his voice. "A meeting place. Big enough for all the believers in Jerusalem."

"The truth you tell!"

"And only the truth."

"Is it far? Where is it?"

Amon grinned. "You're standing on top of it."

Peter and James both looked down at their feet, then back at Amon.

"Under our feet?" Peter looked again at the stones under his sandals, then at the crowded street. "Let us go and sit, so you can tell your story somewhere more private."

They walked around a corner to a small courtyard overlooking a pool and sat under a date tree. "Now, tell us," James said.

Amon explained how his little brother had accidentally discovered the entrance to a cave near the Damascus Gate. How none of them knew it was there, and when they realized it was more than a few feet deep, they got torches and explored. "It goes back almost as far as Antonia is from the gate." Amon said. "There are many little side tunnels and chambers, but the whole center of it is open and huge."

James looked skeptical. "Is it possible you are exaggerating just a bit? It is difficult to believe that a tenth of the city could be built on top of a cave that no one knows about."

"We measured," Amon said. "My friend Benjamin and I got a length of rope, and my brother Jadon helped me. The cave goes back almost seven hundred feet."

Peter and James both raised their eyebrows.

"In all my life, I have never heard of such a cave under Jerusalem," Peter said.

"Nor have I," James agreed.

"It looks like it might have been a quarry," Amon offered. "The stone has been hewn on purpose. It doesn't appear to be natural."

The two apostles looked at each other, then Peter said, "Well, we will have to see if anyone else has heard of this. It won't do much good as a secret meeting place if it's not actually a secret."

Amon got up and started to leave.

"Amon," James called, and waited until he looked back. "Very good work. If it turns out that this cave is as secret as we hope, you have done a great service for the church. Again."

Amon bowed his head, then headed home.

✦ ✦ ✦

Oh yes, obedience can lead to such wondrous things.

If Amon hadn't obeyed his mother and taken his brothers with him, Uri would have never discovered the cave, and the good things to come would have never happened.

God used one simple little act of obedience—Amon's obeying his mother when she told him to take his brothers—to accomplish something no one thought was possible.

Of course, this is just a story. Do things like that happen in real life?

Every day. Far more times than we could ever know of or count.

Obedience to God opens doors we never thought were possible. In fact, if it weren't for simple acts of obedience, the book you're reading would have never existed. The first book in this series, *Jotham's Journey*, was the result of many such acts—not just on my part, but by many others as well. That was true for all the books that followed, including this one.

God can part the waters of the vast sea, protect people from the flames of blasting furnaces, crumble the walls of a mighty city, and raise people from the dead. But much more often, God's miracles are less grand in proportion and are almost always the result of a simple act of obedience on the part of his children.

Chapter Twenty-One

# Uri's Place

What if they're beaten and reveal our secrets?" Amon asked.

Bartholomew looked down as he thought. "All we can do is pray and trust in Jehovah."

Amon already knew this was the answer to his question but was hoping for something a bit more reassuring. Then he stopped and chastised himself for thinking that there was anything more reassuring than being able to trust God.

He was at another meeting of the apostles, who were trying to decide how best to use the cave Amon had found.

"Uri actually found it," he would correct each time someone gave him credit.

But just before the meeting had begun, word was passed through the network that another three men had been arrested by the temple guards.

"These are all good men," Barnabas said. "They will not reveal our secrets unless severely tortured."

"I'm afraid severe torture is exactly what our friend Saul has in mind," Peter said.

The group mumbled agreement. All the apostles were there, plus Amon and his parents, Tamar, Barnabas, and Omar. They were working out the best way to get hundreds of people into and out of the cave Uri had found without being seen. This plan would then be passed on to the congregational leaders—the men and women who kept the individual worship groups organized and informed.

Amon was always amazed at how slowly things happened when many people were in charge of making a decision. Several plans had been suggested, but someone always found something wrong with them.

He was trying to be respectful of his elders but finally decided he just needed to speak up. "What if we held the meetings late in the afternoon?" he suggested.

Everyone looked at him and listened.

"The nonbelievers will all be thinking about the things they did that day, about getting home, about making dinner, counting their money, and so forth. They'll be tired, and there will be many people moving about the streets, so no one will even notice a few hundred extra people moving around, especially if we all take different routes."

James leaned back, tapping his foot on the floor as he considered this. "Go on."

Amon paused, thinking fast now, since that was as far as he had gotten in his plan before starting to speak. He stood and paced in the dim light of the cistern. "We'll call the cave 'Uri's Place' as a code."

Amon's mother smiled at this.

"And we'll make sure people come from different directions, and only a few at a time." He was getting excited now, as his mind found solutions to the problems. "They can wait in the garden." He looked up at the other men.

"Yes. That will be perfect," Peter said.

Matthew cocked his head. "What garden?"

"The garden where the tomb of Jesus sits," Amon said. "It's just across the road from the cave—from Uri's place."

"You mean the *former* tomb of Jesus, do you not?" Peter said.

Amon grinned. "Yes, the *former* tomb." He went back to pacing and continued explaining his plan without revealing to them that he was making it up as he spoke.

They finished making plans for the joint worship service as they shared loaves of bread and bowls of olives. They laughed at themselves when they realized they were in a cistern that would hold enough water to serve half of Jerusalem for a year but had brought none to drink.

Gehazi, the owner of the cistern, kindly fetched some from his kitchen above.

Next, the apostles would convey the plans to the group leaders, who would pass on the plans to their groups. The first joint worship service was set for the day before the next Sabbath. It would be at the end of the week, so other people in the city would be tired and less attentive, many shops would close early to prepare, giving believers a good reason to close their own shops early. The priests would also be getting ready for the Sabbath, so were less likely to be watching the city.

~

Two days later Amon was walking home from a visit to Gamaliel. As he turned onto his street, a squad of temple guards came up from the other direction, headed for his house. This was a sight that frightened almost every Jew, but Amon was especially tense, knowing that Saul was hunting for the Clever One.

Instantly Amon jumped into the shadow of a house and flattened himself against the wall.

The squad stopped in front of his house, and their leader pounded on the door.

Amon's father opened it.

*I should go over there*, Amon thought. But fear kept his feet planted where he was.

The house was too far away to hear what was being said, but it was obvious the guard was demanding something, and Jotham was refusing to provide it. When the guard yelled, Amon could finally understand the words. "Bring him forth this instant," the armored man screamed, "or go to prison yourself!"

In a flash Amon remembered seeing his father in prison, starving, waiting to be executed, and knew he could not allow that to happen again. With no more thoughts of fear, he left the shadows and ran toward the house. "Wait!" he yelled. "I am here!"

Both his father and the guard turned to look at Amon running toward them.

Jotham started to yell something to Amon, but the guard drew his sword and threatened him to be silent.

Amon skidded to a stop a few feet in front of the guard. "I am Amon," he said, panting, "and I am here. Leave my father be."

The guard looked back and forth between Amon and his father as if they had just told him they lived on the moon. "And why would I care if you are here or not?"

Now Amon was confused. "Aren't you looking for me?"

Another look at Jotham, then back at Amon. "No, I am not. I am here searching for a man named Uri, and I was told this is the place where he lives." He looked back at Jotham. "Now bring him out immediately. My patience is at an end!"

Amon's mind still was not comprehending this, but Jotham yelled into the house. "Uri, would you come here, please?"

A moment later, Uri ran to the door. "Yes, Father?"

"Uri," Jotham said carefully, "this man wants to take you away and kill you. Would you go with him, please?"

Uri looked up at the guard. "Yes, I will go with you. But can you kill me quickly so I can be home by dinnertime? My mother is making honey cakes tonight."

The guard stared at Uri, then spoke again to Jotham. "And this is the *only* person named Uri in this house?"

"Yes," Jotham answered. "He is the only Uri in this house, and the only one I know of in the entire city."

The guard stared at the boy again, then ordered the squad to do an about-face and return to the temple.

Amon let out a big sigh and felt his whole body go limp. Back inside the house, Jotham told Uri he didn't need to go with the man and could return to playing.

"He is not going to kill me today?" he asked.

Jotham swallowed hard. "No, not today."

Uri shrugged as he started climbing the steps to the upper room. "Perhaps another day then."

Jotham stared after him for several seconds before whispering, "Perhaps."

Tabitha told Jotham to come and sit, and together they spoke with Amon. "You understand what this means?" his father asked.

"Yes. Someone talked. The guards were looking for someone named Uri and specifically emphasized the word *place*. Someone told Saul of our plan."

Tabitha looked from Amon to Jotham. "But why would they be searching for a child?"

"They didn't, Mother. They must have asked around the city for anyone named Uri, and someone told them that he lives here."

"We should tell James to cancel the plans," Jotham said.

Amon shook his head slowly, analyzing the situation. "No need. Obviously they do not know who Uri is, or what 'Uri's Place' means. But the bigger concern is how they found out. Who talked?"

After some discussion, Jotham sent Jadon to run to the house where James was staying to have him come over.

"This is most serious," the apostle said after Jotham had explained. "Either someone was overheard talking about the meeting, or there is a spy in our group."

"That is my analysis as well," Amon said.

James put his head in his hands and closed his eyes. Amon wondered if he was praying. His eyes were still closed when he finally spoke. "We will go ahead with the meeting as planned. Obviously Saul has nothing more than a name, or else they would have known Uri is just a boy." He looked up at the other two. "I refuse to live in fear. We will worship the risen Lord in faith, using the wisdom of our minds to be as safe as possible, but trusting that Jehovah is in charge when we cannot be."

"Saul's ignorance may be a trick," Amon's father said.

"And we must keep Amon safe in case it is," James answered. To Amon he said, "We will not include you in any more meetings for now, and you must not be part of the preparations for the gathering."

Amon looked at James first, then his father. This wasn't a possibility he'd ever considered. "But I may still attend, correct?"

James raised his eyebrows. "Is there anything on this earth that could stop you?"

Amon grinned. "Only a direct order from my father."

Jotham looked from Amon to the others. "He'll be as safe with us as anywhere else."

~

For the next two days, Amon stayed at home cleaning the sheep pens, making small repairs, and helping his mother. He ached to be a part of the preparations for the meeting but knew it was better if he was not. He put everyone else in danger just being near them.

One day while he worked outside, he looked up to see a man he didn't know standing by his neighbor's house. The man seemed to stare aimlessly but every once in a while would look toward Amon. Later, while Amon worked on the water system on the roof, he saw another man watching, a man he was pretty sure was a temple guard but wore the clothes of a workman. This man, too, seemed to be watching Amon. It gave him an empty feeling in his stomach.

After he saw a third man watching him, a man who didn't belong in the area, he knew someone was spying on him. Could it be Saul? Caiaphas? Pilate?

On the third day, Amon told his parents of his suspicions. After considering his son's story, Jotham said, "You know, son, you've thought this way twice before. We often see what we expect to see. That's how magicians work their magic. Is it possible those men only seemed suspicious because you expected them to?"

Amon rubbed his eyes. "Yes, it might be." He leaned back against the wall and sighed. "Perhaps it was my own fear making me see things that were not there. Again."

"Well, there is no reason for you to feel bad about it," his mother said. "You have many good reasons to expect trouble."

Amon nodded his thanks to her for her kind words. Before he could say anything, the door burst open and Benjamin ran in, out of breath and with panic in his eyes. "I was just stopped by the captain of the temple guard," he wheezed.

"Raphu?" Amon said, sitting up straight.

"Yes. He wants to meet you at the inn tomorrow morning!"

✦ ✦ ✦

Knowing the right thing to do can be difficult. Even when we *want* to obey God, his will isn't always obvious.

Think instead about your own will.

In any particular situation, what is it that *you* want to do? Be honest. Deep in your heart, what is the course of action you'd really like to take?

Now that you have that in mind, what are the other options?

Finally, line up all those possibilities in your mind and look at them carefully. Often it will now be obvious how God wants you to proceed. It may or may not be what *you* were hoping for, but by identifying your own desires, you've made it possible to hear God more clearly.

Amon is scared to meet with Raphu. Every part of him wants to run away and hide. But once he realizes those are his *own* fears and desires and not God's spirit telling him to run, he will be able to hear God's true voice.

It's never easy listening for God's will. But by acknowledging the noise of your own thoughts and fears, you might find it easier to hear God's desires.

## Chapter Twenty-Two

# Raphu

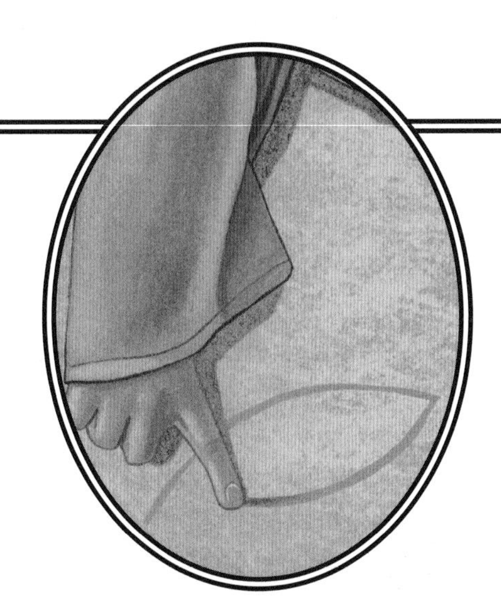

Amon's father was at a stall, talking with a man he knew, a seller of meat. The apostle Thomas had been pressed into service and stood in a doorway across the street. Bartholomew had just returned home from preaching in Samaria and was slowly drinking water from the public well. And Mathias, the newest apostle, sat three tables away dipping bread into olive oil.

Amon stood at the edge of the inn, working up the courage to enter. He saw Raphu sitting at a table, staring into the cup in his hands.

Benjamin's message had prompted a long evening of questions and debates. Raphu had recognized the boy and stopped him as he left the temple. Amon was surprised that Benjamin was even *at* the temple but said nothing. Immediately Thomas, Bartholomew, and Mathias had been summoned, the other apostles being on preaching trips to local villages. They debated what Raphu could possibly want from Amon, debated whether or not it was a trap, debated what should be done.

In the end, it was decided Amon should meet the guard, but that the four men would be close by in case of trouble.

Amon's hands were sweating and his heart pounded. His mouth was dry, and his legs didn't seem to want to hold him up. He should either run home and hide or walk over to the table and sit down, so he did the second of those things. As he approached, he glanced at Mathias to make sure he was still there.

Raphu looked up and smiled as Amon approached. "Ah, my young friend. I am happy you decided to come."

"Why would I not come?" Amon asked as he sat on a stool.

Raphu's long knife lay on the table between them, and Amon wondered if this would be the day he died, and if that knife would be the cause of it.

"I was surprised by the invitation," Amon said, "but there was no reason for me not to accept."

"And yet," Raphu said without taking his eyes from Amon's, "your father, Mathias, Thomas, and Bartholomew are all within ten seconds of the table, should you need help."

Amon felt his face flush. *Of course*, he thought, *Raphu is captain of the temple guard. He notices everything.*

Raphu turned to his right and waived at Mathias, who looked back and forth quickly as if deciding whether he should notice or not. "It is of no importance," he said, turning back to Amon. "You are in no danger, and I have no evil motives."

Amon wasn't so sure about that and said a silent prayer of thanks for his protectors. "Why did you want to see me?" he asked.

"It is a simple matter, I assure you. Saul commented to me yesterday that he hadn't heard from you in a while, so I offered to find you and get a report on your progress in the investigation."

Amon's whole body seemed to let out a sigh of relief. "Oh, yes, I have been very busy," he said. "You can tell Saul that I have eliminated many suspects, but do not yet have a name to give him."

"Excellent." The guard put a handful of parched corn in his mouth. "I know he will be frustrated that there is no news of this Clever One, but he will be happy that you've been working on it diligently and will soon solve the riddle."

Amon pushed back from the table and started to stand, then sat down again as Raphu kept talking.

"But now that I have completed Saul's task . . ." He took a handful of salt from a bowl and spread it on the table. "I have some questions of my own to ask you."

*Why the salt?* Amon wondered. *And what questions does he have now?*

Then, even as he kept talking, Raphu casually reached down and, with his finger, drew an arc in the salt.

Amon froze. He stopped breathing. He stopped thinking. He could only stare at the first half of the fish symbol and wonder what it would feel like to be stoned to death. Sitting across from him was a man who represented every evil thing Amon had come to know in the last several months—men who used their power for their own glory, men who *worshipped* power so they can force the world into their own vision of right and wrong. Often in the name of God when God wants no part of it. Sitting across from him was a man who worked for men who killed people just for thinking differently from themselves. And now this man was trying to get Amon to admit he was one of those who thought differently.

Amon took a breath finally, but a very shallow one. He was still staring at the half symbol on the table, his thoughts spinning around inside his skull. He liked to keep his thoughts neat and orderly, always understanding his world. But this he did not understand, nor did he have any idea what to do.

This was the captain of the temple guard, the defender of all that the Sanhedrin believed in. Had he somehow found out about the secret sign—perhaps through the torture of one of the believers? If Amon now completed the sign, would he immediately be condemned to death?

Amon desperately wanted to ask his father for advice but knew that wasn't an option. He prayed quickly and silently, but the thoughts kept spinning. Amon gulped as sweat trickled down his neck and his mouth went dry. He looked up at Raphu and stared in his eyes, trying to discern his thoughts. Should he complete the symbol and admit to Saul's right-hand man that he was defying the orders of the Sanhedrin? Or should he pretend he didn't know what the mark on the table was about—the mark he himself had invented?

As that last question spun through his mind Amon grabbed onto it and held tight. Deny he knew Jesus? Turn his back on everything he had come to believe since meeting the resurrected Messiah?

Not a chance.

Without thinking of the consequences now, and without even mentally listing all the pros and cons as was his habit, Amon reached over and drew the second half of the fish in the spilled salt. Then he sat back, breathed, and waited for his execution.

Raphu half stood and put his hand up for Amon to grip.

*Is this just part of his act*, Amon wondered, *or is he truly a believer?* Finally he grasped the hand.

Raphu shook it, whispering, "Brother!" Then Raphu erased the symbol with a sweep of his hand and sat back with a satisfied smile.

A smile of victory, Amon realized, of having tricked his enemy into confessing. A smile of hate.

And yet, Raphu's eyes looked so sincere. They were not eyes of victory or hate. They were eyes—

*Eyes!* Amon thought. *Of course, the eyes.*

Months before, Amon had sat at this very table across from this very captain of the temple guard and learned that the man was telling the truth by watching the black part of his eyes. If someone lied, Amon had discovered, the black center of their eyes grew bigger. If they told the truth, the black part stayed the same. *I wish I had thought of that before I completed the symbol.*

Amon felt better now that he had a bit of a plan. He leaned forward and tried to make his breathing normal.

"You are of The Way?" he whispered, barely moving his lips.

Raphu dipped his head ever so slightly.

*His eyes didn't change.*

"How did that come to be?" Amon asked, still in a hushed voice.

Raphu leaned closer, as if to warm himself over the tea in his mug. He spoke softly, with kindness shaping his voice. "After watching what we did—all of us—to Jesus, I began to feel that the priests do not always see God's truths in the Scriptures. Or perhaps they are simply more interested in their own power and pleasure. Either way, I understood for the first time that their words are not always the words of Jehovah." He took a deep breath, as if to give himself a moment, then he looked Amon directly in the eyes. "But then I saw Jesus."

Amon's own eyebrows shot up as he watched the black parts of Raphu's eyes. Still, there was no change.

"I saw Jesus," he repeated, "the man I knew had been killed, walking and talking with his followers in the Hinnom Valley. I watched and listened and saw the wounds in his hands and feet that could only come from a Roman spike. And then I knew."

Amon let that statement hang in the air, watching Raphu's eyes closely before he said, "Knew what?"

"I knew that Jesus is the Messiah, whether the priests can see it or not."

*No change in his eyes.* Amon wrestled with several thoughts at once, then spoke one of them. "How is it you know of the fish symbol?"

At this, Raphu seemed to be a bit sad. "A man I know—a friend—had listened to the teachings of the apostles and led me to The Way. He invited me to some sort of meeting with other believers, a meeting in a secret place, but I realized I could never attend. Not only would my presence put fear and doubt in the minds of the others, but it would put them in grave danger as well. If Saul ever found out that I . . ." Raphu didn't finish his sentence, but the ending was clear.

*Unless it's all a lie*, Amon thought. "Why did you want to meet with me?"

The temple guard leaned in even closer. "To tell you that Saul knows about 'Uri's Place,' and to offer you my help."

Amon kept staring. "What does he know, and how did he find out?"

Raphu shook his head. "An overheard conversation in the street. A whispered secret. I do not know how he knows, but I'm positive he knows nothing else. It's a name associated with the followers of Jesus, but he thinks it is the key to unlocking this mystery."

"He is more right than he knows," Amon replied.

"Do not tell me," Raphu hissed. "If I do not know the truth, I cannot be made to speak the truth. All I know, and Saul knows, is that someone named Uri is part of The Way. Saul thinks it must be the leader of the movement. But I suspect"—he paused and sat back—"I suspect it has something to do with your brother."

Amon asked his next question carefully. "Why did your temple guards come to arrest my brother?"

"I sent them."

Amon held his breath and clenched his teeth. Had the eye test not worked this time?

Raphu explained. "Saul was ranting on and on about finding this man, Uri, and killing him to stop The Way. I knew it was only a matter of time before Saul realized that you have a brother by that name. So, to stop such thinking before it could start, I sent a squad to arrest Uri. I knew that once they saw your brother, they would realize how ridiculous it was to think he could be the leader of a vast conspiracy. And now the idea of him being part of The Way has been considered. And rejected."

Amon released his breath and blinked several times. "Very wise," he said. *Or a very clever way to trick me into trusting you*, he thought.

"I also wanted to offer you some help." Raphu took a sip of tea. "Although I completely understand if you do not trust me and do not want to accept such an offer."

"What kind of help?"

"I have something to show you that you may find of benefit. Will you allow me to take you there?"

Amon hesitated. "Do you think it wise?"

"Today we can be seen together," Raphu said. "Saul knows I am meeting with you. He even thinks it was his idea. But after this, we must not meet often. I will send messages to you through your friend Benjamin. Saul pays no attention to him."

Fear started to creep into Amon's thinking again, but he shooed it away. "Very well, show me what you will."

Raphu stood, paid the innkeeper for the tea, then led the way out of the inn with Amon following.

Out of the corner of his eye, Amon saw his four protectors jump up. Amon motioned behind his back for them to follow.

"I hope your friends can keep up," Raphu said, sounding amused as he walked.

*And I hope I didn't just lure my friends into a trap!* Amon thought.

✦ ✦ ✦

We don't have to live in fear.

But we do. Too often. Too much.

Like the apostles who rejoiced that they were worthy enough to be beaten in the name of Jesus, we could live fearless lives, knowing that God's promises are true and he'll take care of us no matter what.

But that's a tough thing to do, even for a dedicated believer, when we're faced with physical pain, money problems, bullies, people making fun of us, loss of a loved one, and many other situations that come with living in a sinful world.

Amon has a great deal of faith and has even met Jesus for himself. Yet, he's nervous and afraid, because he doesn't know what's going to happen. He's afraid of the unknown.

Jesus knows our unknowns even before we know they *are* unknowns. Believing that truth the next time we're afraid will lead us into God's peace.

Chapter Twenty-Three

# First Church

Raphu led Amon down through the Tyropoeon Valley, past the Hippodrome. Ahead of them, the temple loomed over the tops of all other buildings.

"Do you not attend any meetings?" Amon asked in a low voice as they walked.

"No, I do not. It would be far too dangerous for everyone. My friends of The Way tell me about the sermons and the news, so I can be as much a part of it as possible." He turned down a side street going east, then another going north, then a short alley going west. At the end of the alley, on the north side, was an arched doorway with an iron gate across it. Raphu took out a large key and opened the gate.

Amon glanced behind him, but there were no bodyguards to be seen. He stepped through the doorway.

Inside was a small space that looked as though it might have been a storeroom for urns of wine but hadn't been used in many years. It was dark and dusty, with broken bits of urns lying about, and many bird nests, spiderwebs, and rat droppings.

"What is this place?" Amon asked aloud, but in his mind he was listing the possibilities—*A prison? A torture chamber? A graveyard?*

"It is nothing," Raphu answered, locking the gate behind them. "At one time it was something, but now it is very much nothing." He used the same key to open a heavy wooden door, but inside was just a small closet.

*Strange, to have such a thick door to such a small storeroom*, Amon thought.

The closet was made of wood, and now Raphu turned or pulled on something in the dark. The back wall swung open like a second door. Behind it was another iron gate, which he opened with the same key. He lit a torch that was hanging on the wall, revealing a narrow stone stairway descending into darkness.

"Follow me," Raphu said, "and do not be afraid."

Amon followed but was very much afraid. The staircase went down and down, turning every dozen steps or so. When finally they reached the bottom, Amon figured they'd gone down about the height of a three-story building. Maybe more.

Raphu lit a torch hanging on the wall, then many other torches and lamps on the walls and in alcoves.

As the place brightened, Amon saw in front of him a large courtyard with a tiled floor, one that reminded him of some fine mansion on top of the ground. A large wooden table sat in the center, surrounded by benches and chairs. Urns and bowls and kitchen pots were everywhere. At the far end were two smaller rooms, one higher and one lower, connected by short stairways going up and down.

"Dancin' camels! What is this place?" Amon asked again.

"What it was built for, I do not know," Raphu said. "But now I am the only one who knows of it, and it is a place in which I can torture men where their screams cannot be heard."

Amon sucked in his breath and whipped around to look at the man.

Raphu stared back, then started laughing. "But I would not do that. I am not here to harm you or anyone else. I am here to help you." He swung the key around his finger by its ring a few times. "But that is not what you were expecting, was it?"

Amon stared at the spinning key, then looked Raphu in the eye. "No, it is not. Torture is what my fear was expecting."

Raphu walked over and put a hand on the younger man's shoulder. "Amon, I know you have no reason to trust me. I hope that will change some day. But I only brought you here to offer you this place for secret meetings, worship services, or for hiding from the prying eyes of the Sanhedrin. There are three rooms here, plus a large, abandoned cistern down that narrow passageway there." He pointed with the torch at a corner of the courtyard. "You may use this space however you like, or not at all. It is up to you."

"But you *work* for the Sanhedrin."

Raphu hung his head. "Yes, I work for the high priest, and the temple, and the Sanhedrin itself." He looked up at Amon. "But my devotion has always be to Jehovah, and now to Jesus, and to those who truly seek his way and his will."

"How did you find this place?" Amon asked.

"It is my duty always to make sure the temple is secure. As part of that, I survey the area *around* the temple to make sure there are no threats. During one such survey a few weeks ago, I found the locked door upstairs that seemed to be protecting a small closet. I felt it my duty to figure out why. I had a blacksmith who builds locks examine the door and make me a key, and then I discovered the false wall."

Amon nodded.

Raphu pulled something from around his neck and handed it to him. "This is a duplicate key to the gates upstairs. It is yours to use anytime you have need. No one but you and I know of this place—at least no one I know of. As I said, use it to meet, to escape, or to live, whatever you need. It's my contribution to keeping the Clever One safe."

Amon hung the key around his neck, under his tunic. He still wasn't sure if he could trust the guard and decided to tell only his father of this place, in case it was a trap.

~

"How could it be a trap?" his father asked on the roof late that night.

"Think of it, Father," Amon whispered as they sat in the dark. "I could organize a meeting there of every apostle and leader. All Raphu would have to do is come in with a single pair of soldiers and he could capture the leaders of The Way without even a scuffle."

Jotham leaned back and gazed at the stars. "You may be right. He could even lock the door and leave the apostles in there forever. Or worse. It *sounds* like a very attractive space for meeting but could also be a very attractive trap if Raphu is not sincere."

"That's why I am telling only you for now, and why I told Mathias, Thomas, and Bartholomew that Raphu showed me a storage room. I just can't decide if Raphu is to be trusted."

Jotham stood and stretched. "Well, what you told them was true, but I think you could have trusted the apostles with the full truth. Ready for bed?"

Amon scrambled to his feet. "I'm not sure I'll ever really sleep again."

The next morning Benjamin's father came to speak with Amon's father, asking if Benjamin could stay with them for a time. "My wife and I must travel to Jericho on business, and Benjamin must not miss his lessons." The man leaned in close and whispered, "His rabbi thinks he will soon be ready for his exams."

Jotham agreed, and Benjamin moved in with Amon. The following day was the day before the Sabbath and the day of the first joint worship service. Amon woke up nervous, spent the day being nervous, and was nervous as the plan was put into action.

Because he might be watched, Amon took no part in implementing the plan. He, Tamar, and Benjamin took up a position on top of the wall, just as they often did on any normal day. If anyone looked, all they would see was three friends doing what they always did. In reality, they were sitting directly above "Uri's Place," just east of the Damascus Gate. They could see the road far below, the garden with the former tomb of Jesus, the entrance to the cave, and on the other side, the entire city inside the wall up to the Antonia Fortress.

Amon's job was to sit facing east and watch the road below. Whenever it was clear—whenever there were no Romans or temple guards or citizens coming up the road from the east—he would play with a whitish stick from a sycamore tree. When someone was coming, he'd put the stick down.

Benjamin did the same thing while watching the road to the west of Uri's Place. Tamar had her back to the road and watched the city and the Damascus Gate. She also would play with a stick unless someone seemed to be watching from a window or approaching the gate.

Below, and across the road, the believers very casually wandered into the garden as if looking at a tomb or enjoying a bit of shade. Two ostiaries—from a Latin word Amon had taught everyone for "doorkeepers"—lounged at the entrance to the garden. Whenever they saw all three of the lookouts on the wall above playing with the sticks, they would send a group of believers across the road. A slight path had been cleared through the rocks and rubble at the base of the wall—enough to make it easier for people to get through but not enough to be obvious from the road. The believers would quickly run up the hill and disappear behind the big boulder, where another ostiary waited and ushered them into Uri's Place.

As each family arrived at the garden, the head of the family would make the sign of the fish on their palm so the ostiary would know they were of The Way, just in case some nonbelievers actually did come to visit the garden. None did, as it turned out, since it was late in the day, late in the week, and the people of the city were weary.

The believers had been taught all of this well, and congregations had been given an approximate time to arrive, so that everyone didn't show up all at once. They were also taught that if there were no ostiaries at the garden, or if anything else didn't look right, they should just keep walking and go back home.

Amon's stomach seemed to be full of worms as he sat at his post above the wall. This was all his idea, and if something went wrong, if somehow the temple guards or Romans or Saul found out about the meeting and arrested everyone, hundreds of lives would be put in danger, and it would all be his fault.

*What am I thinking?* he suddenly realized. *Hundreds of lives ARE in danger!*

Amon felt like he might throw up.

But as he and Benjamin and Tamar sat and did their jobs, casually talking and, every once in a while, raising their sticks and swinging them slightly through the air as if just keeping their hands busy or chasing imaginary butterflies, the system worked as well as a well-oiled Roman battering ram. Families of The Way casually entered the garden, gave the sign of the fish, and waited in the shade. When all three of the lookouts had their stick in the air, the ostiaries sent a few of those waiting quickly across the road and up the hill, where they disappeared. From the seventh to the eighth hour of the day, hundreds of people entered Uri's Place in this fashion.

At the eighth hour, Amon and his two friends left their post and went down to the cave as well. Only the three ostiaries, who had all volunteered to keep watch at the entrance, remained. As Amon slipped behind the boulder and entered, he checked to make sure the rope he and the others had installed was still in place. This rope went through iron rings they had driven into the limestone and ran all the way back to the large meeting chamber, where it was attached to a bell. Should the ostiary at the entrance be able to hear them singing, or if danger was approaching from outside, he would pull the rope to ring the bell and warn the worshippers.

When Amon and his friends were about halfway to the chamber, they began to hear voices singing softly. The closer they got, the louder it got, though Amon did not recognize the song. When at last they reached the chamber, Amon stopped, eyes wide, staring. He knew there would be a lot of people here, but there were *hundreds*. Packed in from wall to wall and as far into the cave as he could see. "I can't believe this," he mumbled to his friends.

"I knew there would be many people here," Tamar said, "but there are *so many people*."

"I don't think it's how many," Benjamin croaked. "It's that they are all worshipping *Jesus*."

Amon stood and watched for several moments before answering. "Yes, I believe you're right. We've never seen anything like this before. There has never *been* anything like this before. This is the first time in all of history that a crowd has gathered to worship Jesus together like this."

The chamber in front of them was so full Amon couldn't see the floor except directly beneath his own feet. Some people stood around the outside walls of the chamber, but most sat cross-legged in small groups in the middle. The glow of a dozen torches bounced amber light off the walls, and the music reflected off the rock across and back again, blending all the voices into one. Amon glanced at the alarm bell, saw that it remained silent, and relaxed. The sound had failed to resonate to the surface of the city above.

As the three friends watched, Bartholomew came up to them, putting his arm around Tamar's shoulder. "We didn't even need to say anything. As people gathered from a congregation, they would start singing. Everyone else would join in as they learned the words."

"But where did the songs come from?" Amon asked. "The Way is only a few months old. How is it they know songs of Jesus?"

"They've made them up in their congregations," he said, "just as we did." Tears began to stream down Bartholomew's face. "It is the most marvelous thing I've ever experienced since the night in Bethlehem when I held the infant Jesus in my arms." He turned back to Amon. "And you did this. You made this happen." He listened again to the people singing. "The world will never be the same."

Amon looked out across the worshipping believers, and he could only think of one thing to say. "Dancin' camels!" he whispered.

✦ ✦ ✦

And the world never *has* been the same.

I love going to church and singing songs of Jesus. I am often moved, often brought closer to Jesus, and often learn something about him as I sing. It's a marvelous time.

But I love it even more when I get to worship in a huge crowd of believers or in a special place. I was once in a crowd of one million men singing those songs. It was thrilling to know that every man there held the same love for Jesus in his heart that I did.

And I was once with a much smaller group of about thirty in a cave near Jerusalem, near the place they say Jesus ascended to heaven. We sang those same songs of praise in a place Jesus had surely passed by if not visited, and it was almost overwhelming.

But far from either of those places, I was once in an old Olympic stadium in Moscow, Russia, shortly after the fall of the Soviet Union, singing with a couple dozen believers who had been forced to hide their faith for years or face punishment from the government, just like Amon and the believers of Jerusalem in the story. Their faith was inspiring.

It's easy for us to take for granted the privilege we have of gathering and worshipping Jesus as one body of believers. But such gatherings are vital to our spiritual health and growth as Christians. Such gatherings are where Jesus lives, even if there are only two or three of us (Matt. 18:20). And whether it's on a field, in a cave, or in a stadium, such gatherings are what we call the "church."

Chapter Twenty-Four

# Church

For over an hour the people of The Way sang praises to Jesus. As one song ended, a congregation of twenty or thirty people would start another—one they'd made up. Soon everyone else joined in as the song became familiar. By Amon's count, every congregation contributed at least one song. When the singing finally ended, every soul in the chamber knew at least twenty new songs of Jesus.

"I wish this could go on forever," Amon whispered to Tamar.

By now the three were sitting together at the back of the crowd, which had formed a circle. At the urging of Peter and John, James the brother of Jesus went over and stood on a section of rock that was a few inches higher than most others. This quieted the crowd, and those who weren't facing in that direction turned to do so.

"My friends," he said in a strong voice, "I have been asked to tell you what I know of Jesus, whom we all know to be the Messiah. But what can I say? He was my older brother. And most of us here know what it is like to have an older sibling."

The crowd broke into laughter and several people yelled, "Amen!"

"And if you never *had* an older sibling," James smirked, "just ask Andrew here what it's like."

The apostle Andrew stood at the back, next to his brother, the apostle Peter, and shouted, "Yes, and I can tell you it is not a pleasant experience!"

The adults, including Peter, and some of the older teens laughed again and there were more shouts of "Amen!"

James then became more serious. "I must confess to you now that I did not believe my brother to be anything special as we grew up together."

The crowd went silent and listened intently.

James paced on the small stage of rock. "He was kind, to be sure, and always watched out for me and our brothers and sisters. But the Messiah? No! Never! After he began his ministry, I once heard someone say, 'Can anything good come out of Nazareth?' And that is how I felt. In fact, when we, his family, heard he had gathered twelve followers together and was saying crazy things, we went and tried to stop him. We thought he'd gone mad. This man, my brother, is of my own family. How could he be more than a brother or more than a man? But then . . ." James stopped, his face toward heaven and his eyes closed. "But then I saw my brother crucified. I saw him dead. And I saw him resurrected, raised from death by the spirit of God, and I saw him ascend into heaven, my Lord and Savior, the Son of God, Jesus the Christ!"

All present stood and cheered and shouted and cried and praised God. When it was finally quiet again, and with most the people seated, James paced slowly back and forth across the small space.

"So, is anyone among you in trouble?" he said. "Let them pray. Is anyone happy? Let them sing songs of praise. Is anyone among you sick? Let them call the apostles to pray over them and anoint them with oil in the name of the Lord. And the prayer offered in faith will make the sick person well; the Lord will raise them up. If they have sinned, they will be forgiven. Therefore confess your sins to each other and pray for each other so that you may be healed. The prayer of a righteous person is powerful and effective."

James stepped down from the platform to many shouts of "praise God" and "hallelujah." Several of the other apostles spoke short messages of hope, praise, instruction, and encouragement. After that, Peter announced that the service must end, and reminded everyone to be careful and follow the instructions of the ostiaries on the way out. Finally, he thanked them for their generous contributions of food and clothing, which would be distributed among the widows and orphans. One congregation led the rest in a song of benediction as Amon, Benjamin, and Tamar slipped out and returned to their post.

Back on top of the wall, there wasn't much for them to do. It was almost dusk as the people started exiting the cave, and the rest of the city was indoors preparing for dinner. The ostiaries directed people to go left or right, so there wouldn't be a steady stream in either direction. Most people happily complied, though a few grumbled about having a longer walk home.

~

"I *thought* I smelled peaches!" Amon said as he descended the steps to the kitchen of his house the next morning. His mother and father were sitting at the table talking. Benjamin had left early for his lessons. A bowl of the peaches sat in the middle of the table next to a bowl of almonds, his father just reaching for another handful.

"It is a celebration of the wonderful time we had together with the believers last night," Tabitha answered.

Amon sat and bit into a peach. "I think this should be a new tradition," he said, peach juice running down his chin. "A banquet after every worship service."

After Amon enjoyed two handfuls of almonds and lots of joyous but quiet talk of the night before, a knock on the door interrupted the breakfast. Amon opened it and saw the cheese seller standing there. "Josiah? I am surprised. You have never before come to visit here."

Josiah looked terribly nervous, shifting his weight from one foot to the other, then back again. "I am sorry to disturb your morning," he said, "but I have urgent information for you."

Amon stepped aside, old fears making his stomach quiver. "Come in, please. Sit with us."

The cheese seller entered and sat on the bench closest to the door. "I am sorry to disturb your morning," he repeated, as if he didn't realize he had said that already, "but I came to warn you of a thing. A Roman soldier stopped by my booth this morning." He looked at Amon and added, "A very large Roman soldier."

When Josiah didn't say anything more, Amon's father asked, "And did he buy any cheese?"

"What? No, of course not." He seemed lost in his thoughts, then said, "He was asking questions."

Again there was a pause, and this time it was Amon who prompted him. "What kind of questions?"

Josiah took a breath before answering. "About you."

Amon felt his body go cold. "Why would he ask you about me?"

"He said he saw you talking to me once. It must have been the day after Stephen was killed."

"What did he want to know?"

"He kept asking what kind of man you are. You know . . . 'Is he smart?' 'Is he inventive?'" Josiah leaned in closer and lowered his voice. "And he kept using the word 'clever' over and over."

Amon looked at his parents, whose faces revealed their fear.

"Do you know his name?" Jotham asked. "Have you seen him before?"

Josiah shook his head. "No, I didn't recognize him. But, you know, with their helmets on, they all look alike."

Jotham sighed. "Thank you, Josiah, for telling us. We will have to think much on this news."

Josiah saw the bowl of peaches and seemed to gobble them up with his eyes before standing. "I will go now," he said.

"Have a peach before you go," Tabitha said.

He hesitated, then took one, bowed in thanks, and left.

The door had barely closed before Amon jumped up. "They know!" he said. "Pilate's butchers have figured it out, and any minute they'll be here to arrest me and turn me over to the Sanhedrin."

Jotham drummed his fingers on the table as he thought. "Then we must take action before that happens." He hesitated before finishing his thought. "You must go and hide in the apartment Raphu showed you."

Amon looked up in shock. "Hide where the enemy told me to hide?"

"I don't believe Raphu is the enemy, Amon, and I don't believe you do either. What was he to gain by showing you that chamber and giving you a key?"

"You said yourself it could be a trap—gather all the apostles in one place then lock the door."

Jotham hesitated. "Yes, it is a possibility. But you looked into the man's eyes, and you looked into his heart. What does that clever mind of yours tell you?"

Amon sat heavily on his stool. So much had happened since he had been declared to be a man, so many things had changed. And now the entire Roman legion was searching for him as if he were a country to be conquered. The thought pressed down on him like all the blocks of limestone ever carved out of Uri's Place.

"Amon," his mother said softly. "Whether the weight we carry is a feather or a mountain, the Spirit of Jesus is here to carry it for us. Do what seems right, but do it in the knowledge that it is not your burden to bear."

Amon nodded. "Very well. I will stay in the hidden chamber until Jehovah tells me otherwise."

The door opened and Benjamin walked in looking as dazed as if he had just seen an elephant flying over the city.

"Benjamin," Tabitha said. "What is wrong?"

Benjamin's mouth opened slowly and he whispered, "My rabbi says it is time for me to become a man."

~

The iron door creaked, then three pairs of sandals clopped their way down the narrow, wet stairway, a handheld torch lighting the way. Amon hadn't noticed the moss on the steps before. There must be a hidden spring or stream somewhere under the temple, he decided.

When they reached the bottom, Amon's father could do nothing but stare at first. When he finally spoke, his voice was raspy and quiet. "This has been down here all this time? It's so large. And ornate. It looks like a palace!"

By now Amon had lit the torches down one side of the large room.

"How could this have been here for hundreds of years, and no one know of it?"

Amon shrugged as he lit the other side. "Jerusalem has been here a very long time. It probably holds many more secrets than this."

"We're going to *live* down here?" Benjamin asked.

"Only until it is safe to go up," Amon answered.

The decision had been made only minutes after Benjamin arrived home: he and Amon would come to this chamber to hide for a time. Amon would quiz Benjamin in preparation for his exams, and Benjamin would keep Amon company and, if necessary, slip back out to carry messages from Amon to his parents.

Jotham set sacks of food and water on the table, starting to recover his wits. "Well, I must say, if you have to hide somewhere, this is a very nice place to hide." He looked across the colorful mosaic floor, only slightly dimmed by centuries of dust, and at the fine workmanship of the walls and arches. "Perhaps the rest of us should come down and join you."

Amon finished lighting the last of the lamps and torches. "I do not believe Mother would like to live in a place with no sunlight."

"No, I would agree with that," Jotham said, laughing.

"What will you say if someone comes searching for me?"

Jotham answered so quickly it was clear he'd already thought of this. "I will say that my son is with his best friend, Benjamin, and that Benjamin's parents are away traveling. Both these things are true. And now I must go."

Amon pulled Jotham close, buried his nose in his father's cloak, and inhaled the smell of his home. "Come and get us as soon as you can."

Jotham patted Amon on the back, then climbed the stairs.

Amon listened to be sure the gate, wall, and door at the top closed tightly, and then he and Benjamin set up house. They rolled their beds out in the small room above the main room. They unpacked their food and other supplies onto shelves in a small alcove. Then they brushed off a bench and sat at the table.

"What do you want to do?" Benjamin asked.

"I don't know. What do *you* want to do?"

Benjamin twisted his mouth into a shape Amon couldn't put a name to. "I guess I should probably study."

For the rest of the afternoon, Amon quizzed his friend. When it felt like dinnertime, they lit an extra candle for the Sabbath and said the prayers. They didn't have the proper Sabbath foods but decided Jehovah would understand and ate some bread and cheese. They decided it would be unlawful to clean up the crumbs they'd made until after Sabbath then went to their beds in the upper room. Amon reached over to snuff out the last lamp.

"Wait!" Benjamin said.

Amon stopped. "Wait for what?"

"This is the Sabbath. If you put out the lamp, can we light it again?"

Amon thought. "Probably not." He laid back in his bed. "Good thing you thought of that."

"I've been studying all day," Benjamin replied. "I think I know every word of the Torah by heart."

~

Amon slept fitfully that night, since he was used to sleeping in the fresh air of the rooftop and hearing the sounds of night animals and guards on patrol. Here the only sound was that of distant, dripping water, which annoyed him greatly. When he finally awoke, he didn't know if it was morning or still the middle of the night.

"Are you awake?" Benjamin whispered.

"Yes."

"Is it morning?"

"I don't know."

Amon got up, decided it was okay to light a torch from the lamp since that wasn't really work, and went down the five steps to the main room. He climbed up the long staircase at the other end and quietly cracked open the false wall.

Daylight sneaked in.

He closed it again and returned. "What are you still doing in bed?" he asked Benjamin, loudly. "It's the middle of the day!"

After breakfast they tried to figure out how to fill their time, given that it was the Sabbath.

"What would you be doing if you were at home?" Amon asked.

"Usually visiting you, playing with my brothers, or listening to my father tell stories of the old days," Benjamin said.

"I enjoy my father's stories," Amon said, "now that I know they're true."

"You mean how he and your mother were in Bethlehem when Jesus was born?"

Amon nodded. "I still can't believe that really happened. But it did."

"So tell me! We have all day, you know."

Amon spent the rest of the day telling the stories of how Jotham, Tabitha, Bartholomew, and Ishtar had all lived through exciting adventures which led to them being present for the birth of Jesus.

Another night of dripping water left Amon tired the next morning. When Benjamin asked, "What do you want to do today?" Amon stood and said, "Come on," and grabbed a torch off the wall. "Raphu told me there's a cistern down that tunnel. Let's go explore. Maybe we can find the drip and stop it." But as he approached the tunnel entrance, he heard a sound he hated more than anything and stopped dead in his tracks.

✦ ✦ ✦

Benjamin is preparing to be tested.

In the tradition of his faith, he has reached the age when it's expected for a boy to become a man or a girl to become a woman. He'll have to prove to the rabbis that he knows the Scriptures well and has the wisdom to apply it.

Many Christian traditions have similar times when children are ushered into a more grown-up understanding of Jesus. Sometimes it's a formal ritual, sometimes just a natural process.

Whether your particular faith tradition is formal or less so, there comes a time in each of our lives when we must take our faith in God more seriously. It must become our own, something we not only understand with our heads, but live in our hearts. It's more than just knowing the answers to some questions—it's understanding why the questions exist in the first place and how those questions shape who we are and how we treat others.

Of course, we each have a choice in that process. If we go through it only because it's expected of us, or because we're forced to, we can make it fairly meaningless.

The other option is to learn for the love of Jesus. Learn so that you know and understand him better—the way you might about a good friend as your relationship grows. Learn to know him as well as you know all your other loved ones.

If you do that, there's a future ahead that you can't even imagine.

Chapter Twenty-Five

# The Hiding Place

Amon stopped at the entrance to the tunnel, which was only as wide as a man turned sideways and only as tall as a man hunched over. He handed the torch to Benjamin. "Here. Why don't you go first?"

Amon looked away, silent, as Benjamin stared at him. Then Benjamin said, "Ah, let me go first," and Amon knew his friend had figured out the problem. Amon had tried hard to overcome his fear of rats but still preferred not to run into them without warning.

With Benjamin in the lead, they wiggled and pushed through the narrow passage. About forty paces along they came into a room with a domed roof of hewn rock and a large, empty pool with rounded corners in the floor.

"A cistern," Amon said. "I might be impressed if we hadn't seen so many cisterns in the last few months." He spotted a tiny stream of water coming out a hole in the wall. "Ah! The drip!" Benjamin held the torch as Amon found a small stone and plugged the hole. "Now maybe I can sleep at night."

A ledge ran around the top of the empty cistern, and on the other side lay another passageway.

"Want to explore more?" Benjamin asked.

Amon hesitated, but then said, "Sure."

"We don't have to, if you're worried about rats."

Amon shook his head. "No, I'll be okay."

Benjamin led them around to the other side and into the passage.

This time they had to travel many more paces than before. In places, the walls narrowed so much that Amon couldn't take a deep breath. "Good thing we didn't have a bigger breakfast," he muttered. Soon his arms were covered in scratches, and he saw that Benjamin was scraped up as well.

"Can we go back now?" Benjamin said as they reached yet another narrow spot.

"Just a little farther."

"What if we get stuck?"

"Then someday someone will find our skeletons buried in this tunnel and wonder what two boys were doing under Antonia."

"You're a man, not a boy."

From somewhere in the distance, Amon heard the squeaking of a rat. "Right now I don't feel like one."

They pushed through the narrow spot and around the corner.

Daylight!

They stopped, assessing the danger. The light was glowing from around a corner ahead, but they couldn't see past the curve.

"Should we go forward?" Benjamin whispered.

Amon looked over his friend's shoulder for a long time. "Yes. But slowly."

They inched ahead, the dim light getting a little brighter as they went. When they were close, Benjamin peeked around the corner. "The tunnel just continues. The light is coming from above."

"Keep going," Amon whispered back. They moved forward around the corner and stopped under a vertical shaft going straight up several feet. At the top of the shaft was a grate, and through the holes in the grate came the dim daylight.

"A drainage shaft," Amon said.

A moment later they heard footsteps approaching overhead.

"Put the torch out," Amon hissed.

"But how will we get it—?" Benjamin stopped his question because Amon had grabbed the torch and smothered it on the stone floor.

The heavy footsteps stopped directly above.

"Did you hear that?" a low, gruff voice asked.

"Yeah. Somethin' is down there."

Amon and Benjamin hugged the walls but didn't dare move farther away for fear of making noise.

"Do you smell smoke, like from a torch?"

The other man sniffed. "Nope, but I'm all stuffed up."

"Wanna go down there?"

"No. Do you?"

"Nah. Probably just rats."

Amon stiffened and tried to brace himself against the walls and lift his feet. He couldn't do it. His eyes darted around the floor looking for the rodents.

The footsteps faded into the distance, and Benjamin leaned over to his friend. "Don't worry," he whispered. "I haven't seen a single rat dropping."

Amon exhaled, then picked up the dead torch.

"Lit again," Benjamin said.

Amon stared at him in confusion.

"That's what I started to say. How will we get it lit again?"

Amon searched the floor, found a fragment of jagged rock, and dug into the center of the torch. He found a small ember inside and blew on it gently. Soon the torch erupted into flame.

"Oh," Benjamin said.

They quietly stepped farther down the passage and soon saw the glow of light again. This time it came from a bigger shaft going straight up. The tunnel they were in dead-ended there. They looked up and saw that this shaft was also covered with a grate at the top. Down at their level, where the two tunnels met, there was a bit more space—enough that they could trade places if they wanted to. First Benjamin and then Amon stared up the shaft. It was about as tall as two men and wasn't quite as tight as the tunnel they'd come through.

"Well, I guess we go back," Benjamin said.

Amon heard him but wasn't listening. "Another drainage system," he said. "Rainwater flows in through the grate and down this tunnel to the cistern."

"Great. I guess we go back then," Benjamin repeated.

Amon looked at him as if Benjamin were insane. "Go back? Why? We must see what's up there." He gazed up the shaft again and saw tiny ledges chiseled out on each side all the way up. "Toeholds," he said. To demonstrate, he handed the torch to Benjamin, reached up and stuck his fingers into two of the ledges, then stepped up to a lower one with his left foot.

In a few moments he had climbed up to the top. He tried lifting the grate, but it was too heavy. He planted both feet one ledge higher, then arched his back and pushed with it against the grate. It moved slightly, so he gave one more push and lifted it out of the hole. After that, it was easy to slide it to the side. Amon climbed up and out of the shaft.

Benjamin passed the torch up, then joined Amon. They saw they were now in a larger tunnel. "There must be a whole network of drainage tunnels," Amon said as he led the way.

Each time they came to an intersection, Amon marked the direction they had come from with a splotch of torch soot on the wall. Sometimes they went left, sometimes right, sometimes straight up. All the tunnels had a low roof like the first one, and their backs ached from stooping over.

Amon was sure it had been hours by now, a feeling confirmed when Benjamin whispered, "I'm starving. We should have brought lunch."

Amon sighed. "Yes, we should probably go back so you can study."

~

The following morning, they took a different route. They discovered another cistern and a room full of broken urns. That afternoon, as Benjamin studied, Amon drew out a map of all they had discovered.

The fourth day, they went another new direction, following the tunnels much farther than the days before. They were just about to turn back when they saw light up ahead.

"Wait here with the torch," Amon said, then went forward.

The light came from a slit in the wall.

Amon looked through, then jumped back as best he could.

"What is it?" Benjamin hissed.

"Put down the torch and come," Amon whispered back.

Benjamin did and sucked in his breath when he looked through the slit. "What *is* that?" he asked.

"That's Pilate's throne room."

Benjamin turned to his friend, the light from the slit dividing his face in two. "Pilate's?"

"Yes. I worked many days in that room. It's where I put in the glass windows and where I overheard Caiaphas talk to him."

"Let's get out of here."

"Why?"

Benjamin looked as if he was trying to think up a reason that had nothing to do with being scared. "I'm hungry."

Amon smiled at him. "You always say that."

"I always am."

Amon swallowed. "Yes, I am as well. Alright, let's go."

They started to move. "We should have brought—" Benjamin stopped when he heard what sounded like a large door open and voices entering the room.

Amon went back and peeked through the slit.

Pilate entered and sat on his throne. "Alright, bring in the first one," the Roman leader said.

There were footsteps on the marble floor, then a man's echoing voice said, "This is Citizen Decimus. He is asking for favor from Caesar."

"What is the favor?" Pilate droned, already sounding bored.

"I would like to have my family returned to Rome, Your Excellency. The heat here is too much for my wife and daughters."

Amon could barely understand the man's words, since he stood far back from the throne and his voice echoed in the great hall. Amon put his ear as close to the slit as he dared and strained to hear.

Pilate granted the favor, then listened to a seemingly endless line of issues and requests. Some were lawsuits, while some were criminal matters that usually ended in someone being sentenced to death. Others were mundane business, such as requests for permission to build. In each case, Benjamin and Amon couldn't see the people through the slit. In fact, Amon realized, the slit was cut at such an angle that he could only see Pilate on his throne. "This slit was made by a spy," he whispered in Benjamin's ear. "Someone long ago keeping watch on the governor or king."

Benjamin's eyes opened wide and his mouth dropped halfway open. "Dancin' camels!" he whispered.

Amon was sure it had been well over an hour when Pilate held up his hand and said, "Enough. I am done for today." He started to get up, but the man who introduced each new person said, "Your Excellency, Caiaphas has sent word inquiring about a favor he asked of you on behalf of a man named Saul."

"A favor? What favor?"

Apparently the man shrugged in ignorance because Pilate sat back down and was quiet. "Oh, yes," he said at last. "It is a silly matter, but it comes from a citizen of Rome. Have the first centurion report to me tomorrow at this time. We'll see how clever he is." Pilate chuckled at his own joke, which no one else seemed to get. He stood and left the chamber.

When all was quiet, Benjamin headed back the way they'd come, followed by Amon. They talked little on the trip back and, when finally they arrived at the apartment, scarfed down some bread, olives, and cheese.

It was much nicer being in the large room with all the lamps and torches lit. Benjamin was just stuffing his mouth with bread when Amon said, "We need to go back there tomorrow."

"We whuh?" Benjamin said around the wad of bread.

"They're going to talk about me. We have to be there."

After a short discussion Benjamin agreed. They spent the rest of the afternoon on his studies, and both slept better that night than they had the first few. After packing a lunch the next day, they headed back into the maze of small tunnels. They didn't have to wait long after arriving at the spy hole.

Pilate entered and the assistant's voice announced the arrival of the first centurion.

"Report," Pilate said.

"Your Excellency, I have not yet been able to identify the Clever One as you commanded. I have asked and threatened many, but so far none know the identity of the criminal."

"I must have someone to turn over to this Saul, centurion. Do you not understand? If I don't keep Saul happy, he'll complain to the emperor, and the emperor will be annoyed, and you and I will be transferred to an even worse dust bowl than this just so the emperor doesn't have to deal with it."

"I will increase my efforts, Excellency." Amon could imagine the soldier bowing at this.

"Not good enough. I need the criminal soon. *Today*." It was quiet for a few moments, then Pilate sat upright. "The boy!" he said.

"What boy, Excellency?"

"The one who built the wind machine over my bed and put clear rocks in these windows here. *He's* a clever boy. Just arrest him and give him to Saul."

"B . . . but, Your Excellency, I have no evidence against that boy. I do not even know his name."

"What do I care? Maybe he's not *the* Clever One, but he is *a* clever one, and neither this Saul nor Caiaphas will know the difference."

"Do you think . . . ?"

"Find him!" Pilate snapped. "Find him and take him to Caiaphas and let us be done with this ridiculous business."

The soldier mumbled something else, but Pilate glared at him. "Yes, Excellency. I have been working closely with the captain of their temple guard. I'm sure he knows the boy. I will ask his assistance." The soldier said this with no sorrow in his voice.

As the sandals of the soldier echoed out of the hall, Amon and Benjamin collapsed against the sides of the tunnel. They looked at each other, not daring to speak. Amon pointed down the tunnel the direction they had come, then Benjamin turned and led the way.

It again took the friends a large part of the afternoon to return to the apartment. Once there, Amon was close to tears. "I can't believe this," he hissed. "All the believers in Jerusalem have worked hard these many weeks to keep my identity a secret. But then Pilate comes in and condemns me without even knowing it really is me they've been searching for!"

Benjamin looked around the chamber. "Are you sure people can't hear us through these walls?"

"I was so stupid," Amon raged at himself. "I never should have trusted Raphu. What a *fool* I've been—to think he could be anything but the high priest's puppet."

He ranted for several more minutes until Benjamin said, "Amon? Don't you think we should get out of here?"

Amon's eyes shot wide open. "Of course! That's why he put us in here. It's just a giant rat trap!"

They grabbed their clothes and bedrolls, leaving the food and supplies, and ran for the stairs. They were about halfway up when they heard the iron gate above screech open.

Two sets of sandals clip-clopped down the steps toward them.

Amon and Benjamin flew back down the stairs to the courtyard. Amon's mind raced with possible escape plans. The tunnel! The two *young* men could fit through it, but the two *older* men never would, especially in their armor. He threw down his belongings, grabbed Benjamin by the sleeve, and pulled him over to the tunnel entrance.

"Quick," he said, shoving his friend. "Get in."

Benjamin protested that Amon should go first, but Amon shouted, "Just go!"

Benjamin bent over and his head was just inside the mouth of the tunnel when a voice said, "I thought I'd find you here."

Amon spun around to see Raphu standing there, a smirk on his face, and a large Roman soldier holding a sword behind him.

✦ ✦ ✦

I can't begin to count the number of times in my life that I've made plans that failed. They were good plans, often, and sometimes *very* good plans. Plans that should have worked, should have achieved what I was trying to achieve.

But they failed. Often.

And yet somehow, when they were plans to promote God's kingdom or care for his children in some way, something else happened completely outside of my expectations or control that ended up accomplishing the goal even better than the way I had planned.

Imagine that. God is better than I am at achieving his goals.

Go figure.

It's not that God doesn't ever want us to work and plan for him. It's more that he wants us to understand that *he* is in control. Not us.

All the believers in Jerusalem have worked hard to protect Amon's identity, and up until now, it has worked and worked well.

But Pilate's top soldier, along with the chief guard of Caiaphas, have joined together to capture and punish Amon, though none of the believers ever betrayed him.

What does God have planned now?

That's a question I find myself asking. Often.

## Chapter Twenty-Six

# Betrayed

Amon let out a throaty yell, then pushed Benjamin into the tunnel. He turned back to face Raphu, covering the tunnel entrance with his body. *If I can delay them even a few seconds they'll never get Benjamin*, he thought. "Go Benjamin! Run!" he yelled.

Raphu stood in front of Amon, face twisted, then stepped forward.

Amon looked around for a weapon—*any* kind of weapon. The only thing close was the bag of bread on the table, so he grabbed it and prepared to bash the solider in the head.

"Amon!" Raphu roared, and it sounded like the roar of a lion to Amon's ears. "What are you doing?"

"I am defending myself and saving the life of my friend. You may get *me*, but you will never catch *him* in that tunnel."

Raphu looked at the Roman, then back at Amon. "Well, I guess you can defend yourself against us if you think it necessary, but I'd really rather sit down and plan out how we'll help you escape Caiaphas."

The Roman soldier stepped forward into the light.

Amon blinked several times, had to reroute the thoughts inside his brain, then said softly, "Cornelius?" His head tilted to the side as he stared, then the thoughts fully connected and he yelled, "Cornelius!"

The two soldiers laughed.

"Amon, we are here to help you, not arrest you," Raphu said.

"And just what were you going to do with that bag?" Cornelius asked.

Amon held the bag out in front of him and felt his face get hot. "I just thought you might be hungry?" he said weakly, pulling out a loaf.

The soldiers laughed again.

"Amon? What's going on?" Benjamin's voice came before his head poked out from the tunnel.

"It's alright," Amon said. "This ugly Roman is a good friend."

Benjamin climbed out of the tunnel shaking badly.

Amon went over and put his arm around him. "There is no fear here now. The Romans have come to the rescue."

~

"I arrived a few weeks ago to prepare for Pilate's arrival," Cornelius said, tearing off another piece of bread.

They were all sitting around the table, Amon and Benjamin finishing their late lunch. It had taken a minute, but Benjamin had finally recognized Cornelius as the Roman who had helped Amon save his father from death.

"Soon after he showed up," Cornelius continued, "he ordered me to search the city for someone the Jews call the 'Clever One' and take him to Caiaphas. When I heard what the Clever One had done, I suspected it was you. But I didn't dare come to see you. It would've made things difficult for both of us."

"That was *you* who questioned all the people about me?"

"Indeed," Cornelius said.

"This afternoon Cornelius came to me, pretending to search for you," Raphu said. "When we found out we were both on the same side of this hunt, we decided to work together to keep you safe."

"How did you find out you were on the same side?" Benjamin asked.

Instead of answering, Raphu stretched out his leg and drew half a fish in the dust with his foot. Then Cornelius reached out with his and drew the other half.

Amon looked from one face to the other. "So, you were both only *pretending* to hunt for me."

"That would be true," Cornelius said with half a smile.

"Then let me ask you this thing," Amon said. "Did you—either of you—have men watching me these last few weeks?"

Both men looked at each other, then at Amon. "Guilty," they both said.

"I *wasn't* imagining it."

"Not at all," Raphu said. "We both had some of our best men keeping an eye on you. Me for the last several weeks, Cornelius since he got here. They *thought* they were watching for any suspicious activity on your part. But we also gave them strict orders not to let anyone arrest or harm you."

Amon put his head down on the table. "That is such a relief. I thought I had gone crazy." He raised his head again. "I'm glad you pretended to search for me."

"Yes," Raphu said. "But Saul is *not* pretending and is furious that the Clever One hasn't been found. And that which makes Saul furious makes Caiaphas irritated."

"And that which makes Caiaphas irritated makes Pilate annoyed," Cornelius said, "which is why he ordered me today to find you and turn you over as the Clever One, even though he has no reason to believe you are that man."

"Yes, I know." Amon nodded his head.

"You know? *How* could you know?"

Amon explained how he and Benjamin had been exploring and had overheard Pilate.

"Well then," Raphu said. "What to do?"

Amon pulled another loaf of bread out of the bag, tore off a piece, and chewed. By the time the others had all taken a chunk as well, he had an answer. "Cornelius, you must turn me in to Caiaphas. There is no other way to keep all the rest of you safe."

The others all looked shocked, but it was Raphu who spoke. "Amon, if Cornelius turns you in to Caiaphas, Caiaphas will immediately turn you over to Saul, and Saul will have you stoned to death that very hour. There is no way we're going to allow that to happen."

"I'm afraid you have no choice," Amon said. "There is nothing else you can do." And then he explained why.

~

An hour later Amon and Benjamin had left the safety of the apartment, and Amon was knocking on Saul's door. Benjamin had taken all their belongings and gone back home to explain everything to Amon's parents. The two soldiers—one Roman and one temple—were on their way to see Caiaphas, the chief priest. The door opened and Saul talked to Amon as if they were in the middle of a conversation already.

"And that's only the ones we know about," Saul said. Then he turned away from the door, leaving Amon standing there.

Amon entered and closed the door behind him. It was dark inside, since his eyes were still used to the bright sunlight, and all the shutters on the windows were closed. There was a foul smell in the air, and every surface was piled with open scrolls, plates of half-eaten food, and empty urns of drink.

Saul himself was even more of a mess than before. His eyes seemed to disappear in the black pits of their sockets, his beard hung like dried seaweed from his face, and the stink in the room came from Saul's body.

"There are more of them, I know," Saul ranted as he paced. "They're hiding, like rats. They come out in the dark and eat away at what is good and right, stripping the wood from everything that makes us who we are!"

Amon realized the words made no sense but knew what he had to say. "Then we shall find them," he said. "Together. We shall find them, and we shall do what must be done to bring our world back to order."

"Yes!" Saul screamed. He turned to his young friend and said it again. "Yes. You are such a good friend and ally, Amon. We shall face this menace together."

For almost another hour Saul spouted nonsense and paced furiously.

Amon sat in a corner and waited.

At one point, his older friend jumped at him and put his face close. "Did you hear? Now they've spread to other cities as well. To Bethlehem, Hebron—even Damascus. We must act now, or soon they will cover the whole world!"

"Yes," Amon said. "Something has got to change."

At that, Saul became giddy, describing how the followers of Jesus would be found and slaughtered, like lambs for the sacrifice. "We shall dig out every last one of them, you and I, and save their souls by destroying their bodies."

Amon heard the pounding feet of a squad of soldiers coming up the road from the Tyropoeon Valley. The ground actually shook as they approached, then a loud banging rattled the door.

Saul opened it and Raphu, captain of the temple guard walked in.

Amon thought Raphu looked as though he had aged a dozen years in the hour since they'd seen each other. "By order of the chief priest Caiaphas," he bellowed, "I am here to arrest the criminal Amon, son of Jotham, for subversive acts against the temple and the laws of Jehovah."

Saul looked from Raphu to Amon and back again. "What are you talking about, Raphu?" he said in a daze.

Raphu took in a deep breath, then spoke reluctantly. "Amon is the Clever One we have searched for these last many weeks."

Again Saul looked at Amon, then back at Raphu. "Why do you say these things? What evidence do you have?"

It was the most rational thing Amon had heard Saul say since his arrival.

"A Roman centurion has informed the chief priest Caiaphas of these facts even within the hour. Caiaphas then ordered me to make the arrest."

"A *Roman*?" Saul said. He stared at Amon, who watched Saul's eyes doing their nervous dance. The black center parts of those eyes were huge in the dark room, and Saul blinked erratically as if batting out some message. Then, still staring, he whispered, "Amon?"

Amon had been waiting for this question and had thought carefully about his answer. He stared back. "I *am* who I always have been, Saul."

Saul stopped blinking and seemed to search inside Amon's head. Then he burst out laughing and said to Raphu, "This is nonsense. You go back to Caiaphas and tell him I will personally vouch for Amon, son of Jotham. There is no possibility that he is the Clever One. And tell that Roman to go back to his keeper and stay out of our business! These matters are for the Sanhedrin to worry about, not some puppet of Rome."

Raphu bowed his head in obedience. "As you say." He backed out of the door and the squad of soldiers rumbled in retreat toward the temple.

Amon tried to hide the fact that he was greatly relieved. His plan had worked, but it had been a dangerous one that relied on Saul's belief in his young friend.

As soon as the door closed behind Raphu, Saul let out another loud laugh and began pacing again. "Can you believe it? My friend Amon being the Clever One! Not that you aren't clever in your own way, but to think you could—" He laughed so hard he couldn't finish his sentence. "Oooh, I sometimes wonder how our kind can survive when our highest leaders are so tied to the dogs of Rome!" Saul continued on for several more minutes, making less and less sense as he rambled on. Suddenly he froze, his eyes blazing. "I know what I shall do!" he hissed. "Yes, it all makes sense now. The road ahead is clear."

Amon wondered what in the world Saul was talking about but kept silent.

"I shall travel the same length these lies have traveled and go where they have gone." He was pacing again, staring into the ceiling as if actually seeing there the commands of God. "Damascus! Yes. Damascus. I shall go there and stop the spread of this evil."

Amon wondered exactly how Saul intended to stop the evil. He didn't have to wait long to find out.

"I will hunt down the followers of Jesus," Saul said, as if answering Amon's question. "I will arrest them all, and if they confess, I will bring them back to Jerusalem for trial. But for those who refuse to admit their blasphemy . . ." He stared at the shuttered window as if he could see all the way to Damascus. "Immediate death. Stoning shall be their salvation."

Then Saul turned slowly toward Amon, stared him in the eyes once again, and said very softly, "And you, my friend, shall go with me!"

✦ ✦ ✦

The funny thing is, the whole time, Amon thought it was all *his* idea.

Even though it was made in haste, the plan Amon had come up with worked perfectly and accomplished exactly what he set out to accomplish.

But then the twist in the story—the plan had worked so well that he found himself bound to Saul in a way he not only didn't predict, but that put him in a terrible position: he will now be one of Saul's party traveling to Damascus to persecute believers in Jesus.

That wasn't what Amon had planned at all.

That's the thing about believing and trusting in God—you have to accept that his ways really are *not* our ways and be willing to follow him regardless.

As often as I've seen my plans fail, I've seen God's plan work out perfectly, better than I could have hoped for or accomplished myself.

But not at all the way I had imagined.

It's not as though God is leading us around on a leash like a dog. It's simply that he is so much *more* than we are. He can see the paths into our future better, and farther and in more detail, than we ever could.

And he knows which one is best for us to take.

Even if it leads to Damascus.

Chapter Twenty-Seven

# Strategy

There was a lot of screaming.

Most days no one even noticed it, Amon knew. It was just there, always in the background, something to be ignored. In a city like Jerusalem, there wasn't a lot of privacy. Even with the shutters closed on all one's windows, the coverings left many cracks and gaps, so that anyone walking by outside could hear everything that was going on inside. Politeness dictated that residents simply ignore it and walk on, and never mention or ask about what was heard.

On this particular walk he heard several babies crying, a man and woman fighting over money, a woman and her teenage daughter arguing, and a small boy throwing a temper tantrum.

The world, it seemed, had become very dark and nasty.

Even though his plan seemed to have worked, Amon still searched with his gaze the shadows of every building and around every corner. Would the temple guards or Roman legion yet surround him suddenly, put him in chains, and carry him away to be stoned?

Then again, maybe that would be better than the fate that apparently awaited him: traveling to Damascus with Saul and ruining the lives of innocent people.

He trudged up the hill, a lump of fear growing in his chest. He half expected to see his house surrounded by soldiers. That there were none only meant they had been delayed. Surely his plan could not have worked so well as to put an end to the chase.

When he pushed the door open and walked in, Amon's parents engulfed him in hugs and kisses. "We were so worried about you," one of them said. "Tell us what happened," said the other.

He didn't really know which one said what. Then he noticed Tamar and Benjamin standing in front of him, grinning.

"It worked, didn't it," Benjamin said as a statement rather than a question. "I kept telling them it would work, because your plans *always* work!"

"Yes, it seems that my plan worked. At least for now."

His father took a step back, a questioning look on his face. "Then why are you so glum?"

Amon sat on a stool at the table. "Saul is going to Damascus to kill Jesus followers and has ordered me to go with him to keep records of those convicted."

Instantly everyone else joined Amon in his glumness. Silence followed, followed by more silence.

"Aren't you going to say something?" Amon finally asked.

Jotham drew a breath. "I'm not sure what to say. I don't want you to go, but suspect you have no choice. I want to save the believers in Damascus, but don't know how do to that. Do you have any ideas?"

"I've never even been outside of Jerusalem," Amon said. "Since I was five, I mean. I've lived here all my life. And I don't want to leave."

His mother looked at his father, then back to Amon. "That's our fault," she said quietly. "We kept intending to take you children on journeys, at least to the nearby towns, but you were always so busy with Gamaliel and all your inventions. We should have taught you more about the world outside Jerusalem."

"Do you think you have any choice in going?" Jotham asked.

Amon stared out the window at the street. "Maybe. But it doesn't seem so."

They talked it over for much of the afternoon. Benjamin's parents stopped by to say they were home, then took Benjamin with them. Tamar made dinner so Tabitha could stay with Amon. But it wasn't until late that night, when he was up on the roof and supposed to be asleep, that Amon finally prayed about going to Damascus.

"Jehovah, I am so scared, and I don't know what to do. Please, get me out of this journey. Let me stay home with my family, where I'm safe." He took a deep breath, then whispered into the night, "But I will do whatever you want me to do and go wherever you want me to go."

With a jolt he suddenly realized that was the same prayer Jesus had prayed in the garden of Gethsemane the night before he was crucified. If Jesus could pray that prayer, then maybe—

"Now that is a sight that makes me happy." His father's voice, shooting out of the darkness, startled Amon. "Sorry. I should have made some noise coming up the stairs." He was actually speaking softly, since the other boys were asleep, but in the still night air it sounded like the roar of a lion.

"What makes you happy?" Amon asked, his heart pounding from the shock.

"Seeing you pray," his father answered. "I assume you were praying about the trip?"

Amon nodded.

"And what are you praying? That Jehovah not make you go? Or that you're willing to do his will?"

"Both," Amon said quietly.

Jotham laughed softly. "A good prayer. Tell me, what troubles you the most about traveling to Damascus?"

"Mostly the purpose of the trip, of course. But also, I'm just . . ." He looked away so his father couldn't see tears forming in his eyes. "I'm just . . . afraid."

"Ah, I see," Jotham said, sitting. "Being away from home is a new thing for you."

Amon looked his father in the eyes. "When you were only ten years old, you went on a long journey all by yourself and survived. Yet I am thirteen and afraid to . . ." His voice faded off, too embarrassed at his own feelings to finish the sentence.

"Amon, I grew *up* in a family that did nothing but travel. It was simply our way of life. It was nothing new to me. And besides, I was terrified the entire time I was away from my father and mother."

"You were?"

"Of course. There is no shame in fearing something you've never before experienced. But do not let that fear dictate your actions." Jotham shifted closer and put his hand on Amon's shoulder. "Now, as for the other thing, I too would hesitate to be a part of Saul's plans. Especially when you are one of the people he would kill if he knew your true heart. But think this way for a moment. Perhaps Jehovah is sending you to help *protect* those people. Perhaps you will be the one to save them."

Amon shook his head. "I do not feel this is so, but perhaps."

"If I were you, I would pray for such an opportunity."

"Maybe *you* should go," Amon said, hope lifting his words.

Jotham smiled. "I was not invited."

Amon's hope fell back to the floor. But before he could say anything, he noticed a dark figure moving through the shadows of the street below. The figure stopped and seemed to be checking every direction, then crossed to the front door of Amon's house directly below where Amon sat. There was a quiet knock.

Jotham and Amon looked at each other in surprise, then raced down the steps as quietly as they could. Jotham cracked open the door, using his foot to block it in case the figure had evil intentions. The figure pulled back his hood, and Jotham saw that it was Raphu. He opened the door and gestured the temple guard in.

"Greetings my friends," Raphu said, as Jotham closed the door. "I come with news."

They all sat at the table, and Jotham said, "Tell us!"

"Saul went to Caiaphas this evening and got permission to arrest believers in Damascus. Saul is anxious, and he wants to leave at first light."

"Tomorrow?" Amon choked. "How can—?"

Raphu shook his head. "It is madness. Even now my men are scrambling to assemble all the supplies. It will take them most of the night, and they will get no sleep. But Saul will not be swayed—he is determined to kill as many Jesus followers as possible as soon as possible."

Amon laid his head on his arms on the table. "Then I must go with him," his muffled voice said. "There is no time to do anything else."

"I fear that is true," Raphu said. "But that is why I bring my news. I have been ordered to accompany Saul on this trip."

Amon's head snapped back up. "Really? You're going too?"

Raphu nodded once, slowly. "So you will not be the only one of The Way on this journey. I will be there to protect you if things go badly."

Jotham laid back on the bench, arms and legs falling limp, staring straight up at the ceiling. "Well now, there's an instant answer to prayer if I've ever heard one."

Suddenly the thought of what lay ahead wasn't nearly so frightening. Amon sprung back up and started quizzing Raphu about the trip. Even as they talked, a messenger from Saul arrived to say the mission would be leaving from the temple at sunrise, and Amon was expected to be there. He was also expected to bring quills and parchment for the keeping of records.

Raphu left to attend to his own matters, then Jotham woke Tabitha. Together they spent the last hours of the night packing Amon's clothes, preparing food for him to take, and giving him much advice about everything from blisters on the feet to not drinking from an unfamiliar pool.

Just before sunrise the other boys, Tamar, and Bartholomew were awakened, and they all left for the temple. On the way, Amon stopped at Benjamin's house to tell him the news and he, too, followed.

Amon was still shaking inside—as much from the thought of leaving home as from the purpose of the trip—but knowing his friend and fellow believer would be along helped him keep his feet walking forward. They arrived at the meeting place on the Tyropoeon Valley side of the Temple Mount.

The others were already waiting. The traveling party consisted of Saul, Raphu, six other temple guards, and a man Amon didn't know.

"This is my friend from Tarsus, Nimrod," Saul said.

Amon had never heard of Nimrod and didn't like the look of him. He was taller than anyone else in the party and very thin. His face was long and straight, and Amon was pretty sure it would crack and fall to pieces if the man ever let a hint of a smile show. Still, Amon walked up to greet him.

Nimrod just stared at him with cold eyes.

Amon abandoned his attempt and lined up in front of Raphu.

The sun peeked over the top of the Mount of Olives.

"We must depart," Saul said loudly enough for all to hear.

Families said goodbye to the soldiers, a young woman with a kind face said goodbye to Nimrod, though his face remained rigid even for her, and Amon's family and friends all hugged him. Jotham also locked arms with Saul and said something to him which Amon could not hear.

Saul replied to Jotham quietly, then in a loud voice said, "We depart!"

Saul and Nimrod led the way up the street. Amon was a few feet behind them, Raphu a few feet after that, then the six soldiers marched in a double column. All the family and friends followed along behind, waving and yelling various forms of "Goodbye!" as far as the Damascus Gate. As the travelers passed through the gate, their friends and family stopped, and that's when Amon felt the first pangs of terror.

He was away from his family for the first time ever, following a man who would surely kill him if his secret ever got out.

The line of men climbed the short hill to the north of the city and into the sunlight. There were several ways to get to Damascus from Jerusalem, but only two that were commonly used. Saul had chosen the route that would take them across the spine of the Judean hills, north toward Galilee, then east and north to Damascus. Raphu explained it would take seven days of walking to reach the great city, plus a day of rest for Sabbath, which meant Amon had only eight days to think of a way to change Saul's mind and make him a believer.

It was an impossible task.

✦ ✦ ✦

It's always scary to do something for the first time: the first day in a new school, the first time behind the wheel of a car, the first time you walk into a new job. But the first time you're away from your parents is probably the scariest of all.

What makes these "firsts" so scary?

Simply the fact that you don't know what to expect or what to do. You don't know what will happen or how to react if something goes wrong.

You just . . . don't . . . know.

But God does.

God's been there a million times before. He knows the people, he knows the circumstances, and best of all he knows what's going to happen.

So why doesn't he share that information? I've often wondered why God doesn't just tell us what's ahead and how he's going to take care of us, so we can relax and enjoy the ride. "Faith," I suppose, is the answer. How would we ever build our faith if we didn't have to trust him without knowing where he's leading us?

Amon is scared right now. He's never been away from his home or his parents, never really been away from Jerusalem. But most of all, he doesn't know how God is going to work in this situation.

His fear, and ours, is understandable.

But oh so unnecessary.

"'For I know the plans I have for you,' declares the LORD, 'plans to prosper you and not to harm you, plans to give you hope and a future.'"

Chapter Twenty-Eight

# The Road to Damascus

Amon glanced over his shoulder and saw Jerusalem—and his home—fading in the distance. Looking ahead again he saw only a rough, mountain road, Nimrod, and Saul. Saul and his friend were deep in discussion about something. Probably the best way to track down Jesus followers. If it wasn't for Raphu nearby, Amon would be decidedly more frightened.

Raphu had said it would be an eight-day trip to Damascus, which would require walking through almost all the daylight hours every day except the Sabbath. Each man carried his own food, and the soldiers were also weighed down with chains to restrain any Jesus followers Saul arrested.

*I only have eight days*, Amon thought, *to open Saul's eyes to Jesus.*

After a stop for a midday meal, the group started up a hill. Nimrod and Saul were still deep in discussion and started pulling away. Amon was next in the line but falling farther behind. The temple guards with their chains and other heavy supplies were slowest. As the afternoon wore on, and Amon was trying to get his legs to keep moving, Raphu caught up to him. "How are you holding up, my friend?"

Amon gave him a sideways look of pain. "I thought I was strong after walking up and down the hills of Jerusalem every day. I was wrong."

Raphu laughed. "You are doing better than I expected. But I must tell you, it will get worse before it gets better." Then, with Saul far ahead of them and the other guards far behind, Raphu said in a whisper, "I want to talk to you about Damascus."

"What about it?"

"You know why we're going there."

"Yes."

"Our warrant from Caiaphas says we are only to arrest any believers we find and return them to Jerusalem for trial. But I do not believe that is Saul's intent. I believe he intends to hold court himself if he thinks there is clear evidence."

"What kind of evidence?"

Raphu let out a disgusted snort. "If he catches someone in the very act of worshipping Jesus, or if someone stands on the street preaching in his name. I believe, in that case, Saul intends to find those people guilty then and there and immediately have them stoned to death."

Amon winced at the thought. He didn't tell Raphu that it made him sick in his stomach.

"But the same fate awaits us," Raphu said, "if Saul finds out you and I are followers of Jesus."

"Yes, I already figured that out."

"Then I want you to know," Raphu said with quiet force, "that I am not going to allow any of that to happen."

Amon looked at him, curious. "What could you do to stop it?"

"The warrant." He patted his chest. "I carry the parchment with the order from Caiaphas. If Saul gets out of hand, I will use it to control him. Those guards behind us move at *my* command, not Saul's." Raphu lowered his voice again, even though there was no one close by. "Praise Jesus in your heart, but keep your mouth closed, and all will be fine. At least on this trip."

Amon managed a bit of a smile. "Do you know this friend of Saul's, Nimrod?"

Raphu shook his head. "No, he is a mystery to me."

"Well, I have a feeling he's on this trip to do whatever Saul wants done."

Raphu remained stoic. "My men and I can control even him, if it comes to that."

Amon's body physically relaxed a bit. He hadn't realized how tense he was. Then he admitted to himself he hadn't just been tense—he'd been terrified since the moment he heard he was to go on this trip.

Raphu drifted back to his men, where he took turns carrying the chains for one and then another to give each a break.

Amon actually began to enjoy traveling and studied the many villages and vineyards they passed. That evening they camped atop a hill with a view of the Mediterranean Sea far to the left and the Jordan River far to the right. A nearby spring and pool gave Amon a chance to soak his sore feet. After a dinner of bread and smoked fish, he was instantly asleep.

The next morning Saul preached what sounded like a sermon before they departed. "Today we enter Samaria," he said, making it sound as if it was a particularly disgusting place. "We must take care not to defile ourselves by touching any Samaritan or anything that any Samaritan has touched."

Amon desperately wanted to point out that Jesus had sat with a Samaritan woman and had even told a story about a Samaritan man being kind to a Jew, but decided this wouldn't impress Saul at all.

The trek across Samaria was easier, both because the route they took kept them on top of the hills and because Amon's legs were becoming accustomed to the hard work. Though they passed many Samaritan settlements and travelers, Saul made sure to not even look at them. "We are to be separate from the Gentiles," he kept saying.

Amon thought this strange, since Jews and Samaritans had been working and trading together for many years.

The group camped by a stream in the hills for Sabbath, which gave them all time to recover from the first two days of their journey.

Late in the afternoon of the next day, the travelers reached the top of a steep hill overlooking a large valley. They all dropped whatever they were carrying and rested. Amon was panting hard from the climb and bent over at the waist to catch his breath.

"The Jezreel Valley," Saul announced.

The others seemed to be happy about this, but Amon wasn't sure why until Raphu added, "The Sea of Galilee is just on the other side of Mount Gilboa there."

Amon looked across the wide, green valley. It was an inviting change to the dust and scrub brush of the hills. Hopefully they'd be able to swim in the lake before dinner.

Most of the group stood at the edge of the cliff and stared out at the rich lands below until Saul said quietly, "Hold. What is that I see?" He pointed to a large group of people and animals traveling south along the Jordan River, toward Jerusalem. "Raphu!" Saul yelled. "Look at this."

Raphu ran forward. He looked, then called behind him, "Obed! Your eyes are the best of us. What do you see?"

His second-in-command ran forward and leaned over the cliff edge so far that Amon feared he might fall. "A large party of Greeks," he said. "Heavily armed."

Saul scowled, thought for a long moment, then turned to Raphu. "You will return to Jerusalem at once. Take nothing, move fast. You must warn Caiaphas, then take command of the guard to protect the temple."

Raphu stared at Saul, eyes wide. The rules of command were clear, and he was bound by oath to obey Saul. But Amon knew he would be in terrible danger if Raphu left the party. "I should send Obed," Raphu said. "I will be needed in Damascus."

Saul shook his head. "No, the safety of the temple is the only issue of importance. Nimrod will take command of your squad, and Obed can handle the daily supervision. Go. Now. And take nothing but water. You must reach Jerusalem long before the Greeks. Once matters are settled there, return and join us in Damascus."

Raphu looked around, helpless, knowing he was stuck. But then he saw the terror on Amon's face and knew the younger man was in much danger. "Amon," he barked, "come and gather my baggage. You will carry it to Damascus for me."

Amon understood Raphu was sounding gruff just to hide their secret.

Once they were away from the rest of the group, Raphu's attitude changed. "You are in grave danger," he whispered as he loaded Amon with a bag of food and another of personal items. "You must take extreme care. Speak very little, and when you do, use only the words Saul wants to hear." Raphu looked behind them to make sure no one could hear. "When you get to Damascus, do not object to anything Saul says or does. But if you must, sneak away and find the home of Judas on Straight Street. He is a believer and will help you." He finished adjusting the new weight on Amon and grabbed him by the shoulders. "If Saul doesn't find him and kill him first."

Amon's whole body trembled.

Raphu reached in his bag and pulled out a loaf of bread. "I'll eat this on the way." Then he looked at Saul and shook his head. "The man is no general, that is for certain," he said. "You don't send your most experienced soldier to carry a message." He bent down and adjusted his sandals. "Perhaps," he whispered to Amon, "I will forget to give Saul the warrant from Caiaphas."

They returned to the rest of the group.

"Give the warrant to Nimrod," Saul commanded.

Raphu's shoulders drooped just a bit, but he complied.

"Now go," Saul ordered. "You must reach Jerusalem ahead of the marauders."

Raphu tried to hide his disgust, then without another word, took off at a run down the hill they had just climbed.

Alone now with a group of men who would gladly kill him if they knew what was in his mind and heart, Amon tried to control his shaking.

Saul didn't seem to notice. "We will continue down to the valley and then camp for the night," he announced.

The next day started with an easy walk around Mount Gilboa and across the valley to the far side of Galilee. Amon amused himself by thinking maybe he should explain to Saul some of the sayings of Jesus.

But then the day turned difficult—climbing the long, steep hill to the Golan Heights overlooking the lake. Amon kept daydreaming about having one of Yasmin and Zana's camels and realized the caravan of his Persian friends had probably traveled this exact road not long before.

It was about halfway up the giant hill that a thought first tickled the insides of Amon's brain. He tried to brush it away, but it kept coming back. *Perhaps I should try talking to Saul*, the thought said.

Each time the thought returned, Amon reminded himself he was under orders from Raphu to keep silent. *But is Raphu my master*, another side of his brain would argue, *or is God?*

They finally reached the top of the hill and collapsed in exhaustion. All of them heaved deep breaths of air and dripped with sweat. The heat of the afternoon desert was suffocating, and Amon looked back at the Sea of Galilee far below, longing to jump in its cool waters.

But there would be no swimming or even bathing from this point on. There was nothing but desert heat and dusty roads ahead.

And nothing but cruel death and violent persecution in Damascus.

Amon shuddered at the thought. It was time to take action.

✦ ✦ ✦

Alone.

For most people, including Amon, it's a place we'd rather not be. Even if we're around other people, if we don't know those people, we can feel very alone, and lonely.

When you think about it logically, that's kind of a silly reaction, isn't it? If we understand that Jesus is alive, if we know him as our best friend, and if we believe he really is God with all the power of God, how can we ever say we're alone? Why would we ever be afraid?

Maybe if we think about it another way, it will make more sense. Imagine for a moment that Superman really exists—able to fly, deflect bullets, and leap tall buildings in a single bound. And besides all that, he's a really nice guy who calls you his friend and likes being with you. If you and Superman walked into a new place or even a dangerous situation, would you be afraid? Of course not. You have Superman by your side.

That's how we should feel about Jesus. And it's not just a mind trick. It's not just something we can *imagine* to make us feel better. It's true!

If it came down to it, who would win an arm-wrestling match between Jesus and Superman?

One of them is a super man.

One of them is a super God.

There's no question who would win. And that super God is actually, really, lovingly by our side every time we find ourselves "alone."

Amon is still trying to learn this. So am I. But I keep practicing and reminding myself, and like anything else we practice, it gets easier and easier with experience.

## Chapter Twenty-Nine

# The Debate

Darkness swept across the high plateau and brought with it the chill of night. The travelers had only walked another hour after cresting the ridge, then set up camp to the side of the road. They all sat around a small fire now, taking in a bit of warmth before going to sleep. It was then that Amon took action.

Everything down to Amon's fingertips was shaking, not from cold but from nerves. And fear. *I must say this very, very carefully*, he thought. Finally, in the quiet of the dark desert, he spoke. "Saul, why is it that these Jesus followers believe him to be the Messiah?" Amon kept his eyes fixed on the ground, not daring to look.

Saul was silent for what felt like the length of a harvest season. Finally, he spoke. "That is a fine question, Amon." He sounded to Amon like the Saul of old, the Saul with whom he had debated many points of law and the Torah on many occasions.

Amon silently started to breathe again.

"I believe they would say he fulfilled many of the prophecies about the Messiah, and that, in some way, he spoke into their hearts and proved himself to them."

Amon looked up. "And do you think he really did fulfill any of the prophecies?"

Saul took a sip of water, an amused smile on his face. "You know as well as I, Amon. You have studied the Scriptures and can decipher truth from lie."

*Careful, Amon*, he thought to himself. *Be very careful*. "Of course," he said aloud. "I just wanted to hear your thoughts."

Saul gave a sigh, as if Amon were asking if birds could fly. "The problem with prophecy is that it must be fulfilled completely, not just in part. The prophets say that the Messiah will bring world peace and end all hatred, oppression, suffering, and disease. 'Nation will not take up sword against nation, nor will they train for war anymore,' Isaiah said. Do you see that happening? Even now a Greek army descends on Jerusalem to destroy the temple. Does that sound like peace?"

Amon watched two camel spiders fight over an ant hill as he thought. "I think the believers would answer that the death and resurrection—I mean, the *supposed* resurrection—of Jesus of Nazareth proves he is of God and will accomplish those things in the future." Amon felt he was safe in making this argument because in a debate, as he and Saul had so often practiced, a person argued the side they were on whether they actually believed that thing or not.

"A fine point," Saul said. "But Scripture also tells us the Messiah will spread universal knowledge of Jehovah, which will unite all humanity. 'The LORD will be king over the whole earth. On that day there will be one LORD, and his name the only name.' I do not believe anyone would claim that all humanity is bowing to God because of some carpenter from Nazareth."

The debate had gone as far as Amon dared for one night. "You defend your position with honor, as always. I will think on these things."

~

The next day, as they plodded along the rocky desert road, Amon repeated Saul's point back to him, then asked, "But that would not happen in a moment, would it? Would not it take some time, maybe even decades, to bring the word of God to all the people on earth?"

"Not for Jehovah," Saul argued. "Is he not all-powerful, all-knowing? Can he not make himself known everywhere to everyone all at once?"

Amon wanted to shout out his answer, but reined in his passion and waited several minutes, as if thinking. "Of course," he said at last, "but has not God always in the past used *people* to tell his story? Is that not true of Noah, and Abraham, Moses, Esther, and David? Has he not always appeared to one, who then tell the many?"

"A good analysis of the past," Saul replied. "But the prophet Elijah flew to heaven on a chariot of fire for all to see. Do you think the Messiah will do less?"

"Certainly not," Amon agreed. "But I have heard that some Jesus followers believe they saw Elijah standing with Jesus at an event they call his 'transfiguration.' Surely that would be a sign that Jesus really was from God."

Saul seemed to be getting a bit annoyed. "Nonsense. Perhaps if such a thing had actually happened, you would have an argument there. But since it did not, since we only have the word of fanatical followers to believe, it surely did *not* happen!"

The debate continued around the fire that evening. At every point Amon made, Saul seemed to get more irritated and frustrated. *This is not unusual*, Amon kept thinking. *We both get that way sometimes during debates.*

Amon awoke on the eighth day of their journey—the last day—to a feeling of absolute dread. Not dread, he decided after a time, but terror: *I have less than a day to change Saul's mind.*

Both were silent during the morning of walking. Amon imagined Saul was planning out what to do first when they arrived at Damascus. Amon himself was praying and thinking about how to convince his friend that Jesus was "the way, the truth, and the life." Just before they would stop for the noon meal, he spoke. "If you grant all my previous arguments and consider again the ancestry and birth of Jesus, does it not make sense that he could be the Messiah?"

Saul laughed loudly and looked back at his young friend. "Amon," he shouted. "Have you suddenly become a Jesus follower yourself?"

Amon's insides froze even as he walked. Had he gone too far? Was he now to face the wrath of Saul?

"No," Amon protested. "Of course not. I am merely debating." Instantly the words of his friend Simon Peter came to his mind as he remembered how Peter confessed to denying Jesus the night before his crucifixion. Amon felt a terrible surge of guilt, but the debate built over the noon meal, and he had no more time to think about it.

As they started out again, Saul announced that they were about two hours from Damascus and that their work would begin the moment they arrived.

Panicked now, Amon pressed on with the debate, becoming less and less careful about his words.

"He didn't even follow the Torah," Saul scoffed. "He healed on the Sabbath! He picked and ate fruit on the Sabbath! How can you call one 'Messiah' who does not even follow the laws of Jehovah?"

"Jesus came to *fulfill* the law, not to abolish it," Amon shouted at Saul's back.

"And yet his followers interpret the Scriptures incorrectly to suit their own needs," Saul yelled over his shoulder.

The debate grew louder as they tossed angry words back and forth, no longer debating but full-out arguing. Saul, in a rage, stopped and spun around. "If the believers are so sure of their 'Messiah,' then why do they hide? Why don't they come out in the light and proclaim their beliefs to all who can hear?" He took one more deep, angry breath and screamed, "Why do they hide behind the Clever One? And why are you so anxious to defend them?"

Without thinking, without even meaning too, Amon stared Saul directly in the eyes and screamed back, "Because I *am* the Clever One!"

Suddenly, the earth was silent.

The wind seemed to stop blowing.

The dust seemed to freeze in midair.

All creation seemed to stop breathing, stop moving, stop . . . living.

The anger on Saul's face slowly melted into confusion. Like a fish out of water, his mouth opened and closed without sound. He stared at Amon for long seconds, then uttered, "Amon? What is this you say?"

Amon, once again in control of his mind but no longer caring about his body, marched up close to his friend, stared him in the eye, and said very quietly and very forcefully, "I . . . am . . . a member of The Way. And I am the Clever One you have been seeking. I will no longer hide this truth, and I will no longer be frightened. I am a follower of Jesus the Christ, whom I know to be the Messiah."

Saul slowly shook his head but was otherwise frozen in place. "No," he wheezed. "No, this cannot be. You—you have hunted the Clever One—"

"You asked me to search for him, and so I did. I searched my heart, I searched my mind, I searched my conscience, and each time I searched, I found only logic and truth in my beliefs."

Saul was still shaking his head and staring. "But . . . *why*, Amon?" he whispered. "Why would you betray me?"

Amon closed his eyes. Did he really have the courage to speak his convictions? He slowed his breathing, then opened his eyes and spoke with all the love he had for his "brother." "Because, Saul," he whispered back, "Jesus . . . *is* . . . the Messiah."

Saul's confusion slowly dissolved into hurt, then the hurt dissolved into anger, and the anger became resolve. "Very well, then. If you have abandoned me and Jehovah, then you must face the consequences the same as every other heretic. The same as that blasphemer Stephen." His eyes finally broke away from Amon and found the temple guards. "Bind him," he barked.

Amon's eyebrows shot up and his knees weakened.

"We will continue to Damascus, and when we get there, we shall—" Saul hesitated, as if now finding it difficult to say the words. Then he threw his shoulders back, stood up straight, and said loud enough for all to hear, "We shall do what must be done in the name of Jehovah." Then he bent and picked up a rock. "And I shall cast the first stone!"

Saul spun around and started up the road again as the guards grabbed Amon's arms.

Having just been sentenced to death by stoning, Amon struggled with those who would bind him, even as his attention remained on his friend. "Saul! Saul! Why do you not see? Why do you hate the truth and cling to lies?" Saul was twenty steps up the road, and Amon yelled louder. "You have been blinded by religious rules made by men, not God."

Saul spun back around, dust flying off his feet, hatred on his face. "It is *you* who are blinded! It is you who believe in a false prophet and follow a man who is *dead*."

At that moment a bright light blasted down from the heavens, so bright it was as if the sun itself hovered just above the trees.

Saul screamed as one struck by an arrow and fell to the ground. He grabbed his eyes tightly and rolled in the dust. "I can't see!" he screamed. "I can't see!"

✦ ✦ ✦

What in the world was Amon thinking?!?!?! (Note: you should never use more than one question mark or exclamation point when writing, and never combine the two. But in this case, I felt it necessary to convey my level of exasperation.)

Raphu has been working hard to keep Amon safe and told him how to escape danger once they reach Damascus. But did Amon listen?

No!

He opened his big mouth and had to keep pushing and prodding until he pushed Saul past the breaking point. And now look where he is.

Wait a minute.

He's on the ground. Free from his chains. With some kind of angel or something shining down over him from heaven.

Maybe he's not in such a bad place after all, despite his foolishness.

Wait another minute.

Maybe it wasn't foolishness. Maybe Amon was following the leading of the Spirit in trying to convince Saul. Maybe he was right to follow his spirit-filled heart instead of the commands of Raphu. Even if, maybe, he did take it too far.

What in the world are *you* thinking?!?!?!

You need to get out there and tell others about Jesus!

Chapter Thirty

# Saul

Amon lay with all the others facedown in the rocky dirt, the large bindings slipping from his small wrists. He covered his head, hiding from the light that shone from heaven.

A sound, low and booming, came from the clouds, as if a voice were speaking from inside a tent or building, but he could not make out the words.

Amon peeked and saw Saul frantically rolling on the ground, looking toward the sky but with his eyes closed, as if searching only with his ears. "Who are you, Lord?" Saul yelled.

The voice rumbled again, and again Amon could not understand the words. The muffled voice rolled across the land like thunder.

And then it was over.

The light faded. The last of the voice echoed off the hills. And suddenly it was silent, except for the screaming of Saul.

"I can't see!" He said over and over, lying in the dirt, holding his eyes. "I can't see."

Amon raised his head slowly and looked around. Everything seemed normal, except that everyone was on the ground and Saul was weeping.

Amon and Nimrod both jumped up, ran to Saul's side, and stood before him.

The man who had just condemned Amon to death lay on the ground in a heap, covering his head with his hands.

It was Amon who finally spoke. "Saul, what is it? What happened?"

Saul only wailed, hysterical, crying out the name "Jesus" over and over, as if calling upon the Messiah to rescue him.

Only inches away from Nimrod, Amon looked up into the man's face and wondered if he would report Saul's cries to the Sanhedrin.

Nimrod pierced Amon with his gaze, then lowered his eyes to the ground.

Amon's gaze followed.

With the toe of his sandal, Nimrod drew in the dirt an arc in the shape of half a fish.

Lightning flashed through Amon's body. Could this sour man really be a believer? Or was this just a trick? But he had wondered the same thing about Raphu, and that seemed to turn out all right. With his own toe, Amon completed the fish symbol.

Nimrod looked at him and smiled. "Brother," he said, "I am honored to meet the Clever One. Now, let us take care of our friend."

Together they lifted Saul to his feet, still sobbing.

Amon asked the soldiers who had gathered around them, "Did you see the light? And hear the voice?"

The soldiers all nodded, still numb from the experience. Then they all started down the road toward Damascus. Amon and Nimrod supported Saul the entire distance, and for the entire distance he stumbled along, crying out that he couldn't see, and that he was sorry.

As they neared the city, Nimrod said, "Where should we go? I don't believe the host Saul arranged for us will be very receptive to his current condition."

Amon silently thanked Raphu for the information. "A friend told me of a man named Judas on Straight Street. I believe we will be safe there."

They entered through the city gates and many eyes watched. Some were just curious, but many scowled at the suspicious sight—surely there was some evil afoot, the eyes seemed to say, for a man to be acting this way.

Amon was about to ask one pair of eyes for directions to Straight Street when he saw the straightest street he'd ever seen running right through the city. "That's got to be it," Amon said.

"Agreed," said Nimrod. "But how do we find the house of Judas?"

"Judas, you say?" The voice had come from behind them and belonged to an old woman tottering along while carrying a basket. "I'll take you to him."

"Thank you," Amon said, and they followed her halfway up the street.

She stopped at a door and knocked twice.

The door opened a crack. An eye looked out, saw who it was, then opened it. In two beats of a heart, the man inside the house sized up the situation and said, "Come in, friends."

"Are you Judas?" Amon asked.

"I am. How do you know me?"

"Raphu, captain of the temple guard, told me you would help us."

"And that I will. Is Raphu not with you?"

"No. He had to return to Jerusalem."

"Then what shall we do with *them*?" Judas asked, pointing to the six temple guards outside the door.

"Oh," Amon said. "I'd forgotten."

He looked at Nimrod, who shrugged. "I think we'd better invite them in."

Saul was still crying and shaking uncontrollably. He was mumbling under his breath, but the words made no sense.

"We'd better move him into the storage room, in case someone comes to the door," Judas said.

The others agreed and fashioned a bed for Saul out of sacks of grain.

A knock on the front door interrupted their work.

Amon closed the door to the storage room, then Judas opened the front door.

The man standing there seemed to be wearing all the dust of the desert and was panting like a dog in a drought.

"Raphu!" Amon exclaimed with relief.

"My friends," Raphu said as he stepped inside. He looked around, heard Saul wailing and babbling behind the door, and said, "It would seem I missed something."

Judas fetched Raphu some water as Amon sat him on the floor and quickly caught him up on the events of the day.

"A light, you say? And Saul blind?"

As they talked, Nimrod came and knelt next to them, whispering. "I think we need to do something about *them*." He nodded toward the six soldiers, still standing against the far wall.

Raphu looked at Nimrod, then at Amon.

"He's a believer too," Amon explained of Nimrod.

Raphu shook his head to clear the windstorm of his thoughts. "I'll talk to them," he said of the soldiers. "But first, show me Saul."

All that night and all the next day and for two more following, Saul remained in the dark storeroom. He refused to eat, refused to talk, constantly mumbled and wailed.

On the third day, there was another knock on the door. When Judas opened it, a short, plump man waited there. "My name is Ananias," he said. "I'm looking for a man from Tarsus named Saul. I know he is here praying."

All the men were suspicious, but Amon gestured toward the storage door, opened it, and stepped in.

Ananias came to the door and stopped, staring at the empty hulk of a man lying on the grain sacks. He hesitated, then took a deep breath.

Instantly Saul was alert. "Who's there?" he asked. "Who is it? Ananias, is that you?"

"Yes, it is I."

Amon and Nimrod looked at each other as if to say, "I wonder how they know each other?"

"Brother Saul," Ananias said, "the Lord Jesus, who appeared to you on the road as you were coming here, has sent me so that you may see again and be filled with the Holy Spirit."

At that moment scales like that on a fish fell from Saul's eyes. "I can see," he gasped, blinking at the light even though it was a single oil lamp. He stood and praised God and hugged Amon, Ananias, Nimrod, and everyone else in the house. "Quickly," he said when all had been greeted, "you must baptize me unto Jesus."

The others looked around until Amon said, "But we have no other apostle here who can baptize you."

Saul put his hand on Amon's shoulder. "My friend, you do not need to be an apostle to baptize someone. You just need to have a heart fully committed to Jesus."

They stepped outside the back door to a large watering pool. Amon shooed the goats away, then, for the first of many times in his life, Amon performed the ceremony of baptism.

Back inside they sat down at the table, and Saul said, "I'm starving. Judas, is there any food in this house that I haven't slept on?"

The others laughed, and soon Saul started stuffing bread and olives into his mouth.

Amon rested his head on his hands and stared at Saul. *This is the man who was ready to stone me*, he thought. Aloud he said, "Saul, can you tell us what happened out on the road three days ago?"

Saul leaned back and finished chewing. "After the light appeared, I heard a voice," he said. Then he looked at the others. "Did you not hear it?"

"We all heard a voice speaking but could not understand the words," Amon answered.

Saul took a sip of water. "The voice said, 'Saul, Saul, why do you persecute me?' 'Who are you, Lord?' I asked. 'I am Jesus, whom you are persecuting. Now get up and go into the city, and there you will be told what you must do.'" Saul stared straight ahead, unblinking. "But all I could think of was that I had just been in the presence of God, and I was so ashamed of what I had done."

The house was silent after Saul finished his story. Then Nimrod began to pray, thanking God for bringing Saul into The Way.

Through all of this, Obed and the other five guards sat on the floor by the wall, looking puzzled. When the prayers came to an end, Obed asked, "Could one of you please tell us what's going on here?"

The believers grinned, then spent much of the day explaining it all to them. By evening, all six temple guards had come to believe and were baptized by Saul into the faith.

When morning broke, Amon stretched and sat up in the corner he had claimed for his bed. He saw the others stirring as well but didn't see Saul. He quickly determined his friend was not there and woke the others immediately. A search party was established, with Raphu taking charge. They all went out into the city in pairs, searching in different directions. Soon Amon and Nimrod found Saul standing at the back of a synagogue, preaching the good news of Jesus, the Messiah.

"Saul," Nimrod hissed. "You must stop this and come back. This is very dangerous!"

Saul didn't argue but didn't stop preaching either. All the way up Straight Street, he loudly proclaimed his message of hope but got mostly scowls in return.

The next day Saul again went missing, and again they found him in a synagogue. This time he was at the front, preaching more boldly.

A crowd gathered, and Amon heard one man say, "Isn't he the man who raised havoc in Jerusalem?" Another asked, "Hasn't he come here to take the followers of that carpenter as prisoners to the chief priests?" A third said, "I don't know, but what he's saying makes a lot of sense!"

Every day Saul would sneak out of the house, and every day they'd find him preaching in one of the synagogues, or on the street, or anywhere people would listen.

"If this keeps up," Nimrod said one afternoon, "he's going to make a lot of people mad."

"Maybe so," Amon answered, "but he's making an awful lot of people believers!"

As Amon walked through the city, he heard more and more people arguing about Saul and his message of salvation through Christ. Some people were convinced by Saul's words, others thought them to be blasphemy. One afternoon, Amon heard some talk among Saul's opponents and ran back to warn him.

"Saul!" Amon yelled as he burst through the door of Judas's house. He looked around but saw only Nimrod at the table, writing. "Where is he?"

Nimrod looked fairly disgusted. "Where do you think?"

"Help me find him. He's in terrible danger!"

Nimrod dropped his quill and left with Amon. They found Saul on the other side of the city, preaching to a small group of men and women at the corner of a street.

He had just told them of the resurrection when Amon walked up and whispered in his ear. "Saul," Amon whispered. "I have just heard of a plot to have you killed."

Saul looked as interested as if Amon had announced he was wearing sandals today. "I am not surprised," he said.

"We must take you and hide! They're watching the city gates, waiting to capture you when you leave. If you keep preaching, they won't have to wait that long."

Saul let out a sigh, as if this were just another small annoyance, like a sore toe or empty flour jar. "I follow the will of my Lord," he said, "not the plans of men. If they want to kill me, they'll have to wait until God is finished with me."

Over the next few days, the anger in Damascus grew. Finally it was Nimrod who convinced Saul. "I believe Jehovah would tell you your work here is done. The entire city has heard your message. Many have believed, and those who have not probably never will. It is time to take your ministry back to Jerusalem."

"Perhaps you are right," Saul said. "Make your plans."

That night Raphu, Amon, and Nimrod, along with the six guards, said their thanks to Judas and Ananias and slipped out into the darkness. Thirty steps from Judas's house, they heard a roar behind them and turned to see an angry mob approaching, torches held high. They started to run but were immediately confronted with a second mob, also yelling for the arrest of "that hypocrite from Jerusalem." They ran down a side street only to be stopped by a third mob.

Trapped, the traveling group surrounded Saul to protect him and backed up against the houses on one side of the street. The guards seemed ready to stand their ground, but Amon kept looking for an escape route.

There was none.

The mobs approached, clubs held high, and Amon quickly prayed for a miracle. Moments before the first club would have smashed his skull, a door opened behind the group.

"Quickly! This way," a woman's voice said. They couldn't see inside the house in the dark but knew there was no other choice. They tumbled in through the door, and it slammed closed behind them. A metal bar was lowered across the doorway, and Amon heard threats and promises of injury from the other side.

As their eyes adjusted to the darkness, the men saw an old woman, too old to be living alone, Amon thought. It was the woman who had led them to the house of Judas when they first arrived in Damascus.

"Come this way, my brothers," she said, leading them to the back of the house. "My back window overlooks the road outside the city." She opened the shutters, threw a knotted rope out the window, and gestured for them to go. "I had a strange feeling you might need an escape route."

"We can never thank you enough for your kindness," Nimrod said.

"It is in the name of Jesus that I do this," she answered. "Now go safely in that name."

The men quickly climbed out the window and down the rope to the road below. When it was Amon's turn, he saw that the ground on this side of the house was much farther down than at the front of the house. He descended the rope, then they all gathered and hurried up the road. When they crested the last hill outside Damascus and looked back at the city for the last time, there were no torches following.

✦ ✦ ✦

All that work for nothing.

Amon spent months trying everything he could to convince Saul that Jesus truly is the Son of God and the Messiah.

He tried logic, he tried Scripture, and he tried using anger and yelling louder. But nothing worked.

Saul simply would not change his mind, no matter what Amon said or did.

But then Saul met Jesus for himself on the road to Damascus.

Saul met Jesus.

Face-to-face, so to speak.

Amon couldn't make Saul change his mind. Jesus had to do that himself.

Sometimes we think it's our job to bring others to Christ, to make them understand the logic of it, put together arguments that will prove it to them. We try beating them over the head with Scriptures or using well-formed arguments. And when that fails, we sometimes get angry and yell a little louder.

I don't think that's what Jesus has asked us to do.

What he's asked of us, I think, is simply to introduce him to others by showing them the same kindness, acceptance, and patience that he has shown us. Without judgment, without condemnation, without membership goals or belt notches in mind.

Our job is to love others as Christ loves us and tell others of our own journey with Jesus.

He'll do the rest.

## Chapter Thirty-One

# New Beginnings

Eight days later the group arrived back in Jerusalem. They came to Saul's house, and as they parted, he hugged Amon and thanked them all. Amon started to walk away as Saul entered, then smiled as he heard him yell, "Who messed up my house?" After that everyone was so exhausted that they went directly to their own homes.

Amon's family and friends rejoiced at his return and listened in awe to his stories of the journey.

"Let me make sure I understand this," Tamar said in front of everyone. "It was a woman who led you to safety in Damascus, and *that same woman* who saved you from a mob that wanted to kill you all, correct?"

Amon tried to make his mouth say something profound to argue Tamar's point, but he couldn't. "Yes," he said finally, surrendering in his soul a mistaken belief he'd believed all his life. "It was a woman Jehovah sent to save us."

Tamar sat back with a smile of victory, arms crossed, and Amon returned to her a nod of concession.

Later that night, as they sat on the roof overlooking the city, Amon's father asked what he had learned in his travels.

"Twice now, God has shown me that he is strong and sufficient where I am weak and unable. Once when I tried to save my father and failed"—he looked at Jotham and smiled—"and once when I tried to save Saul and failed. I think I have learned that I need to believe that God, in his son Jesus Christ and in his Holy Spirit, is both present in my life and watching over the entire world. And he's smarter than me. And stronger. And more clever."

Jotham smiled. "It is a hard lesson to learn, is it not? We want to believe so badly that we can do all things, but sometimes the things that need doing can only be done by God."

Amon nodded, then laid his head on his father's shoulder. "And yet," he said, "it is the most comforting knowledge in all the world."

Once news of Saul's return had spread, and especially that he was now a believer, Jerusalem was in an uproar. Somehow the temple guards became confused, receiving conflicting orders from Caiaphas and Raphu. Everyone was searching for the apostles, some to follow them, some to kill them, and there was still a push on to find and bring to justice the Clever One.

The apostles, with Barnabas, all met once again in the upper room of Amon's house, but they were terribly suspicious of Saul. Barnabas finally convinced them that Saul's conversion was sincere. But meeting in Amon's upper room was terribly dangerous, and Amon asked them to meet with him instead at a special place known only to a few. Based on his previous success in organizing meetings, the apostles agreed.

A day later, Amon and Raphu led the group casually through the streets of the Tyropoeon Valley. They spread out so as not to be in a line but all followed Amon. As they walked, Amon turned to Raphu. "Whatever happened with the Greek group you came back to warn Caiaphas about?"

Raphu laughed. "It turns out they were just traders. They had met a caravan of Persians who had just come from Jerusalem and who told them about Jesus. So they came here to find out about him for themselves."

Amon smiled and said a prayer of protection for Ishtar, Yasmin, Zana, and all of the Persian caravan.

They turned down a small side street, then Amon unlocked and pushed open the heavy wooden door. As the apostles followed him inside, he opened the closet and then the large iron gate.

"Where are you taking us, Amon?" Peter asked. "It feels as though we're headed into the dungeons of Antonia."

"Fear not, my elder," he teased. "We are entering a secret place shown to me by an official of the Sanhedrin."

"That does *not* make me feel better," Peter muttered.

They descended the long staircase and finally arrived in the apartment below, where torches had already been lit. Amon's mother had organized a cleaning party, and the space sparkled in the firelight.

Peter gawked at what he saw. "I always thought paradise was in the sky, not underground," he said.

The others laughed but agreed with the sentiment.

"This is the safest meeting room in all of Jerusalem," Amon said. "You may talk here of anything you like, and no one will hear you or find you."

With the apostles assembled, they all sat at the long wooden table. By now everyone just assumed James would be leading them, so he stood at the end. "Now Saul," he began, his knuckles tapping the table, "explain to us why you believe Jehovah would have us take the message of the Messiah to the Gentiles."

Amon listened to his elders talk, and thought, *This is going to be a very long debate.*

Soon after that meeting, Benjamin went before a council of rabbis and completed his exams. He passed without question and was declared to now be a man. The first thing he did was talk to his parents that night and lead them to a belief in Jesus as the Messiah.

Tamar still annoyed and teased Amon on a daily basis, and their friendship grew even as she traveled with her father to distant cities to preach.

One afternoon Amon stopped by Saul's house to see how he was doing.

"I am well," Saul said. "I am preaching by the grace of God, and so far the Sanhedrin has not figured out what to do with me."

"Then my quest is truly at an end, though I had nothing to do with fulfilling it."

"Quest?" Saul asked.

"Long ago I made a vow to bring you to Jesus no matter what it took. Now you have come to know Jesus, even though it was not I who brought you there. I am most happy."

"Amon," Saul said slowly, "do you really think that the friendship you showed me, the way you stood by me, and the things you said to me made no difference? Jesus appeared to me, yes. But it was you who opened the door."

Amon was speechless. "Saul . . . Saul . . ." was all he could say.

"And that's something else I've been meaning to talk to you about, Amon. I think, from now on, you had better start calling me 'Paul.'"

~

That night Benjamin the Man stayed with Amon. Even though the weather was turning and the air was chilled, they rolled their beds out on the roof of the house. Amon pulled his scratchy, gray blanket over his legs, then lay back, put his arms behind his head, and looked up at the stars. "You know," he said, "it occurred to me that if Stephen hadn't been killed by the Sanhedrin, the believers in Jerusalem never would have fled to cities all over the world. And if believers hadn't fled to cities all over, the rest of the world might never have heard the good news of Jesus."

Benjamin also looked heavenward, his breaths coming slower and more shallow moment by moment. "So, are you saying that the persecution of believers by Saul and the Sanhedrin was a good thing?"

Amon rolled over on his side and looked his friend in the eye. "No, not really." He paused to organize his thoughts. "I guess I'm saying that God really can use anything for good, even the murder of one of his children." He settled onto his back and looked up at the stars again. "I remember saying it should take about a year to tell the whole world about Jesus. I now believe that maybe I was wrong. I'm guessing it might take many, many more years. Maybe even decades. Maybe even centuries."

Benjamin sighed softly. "Well then, I guess we'd better get started."

"Yes," Amon said with his own sigh. "But first, maybe we'll rest for a week or two. These last few months have been very exhausting."

Benjamin curled up on his side, the edge of sleep drawing close. "At least the good news is on its way to Persia."

"True," Amon mumbled, his own speech getting sluggish. "Maybe someday you and I and Tamar can help it travel to new places as well."

And though he did not yet know it, Amon had just foretold his future, and the many adventures that awaited him there.

✦ ✦ ✦

Once we humans had turned our backs on God and chosen to live our own selfish lives, God knew there was no way we could ever return to him on our own power. There was no way we could ever obey all the laws that would allow such a return.

God's solution was to send his own son, Jesus, down to live with us for a while, to show us what an unselfish life looks like. To teach us.

But that still wasn't enough. It was impossible for us to repent from our sins on our own power.

So Jesus gave us the ultimate example of a selfless life by dying for our sins. He not only erased our guilt, he demonstrated for us how we were intended to live from the start.

But not everyone got the message. It was hard for many to believe, and in their unbelief, they tried to destroy the believers and eradicate the new church.

Life was difficult—and dangerous—for the first members of "The Way," the first followers of Jesus.

That hasn't changed a lot.

In most places on earth, we don't face a death sentence because of our beliefs, but we do face a lot of anger and ridicule and other forms of persecution.

Maybe sometimes we deserve that when we try to convince others in our own power instead of allowing God's Spirit to work. When we're only concerned about our own rights, making sure everyone looks and acts like *we* think they should look and act. When we think it's our job to judge and condemn others because they don't believe exactly as we think they should.

Our job is to act as if Jesus was living right there inside us. Because he is. His Spirit entered believers on the day of Pentecost and has never left us since then. All you need to do is ask to be a part of that community. It's open to everyone. And it's free to us because Jesus already paid the price of admission.

The early church faced some tough times. So do we. They survived and thrived because they kept pushing one simple message: Jesus is the Messiah.

So can we, if we continue to carry that same message into the world.

Appendix

# Read the Real Story

Amon and his friends and family are all fictional characters. But most of the rest of this story is true. If you haven't already, you should read it for yourself in the book of Acts, chapters one through nine.

## *The Archaeology of Amon's Secret*

Two thousand years is a very long time.

We can't imagine living without cars, airplanes, telephones, or electricity, but it was just over a hundred years ago that those things were only a dream. Less than *three* hundred years ago, the United States didn't even exist and many countries were ruled by kings, tsars, and emperors.

Two *thousand* years is a very, very long time. But that's when Jesus lived, and when he walked the streets of Jerusalem—the very same streets you can walk today if you happen to visit there.

Except that they're not.

Because it *was* so long ago, the streets Jesus walked on—and the buildings he visited and gates he passed through—are completely destroyed or buried far below what we see today. In some cases, those streets are a dozen feet or more under their modern-day versions.

**Walls & Gates:** Jerusalem's walls, gates, and buildings were destroyed and rebuilt so many times over the centuries that we aren't even sure exactly where they were in Jesus's time. Rebuilding the city has been pretty much a constant job over the last two millennia—and even long before Jesus arrived. Much of the time, the *new* was simply built on top of the rubble of the *old*. Scientists called *archaeologists* have spent the last couple hundred years trying to piece together that puzzle by "excavating" (digging) through the ruins and have made much progress. But there are still many pieces missing. We simply cannot say for certain exactly where every inch of the wall was at any given time, and experts have differing opinions on exactly which gates were in use at the time of Jesus.

And then there are the names. Even if we can be certain that a gate existed, different people called that gate by a different name at different times and for different reasons.

Thus, when the Bible says that a person walked through this or that gate, or went to this or that place, we often still don't know exactly where that was. In the story of *Amon's Secret*, it's doubtful that I've used all the names that Jesus would have called each of the gates. I simply chose one of the names that seems most descriptive or is in most common usage today.

**Daily Life:** Just as we don't know exactly where everything talked about in the Bible was located, there is much we don't know about how things happened, how people lived, or in some cases, exactly who a particular name in Scripture refers to.

Don't get me wrong—the Bible is *very* clear about the important things: There *is* a God, Jesus *is* his son, Jesus died for our sins and was resurrected on the third day so that you and I can live with him for eternity, and God sent his Holy Spirit to help us know him and live the example of unselfish love that Jesus showed us.

It's just some of the details about life in Jerusalem we don't know for sure.

Because of this, *Amon's Secret* was written with a lot of speculation. But it was also written in the light of many discoveries made by the archaeologists, including some made very recently, as well as discoveries all over the Middle East.

For example, in *Amon's Adventure* as well as *Amon's Secret*, Tamar and Amon encounter things like coconuts, chocolate, and glass. We don't *know* that those things were actually available in Jerusalem at the time of Jesus, but we do know that those things were all known, and even popular, in other countries in that part of the world. Since we also know that there were many traders crisscrossing the region, carrying goods and knowledge from one side of the known world to the other, and since Jerusalem was a crossroad for much of that traffic, it's *plausible* (reasonable) to believe that those products were known at least to the wealthy merchants of Jerusalem.

Below are some of the other things described in *Amon's Secret* that are either known or are plausible based on actual archaeological discoveries.

**Sign of the Fish:** Numerous archaeological finds have established that "early Christians" used the symbol of the fish just as Amon describes, both with and without the acrostic. These symbols have been found on pottery, buildings, tombs, and in caves. However, the exact definition of "early" is hard to pin down. Most sources simply indicate first and second centuries AD. The question, then, is *how* early in the first century (the time when Jesus lived and the story of Amon is set)? While there's probably no way we'll ever know exactly when the fish symbol was used by Christians, it's completely plausible (at least in this author's mind) that "early" could include the mid-30s. But even if it wasn't used by the very earliest Christians, Amon's use does demonstrate exactly *how* it was used—based on archaeological finds.

**Binary Code and Flags:** As far as I know, this is completely an invention of my own mind. Scripture tells us of the initial joy of the new Christians, followed closely by their persecution. But it also tells us that believers continued to meet together. In trying to fathom this, I imagined myself a believer in Jerusalem at that time. The Sanhedrin—and especially Saul, apparently—was actively hunting down believers after the incident of Pentecost. It would seem to me that believers wouldn't be shouting down the street, "Hey, Joe! Wanna come to a meeting of the Jesus Followers this afternoon?"

Probably the believers simply whispered such news mouth to ear. But wouldn't it be fun, I thought, if a "Clever One" among them devised a more central communication system? (Yes, I am a child of communication and media, so where else would my mind go?) The fact is that people were experimenting with forms of binary code in India and China at least as early as the second century BC. So who's to say that a clever boy in Jerusalem couldn't have done the same thing?

One thing I've learned very clearly in many decades of studying history is ancient people weren't dumb. They had minds that worked like ours, only with less (or at least different) information and technology. They figured things out just like we do. And just like many of the things you and I do in a day never get written down, neither did theirs. That doesn't mean those things didn't happen. For academic work, we must look for evidence of any claims, and label speculation as such. But for fiction writing I think the "plausibility" standard is sufficient.

Bottom line, Amon's binary system is fictional and just for fun, but it's certainly plausible.

**Uri's Place:** This one is real, and you can even travel to Jerusalem and take a tour of it. Of course, it was never called "Uri's Place" except in this story. But the fact of its existence, as well as the way in which it was discovered, is real. Today, scholars and tourists alike usually refer to it as "Zedekiah's Cave" or "Solomon's Quarry." As described by Amon, it was indeed excavated from underneath the city of Jerusalem, almost assuredly to provide stone for building. It is said that the stones for the still-existing Western Wall of the Temple Mount came from this cave.

It's thought that the original excavating was probably done at Solomon's command. Regardless, in times prior to Jesus, someone dug a huge cave under Jerusalem. Did the people of Jesus's time know about this? Impossible to say, since there's no record of it. What we *do* know is that knowledge of the cave was lost, probably until an American missionary named James Turner Barclay went searching for it based on rumors in 1854. When his dog suddenly disappeared, Barclay discovered a small opening in the sealed-off cave, an opening created by a heavy rainfall. Whether or not the cave was ever used by Christians hoping to remain anonymous, we don't know. But it's plausible.

**The Tomb of Jesus:** No one knows exactly where Jesus was buried. In the modern city of Jerusalem, there are at least two different sites that believers claim are the location of his tomb, but no one knows for sure. One of those sites happens to be across the street from Zedekiah's Cave, known in this book as Uri's Place. So while the depiction of the tomb as across the road from the cave is accurate as far as some of today's speculation goes, we don't know if that was really true.

**Cisterns:** The ground beneath Jerusalem—and throughout the region—hides many cisterns, just as described in this story. Archaeologists have discovered dozens, and it's speculated that even more are as yet undiscovered. Not only were they as large as the ones in which Amon had the congregations meet, some were enormous. One such cistern was discovered under the Temple Mount and is calculated to have held over two million gallons of water.First it was a rock quarry where stone was harvested to build the temple, then the hole was plastered over for use as a cistern. Another, discovered only in 2014, is just outside the Temple Mount and held 32,000 gallons.

Why so many cisterns? Israel was a very dry country, especially before the days of water pipes, irrigation, and indoor plumbing. Rains were sufficient during part of the year, but during the dry season Jerusalem had to rely only on springs. To make sure they had a constant supply of water, people carved cisterns out of the limestone beneath their feet.

Just as Amon learned, sometimes those cisterns would leak. That's when the experts were called, who would reline a cistern with lime plaster.

Eventually, though, some cisterns were so cracked they couldn't be repaired. In that case alternative uses were found for those big chambers in the ground: as storage rooms, prisons, and as hiding places. One such chamber is called "Jeremiah's Cistern," and is believed to be where the prophet was imprisoned for a time (Jeremiah 38).

Do I *know* cisterns were used by believers to meet in the early days of the church? No.

But we know cisterns did and do exist just as described, we know they were used for many things including hiding, and we know that those early believers had to be careful where they met. It seems plausible they could have met in old cisterns.

**Underground Passages:** Tunnels and chambers have been discovered under much of Jerusalem, especially around the Temple Mount—the base on which the two temples of Solomon and Herod were built. Politics and religious differences often get in the way of excavations here, but we do know that many passages exist under and around the Temple Mount.

**Pool of Siloam:** Rediscovered only in 2004, the pool existed much as described in the story. The pool was in a trapezoid shape and had stone steps on at least three sides.

**Herod's Theater and Hippodrome:** Yes, they really existed. No one's exactly sure *where* in

Jerusalem the two buildings stood—when the Romans destroyed the city in 70 AD, they left very little standing—but we do know from written accounts *about* where they stood. We also don't know exactly what they looked like, since we only have descriptions, not drawings or carvings, of the buildings.

**The Apartment:** My name for the three rooms discovered in 2019, deep underground and 120 feet from the Temple Mount. Dated to about the time of Jesus, it consists of a large central room, currently referred to as a "courtyard," and two smaller rooms above and to the side reached by stairs carved out of the rock. As of this writing, no one has figured out who created the underground rooms or why, but it's certainly plausible that others throughout the last 2000-plus years have converted the rooms to their own use, just as Amon did in this story.

Jerusalem is an absolutely fascinating place—certainly for its religious history and spiritual meaning for three religions, but also for its history, culture, architecture, and its amazing archaeological sites.

Enjoy these family stories!